## COLLABORATION IN THE FEMININE

*No book is produced without the support of many people.
We would like to thank all the collaborators who have made
the publication of these texts and this anthology possible:
Shonagh Adelman, Barbara Brown, Jessica DeVilliers, Jill G. Didur,
Ruth Frost, Maureen Hole, Chris Jackman, Adeena Karasick,
Jane Kidd, Trish Matson, Maureen Nicholson (with* Tessera*)
and Louise Azzarello, Karen Farquhar, Liz Martin
and the other women from Second Story Press.*

CANADIAN CATALOGUING IN PUBLICATION

Main entry under title:

Collaboration in the feminine : writings on women and culture from Tessera

ISBN 0-929005-57-0

1. Canadian literature (English) - Women authors - History and criticism.*
2. Canadian literature (French) - Women authors - History and criticism.*
3. Canadian literature - 20th century - History and criticism. 4. Feminist literary criticism - Canada. 5. Feminism and literature - Canada. I. Godard, Barbara.

PS8089.5.W6C65 1994    C810.9'0287    C94-931086-7
PR9188.C6C65 1994

Copyright © 1994 by Barbara Godard

Second Story Press gratefully acknowledges the assistance
of *The Canada Council* and the *Ontario Arts Council*

Printed and bound in Canada

Published by
SECOND STORY PRESS
*720 Bathurst Street Suite 301
Toronto, Ontario
M5S 2R4*

# Contents

Introduction: Women of Letters
*Louise Cotnoir, Barbara Godard, Susan Knutson,
Daphne Marlatt, Kathy Mezei and Gail Scott*
9

"Wholeness, Harmony, Radiance" and Women's Writing
*Lorraine Weir*
20

The Doubly Complicit Memory
*Louise Dupré*
26

Red Tin + White Tulle
*Gail Scott*
34

re
*Lola Lemire Tostevin*
40

Writing our Way Through the Labyrinth
*Daphne Marlatt*
44

Certain Words
*Nicole Brossard*
47

Theorizing Fiction Theory
*Barbara Godard, Daphne Marlatt, Kathy Mezei and Gail Scott*
53

It Was Not a Dark and Stormy Night
*Smaro Kamboureli*
63

Impunity: Distance as an Ethic
*Line McMurray*
68

Ritual
*Anne-Marie Alonzo*
78

Gnosis
*Donna E. Smyth*
81

Mother Tongue and Women's Language
*Madeleine Gagnon*
88

Diction Air
*Jam. Ismail*
96

Is Feminist Theory Anti-Feminist? (Reprise)
*Valerie Raoul*
103

Power, Ethics and Polyvocal Feminist Theory
*Kathleen Martindale*
108

In Conversation
*Barbara Godard, Susan Knutson, Daphne Marlatt,
Kathy Mezei and Gail Scott*
120

What We Talk About on Sundays
*Nicole Brossard, Louky Bersianik, Louise Cotnoir,
Louise Dupré, Gail Scott and France Théoret*
127

What? You Too?
*Lise Gauvin*
136

Doing Time
*Persimmon Blackbridge, Michelle Kanashiro-Christiansen,
Geri Ferguson, Lyn MacDonald and Bea Walkus*
140

Suzanne Lamy: "Talking Together"
*Sherry Simon*
148

Vers-ions con-verse: A Sequence of Translations
*Barbara Godard, Susan Knutson, Daphne Marlatt,
Kathy Mezei, Gail Scott and Lola Lemire Tostevin*
153

Coming to Terms with the Mother Tongue
*Dôre Michelut*
162

S(m)other Tongue?:
Feminism, Academic Discourse, Translation
*Pamela Banting*
171

To Speak without Suffocating
*Louise Cotnoir*
182

Incredulity Toward Metanarrative:
Negotiating Postmodernism and Feminisms
*Linda Hutcheon*
186

Whose Idea Was it Anyway?
*Marlene Nourbese Philip*
193

Self-Representation and Fictionalysis
*Daphne Marlatt*
202

Tell Tale Signs
*Janice Williamson*
207

The Pornographic Subject
*Claudine Potvin*
214

The Subject at Stake
*Carole Massé*
218

Power or "Unpower" of the Fictional Subject:
A Letter to Lise Gauvin in Reply to "What? You Too?"
*Monique LaRue*
221

Imagine Her Surprise
*Susan Knutson*
228

Writing the Risk In, Risking the Writing
*Kathy Mezei*
237

Other Orthodoxies or The Centring of the Margins:
A Dialogue
*Sarah Murphy and Leila Sujir*
247

Opening Up to a Lot of Pain
*Busejé Bailey*
256

Women of Letters (Reprise)
*Barbara Godard*
258

Contributors' Notes
307

## INTRODUCTION

## WOMEN OF LETTERS

*Louise Cotnoir, Barbara Godard, Susan Knutson,
Daphne Marlatt, Kathy Mezei and Gail Scott*

In 1983, when I participated in the Women and Words conference in Vancouver, the project of *Tessera*, a bilingual, pan-Canadian periodical offering a space for women's thinking and writing, seemed to me completely Utopian ... Who would have thought that one day I should be one of its artisans! Still, for five years now I have had the pleasure and privilege of being "directly" involved with the production of *Tessera*.

What I have found most valuable in this unusual experiment has been above all the enthusiasm, the tenacity and the great generosity of all the co-editors. Throughout a decade, their animated words have elaborated a feminist discourse on all the questions of the moment and even imagined the future! Each in her own way has shaped the periodical to the image of multiple, pluri-elle women. Together these women have contributed to the opening of a scriptural space where other writings in the feminine have come, will come, to inscribe themselves. For each of us may keep memory alive because of *Tessera*. From its beginning, the periodical has known how to harmonize languages, races, economic situations, ideologies, and through its openness has succeeded in giving priority to what is for me essential, to women and words. *Tessera* links us all as women and has highlighted DIFFERENCE.

♦ Louise Cotnoir, Barbara Godard, Susan Knutson,
Daphne Marlatt, Kathy Mezei and Gail Scott ♦

I am, we are, *women of memory*. By its presence, *Tessera* has and will contribute, I hope, to leaving traces of women's History, Thought and Imaginary. Because we have dreamed, we still dream, of a world where we will be visible and vital, I am, we are *women of words*, and it is undoubtedly on this territory that *Tessera* has and will be for me most necessary. I have discovered in its pages, along with other women, intelligence, imagination, the literary wealth of women, and I have had many amorous encounters with their texts, their hopes and their ideas which each, in her own way, has nourished my reflections, my fictions and my desires.

*Tessera* is also a manifestation of *women of passion*. And it is on this special terrain that the periodical has been so important and generous to me. Because women and their writings deserve my unconditional love which has always been so stingily given them. Women ever loving, never beloved. *Tessera* loves women and their words, *Tessera* believes in their writing. *Tessera* has been for me a fine linguistic challenge, a place of complicities and cognitions, a moment of great happiness in the feminine.

— L.C.

Four on a see-saw. That's how I remember the *Tessera* editorial process. Four we were for four years and then we were five. Even as four, though, we were multifarious, each of us bringing to *Tessera* the charged issues from other feminist reading/writing groups, enriching and complicating the dialogue. Daphne's long involvement with West Coast editorial collectives, Gail, nourished by her regular Sunday meetings with Montreal women writers, I with my feminist reading groups from the Toronto universities, extended by exchange with international feminist theorists at the Semiotics Institutes, Kathy, and Susan, working with similar communities in Vancouver and Nova Scotia. Later still, Louise continued the connection with the Sunday group, contributing new dimensions from her literary friendships in l'Estrie. Our disagreements were legendary: the only certainty was that we would never all think alike. Each decision brought its surprises. We were sustained by our mutual commitment to keep talking

♦ INTRODUCTION: WOMEN OF LETTERS ♦

because the issues mattered. Vitally. Four or more on a see-saw, *une balançoire* ... What a delicate balancing act it has been to keep the discussion going, to keep the ideas in movement — an aerial version of musical chairs — the bodies shifting from side to side, not all heaped on one side in a muddle on the ground, leaving one stuck in the air indefinitely .... Ghostly figures (not angelic, though) flying, leaping, dancing, on a moving platform.

Mobile, this collective has been, a moving force. Shifting from one periodical to another like guerrillas multiplying their effect on a terrain too vast for their small numbers. Strategic interventions to increase the visibility of feminist writing and theorizing. An editorial direction always in movement too, a few boxes on one person's desk with a flurry of texts and letters and, later, faxes circulating around the country as the collective considered submissions, did copy editing, read proofs.

At the time, in the heat of discussion and the sense of adventure in inventing the future, decisions about topics, selections, seemed tentative, searching, passionately argued over. Subject for endless defense or denunciation in our correspondence, matter to be developed in our collective editorials. Looking back on the body of work we eventually published, however, patterns emerge, a certain cohesion around issues such as the gendering of the critical institution in Canada, the crisis in representation, translation as a practice and an intellectual paradigm for border writing, gender and genre, narration especially, the question of the subject and the dominant symbolic order — a number of concerns now identified with post-structuralism and post-modernism. Hindsight is always sharpest. Nonetheless, to find these patterns seems a surprise when our choices were always so urgently debated and majority vote, not consensus, our general editorial practice. I remember tentative articulations struggling to emerge, not fixed or pinned down with the definitiveness of such categories.

Being part of an ongoing debate, participating in the ramifying discussion with the other *Tessera* editors has been very important for me over the years in helping me clarify my own ideas and aesthetics. Knowing above all that the other editors cared passionately about the questions of feminism and writing, that they would read and

♦ LOUISE COTNOIR, BARBARA GODARD, SUSAN KNUTSON,
DAPHNE MARLATT, KATHY MEZEI AND GAIL SCOTT ♦

respond thoughtfully and fully to what I said or wrote, was an enormously empowering experience. I could struggle with other women over poetics, work out my own position, articulate my own voice. Develop a project and put it forward. Having an audience to write for is crucial in making the bridge between private musing and public statement, passing through the requisite forging of a critical idiom in which to communicate. A glorious, flying workshop this has been forming women of letters. With the aim of producing movement, change.

— B.G.

*Tessera*: a matrix, a generous invitation into real readings, into the feminine, and other women's minds.

*Tessera*: warrior readers who are writers, whose justice targets racism, despair, all kinds of shackles; whose healing words repair the damage to life. Manila envelopes of windows onto the world.

*Tessera*: anagram for Teresa [deL], for the precious gifts of feminist minds, for a motherly saint and a Symbolic Mother, and for Tess (who is safe within us).

I am warm-hearted in the gentle brilliance of Marlatt, Mezei, Godard, Scott, Cotnoir. (Y)our Devonian rocks bear women's voices. Tesserae: a place to speak, when messages matter.

— S.K.

The trouble with putting together an anthology from a journal is that it proposes the journal as a crystallized object one can take slices from. How does an editorial collective slice up the object it grew with? (The proverbial snail in its shell.) Choosing what is "best" or even "favourite" begs the question as to what each of us would choose as most important, looking back with the benefit of hindsight. And that of course is intimately connected with what happens to be central concerns for each of us now as theorists/writers/critics. *Tessera* itself, even our individual theoretical development, is an ongoing process, always in flux, always

♦ INTRODUCTION: WOMEN OF LETTERS ♦

provisional, and here we are trying to freeze a selection of timeframes that are moments in that process, marked as such.

Then there is the way in which any journal is an ongoing conversation between contributors, editors and readers within (and shaped by) a certain climate of current ideas. *Tessera* began with conversations, both formal and informal around the Dialogue Conference Barbara organized in 1981. It continued with conversations by mail and phone amongst the four, and later five, of us scattered across the country. Intensive long-distance editing with much debate, not only of individual submissions but of our editorial mandate, what we saw ourselves doing as a collective in an itinerant and then established feminist journal that sought to engage two different cultural milieus, French-speaking and English-speaking. As such, the journal has been a process both influencing and responding to its theoretical environment.

We published a lot of ground-breaking and provocative work. While some of our issues were more focused than others, what most carries that sense of process for me now, looking back some ten years later, is the dialogue beginning in the earlier issues: those instances where women were commenting on writing in previous issues or on problematics in the cultural community at large. This seems evidence of a real exchange of thought, and ongoing collective debate which I wish we had managed to sustain and focus further. We asked for letters but, true to the conversational matrix of *Tessera's* inception, our readers usually preferred to give us oral feedback.

Several thematic concerns recur through different issues, even though we tried to structure each issue around a unique theme. Translation was one such abiding concern, both as literal process and as metaphor for how women are situated vis à vis the dominant culture. Yet again, reading back, what strikes me as ground-breaking over and over again is not so much the content as the form, the innovative structure of much of the writing. Fiction/theory, originating in Québécoise feminist writing, began to move over into English, modulated by an English sensibility. Theoretical writing became a formal adventure. And the sense of exhilaration, of horizons opening up which the Sunday/*la dimanche* group gave me, still hovers around these early issues of *Tessera* as I re-read them.

— D.M.

♦ Louise Cotnoir, Barbara Godard, Susan Knutson,
Daphne Marlatt, Kathy Mezei and Gail Scott ♦

In remembering *Tessera* I come up against something like Wordsworth's spots of time, collective moments and impressions that have remained behind, reflections upon a unique collectivity. We must be careful about remembering for I cannot remember then. I can only be retrospective from the vantage of now.

*spot i*

It was a brilliant move, I think now, for the editorial collective — the original four — Barbara, Daphne, Gail, and me to bring out the first four numbers of *Tessera* as special issues of established journals. This was the collective process with a vengeance for not only did we four need to negotiate with each other over the fraught and fertile boundaries between academic discourse and original writing, and between our different and fluctuating theoretical positions but also with the congenial editors of the idiosyncratic journals (Bless *Room of One's Own, La nouvelle barre du jour, Canadian Fiction Magazine,* and *CV2* for being intrepid, flexible and supportive!). Publishing in this way freed our *Tessera* collective to focus on ideas and exchanges — with each other, with contributors. In the end it is the administrative aspect of journals (which I did for several years from SFU) that wears one down, though I learned a great deal about the business of running a journal from subscriptions to grant applications. Here was an ideal apprenticeship, and it was with some reluctance that I quit these nurturing, maternal locales.

*spot ii*

As I recall (and our calls for papers, Canada Council Grant applications, prefaces will back me up here), for us, in the early 80s *Tessera* claimed two radical objects (which so nicely integrated with my two passions of that time) a) to publish feminist literary theory and language-centred writing focused on the *feminine*, to publish writing which transgressed genre boundaries and which challenged the innumerable thematic studies of images of women in Canadian literature with its shadowing of traditional Canadian

♦ INTRODUCTION: WOMEN OF LETTERS ♦

literary criticism devoted to landscape, weather, survival, b) and to intermingle — with a certain endearing idealism — the writings of English-Canadian and Quebec feminists. Though as Gail Scott later cautioned in *Spaces Like Stairs*: to act as a bridge between two cultures tends to elide difference. Still I think it was important to make public a private dialogue, to begin relationships that continue to this day.

I liked that bumpy ride I had embarked upon, as I and we lurched from one theoretical position and discovery to another, continually jolting my teaching, my writing out of whichever comfortable place it had started to settle into. I expect the rest of the collective might regard the aftermath of our theoretical venturings with a similar and shared cynicism for what seemed startling concepts in 1984 have now become the dry discourse of academic journals. Much of what we struggled with, investigated, argued over, is now commonplace — *un lieu commun* — écriture féminine, binary oppositions, subjectivity, enunciation, the maternal body, whatever. We also now bear the weight of perhaps having slighted the marginalized, of having glided over issues of race or class; we wrote and spoke out of our experience and our knowledge. Did we make claims for universality? — *I don't remember that.* Retrospection must be fair to a past time and place. Reading back over the issues I am surprised by (except for #1) the specificity and localisation of many of the pieces, and in this sense the *Tessera* anthology is a false representation. I am struck by the topicality and foresightedness of our "themes" — Duplicity, Translation, Autograph(e), Narratology, Changing the Subject, Performance.

*spot iii*

I remember with some amusement the difficulty Daphne and I had in translating Louise Dupré's "The Doubly Complicit Memory," how we puzzled over the twists of her *language*, translating from more than one foreign language into another, from a truly *source* language into a target language. Strange how now these ideas are such familiar companions to us, to students, to young writers.

♦ Louise Cotnoir, Barbara Godard, Susan Knutson,
Daphne Marlatt, Kathy Mezei and Gail Scott ♦

*spot iv*

It was during these years that Nicole Brossard's *L'amèr*, translated by Barbara Godard as *These Our Mothers*, Daphne Marlatt's *Anahistoric*, and Gail Scott's *Heroine* (even the titles are punning, parodic, polysemic) were published and seemed to cap, capture the concepts we were working through in *Tessera* about herstory, subjectivity, the deconstruction of the transparency of language. Though things were meant to fall apart, they began instead to fall into place. There was complicity in the air, a joint adventuring forth, a synthesizing through writing. We were never under any illusions that feminism or feminist literary theory would attain canonicity, but slowly it has entered literary discourse, and found a discourse community — with all the inherent dangers of a received discourse becoming hollow, empty of meaning, a playground for academics.

*spot v*

As I remember we met once only, all four, in Vancouver, during the Women and Words conference, a sweltering summer day; we taped our conversation; we were very curious about each other, careful too, later we became more outspoken. We were all mothers, and mothering floated in and out of all our dialogues, ever after a short-hand into our lives. If two or three of us happened to be in the same place, we would confer; otherwise decisions and discussions took place (before e-mail and fax, for us anyway) by letters and Sunday morning conference calls connecting Susan Knutson (who joined us later) in Ste Anne, Nova Scotia, via Gail in Montreal and Barbara in Toronto with Daphne and me in Vancouver. When Daphne and I stepped down in 1989, Gail had already left the collective, each to pursue other urgent projects, and each thinking too that things have their appointed time and space. Yet, as Daphne once said to me, I feel as if I have never really left *Tessera*.

— K.M.

## ♦ Introduction: Women of Letters ♦

I remember my excitement at meeting Daphne, Kathy, Barbara, not long before Women and Words. They were my first encounter with women from "out there," women with whom I could discuss language/writing/subjectivity in *English*. My closest writing relationships at the time were with people of another language, québécoise friends, several of whom could not read my work. Leaning over my typewriter late at night (yellow paper if I recall) I wrote passionately to other members of the new collective about how, for me, the *sine qua non* of *Tessera* had to be critical writing with difference, reflecting new forms, new relations to reading. The other *sine qua non* was that *Tessera* should be a meeting place for women writing in French and English. This latter proved exhilarating, inasmuch as it sought to transcend one cultural gap, and limiting, inasmuch as it so inadequately reflected the Canadian context.

Like most literary periodicals, we started with nothing. Someone — was it Barbara? — came up with the idea of "piggy-backing" on other publications. This gave us the capacity to produce issues, and also to float around from city to city — perfect for our "pan-Canadian" mandate. With the organizing genius of Kathy, we eventually set up an infrastructure in B.C. Hats off to Barbara, too, who doggedly kept *Tessera* going when the rest of the original group had burned and bowed out. It's true that as we became more time-efficient we lost things. Conference calls replaced the letters we used to write, letters that were starting to explore various currents of sympathy and amicable difference. Such as Daphne's and my desire to take on the business of criticism formally — why should one lapse into the pedantic syntax and rhetoric of "academia": we wanted *texts*. Later, there seemed to be an eastern and western current as far as theoretical approaches, Barbara and I leaning perhaps more towards the notions of *différance* than difference. I remember the small tensions in voices over telephone lines as we discussed what articles and why: but also the joys of meeting when we found ourselves, on rare occasions, in the same place. Here I could lapse into lyric descriptions of Daphne's curls, Kathy's smile, Barbara's irony (Susan and Louise came later), over espresso in Montreal's *la Petite Ardoise*, or tea in a Vancouver hotel.

♦ Louise Cotnoir, Barbara Godard, Susan Knutson,
Daphne Marlatt, Kathy Mezei and Gail Scott ♦

I'll add that *Tessera* was not always easy for me. Perhaps each of us felt separate from the others, on occasion, misunderstood, due to regional or other differences. Coming from Quebec and being a former left-wing militant were my two "differences." I never figured out how to articulate a bridge between my materialism (in the Marxist sense) and my interest in the materiality of language with the *Tessera* collective. At the time, creating a common front around *Tessera*'s immediate goals, in the face of suspicion, even hostility from some respected women writers (cf, certain essays in *Language in her Eye*) took precedence. With hindsight, with age, too, I realize the importance of speaking one's differences as we go along. For example, during the discussion about women of colour in that first *Tessera* "talking editorial" — the patronizing tone of which was rightly criticized by *Kinesis* — I remember wondering myself how much the need to translate culturally complexified the process of writing for First Nations women. Marie Annharte Baker, in "Borrowing Enemy Language: A First Nation Woman Use of English," recently published in *West Coast Line* — the best text I have ever seen on the subject of language, writing, politics — shows how damaging the forced transiting of cultures, tongues, can be.

Yes, translation can imply a painful stretching, bending, conceding when it is an everyday necessity, a tool of survival. Women know this instinctively, to varying degrees depending on their circumstance. There are ways in which this applies to the Quebec editor of *Tessera*: she has an extra load, not always acknowledged or understood, of coordinating translating, of writing abstracts of texts not written in English, of convincing francophones to write about themes articulated, often, in another cultural context. The hardest task when I was editor was deconstructing the image of Quebec that prevailed "out there." It was an image of triumphant feminism at a time when women writers in Quebec were in the worst throes of the 80s anti-feminist backlash. I remember asking a francophone woman to write a text about fiction/theory, and she said with some astonishment, "Oh, that's old, the theory's now absorbed into the text."

Odd, though how things come full circle. The notion of fiction/theory has changed the way many women write, regardless of its degree of "absorption" into the text today. The ongoing discourse

♦ INTRODUCTION: WOMEN OF LETTERS ♦

between women working in French and English has somewhat closed the gap, the potential for misunderstanding. More First Nations, African- and Asian-Canadian women are participating. But how well does editorial representation reflect their concerns? Are Maritime women well-enough represented? Working-class women?

I'm hopeful. *Tessera* with its strengths and weaknesses has remained quite flexible, whatever the anti-theory crowd might say. Definitely worthy of celebration. I raise my glass.

— G.S.

♦

# "WHOLENESS, HARMONY, RADIANCE" AND WOMEN'S WRITING

*Lorraine Weir*

> "For if she begins to tell the truth, the figure in the looking-glass shrinks; his fitness for life is diminished."
> — Virginia Woolf, *A Room of One's Own*

In the course of a discussion of aesthetics in *A Portrait of the Artist as a Young Man*, Joyce's hero, Stephen Dedalus, expounds three Thomist principles which he takes to be essential to the work of art. "*Three things are needed for beauty,*" he says, quoting Aquinas, "*wholeness, harmony and radiance*" (Joyce 216). Although few would argue that mainstream criticism is still primarily Thomist in attitude and intent, it is clear that a majority of Canadian critics at least are still haunted by expectations of accessibility, verbal and structural simplicity, "life-likeness," and that contented sense of roundness, repletion which some expect to follow a good meal or a good novel. And it is not only fiction which is subjected to these quaint criteria but poetry as well, despite the fact that many of our most respectable critics cling to antique notions of generic specificity. Poets are congratulated on the clarity, simplicity and appropriateness of their imagery, the measure of all three criteria being finally the critic's capacity to recognize his own world, his own perceptions and attitudes, translated for him by the poet. For Narcissus only one image will do.

It is, however, unlikely that he will drown, for in a patriarchal society his image is writ large and its power to extract conformity evident especially to all those whose images are other. Feminist critics have long held that women's writing presents radically different views of the world and that our capacity as readers to deal with these diverse and often "experimental" texts (texts, that is, which don't conform to mainstream expectations but have — some of them, at least survived anyway) is limited by our training in traditional assumptions about literature. Let me take this argument one step further by asserting that in Canada the Realist tradition[1] grounded in Anglo-Protestant injunctions against ritual, "mystification" in language and doctrine and so on — has assumed the status of smug credo because its simpler manifestations so neatly reflect the image which Narcissus takes to be the "norm." One need not be a Marxist to see further that the norm in capitalist patriarchy is a bourgeois version of wholeness and harmony (though radiance might be seen as rather extreme). Critics as diverse as George Lukács, Ian Watt and Terry Eagleton have enabled us to see the ways in which the rise of the Realist mode in literature and of the middle class through the Victorian period not only coincided with but reflected each other's ascendancy. To put a complex argument very briefly, then, we have in Canada a class of mainstream critics whose ideology is capitalist, bourgeois, patriarchal and, in its origins if not in current practice, Anglo-Protestant.

Narcissus values simplicity and accessibility in part because his life has been made simple through the labour of countless women whose correspondingly complicated lives are incomprehensible to him. His writing is accessible because it reflects the values of the power élite. The hallmark of the patriarchal voice at its best, this ideal of clarity is a false one which drowns in its own submissiveness to reigning power, avoids the struggle toward free speech, and moulds (in both senses) public understanding of texts by excluding from view that which does not give back the required reflection or — as in the case of Margaret Laurence — by assimilating into the bourgeois Realist tradition works which on the surface conform to its dictates. Thus we have the absurd irony of Laurence's novels being elevated in the canon above Alice Munro's "fragmented" fictions despite the fact that the wholeness of the former counterpoints the jaggedness, incompleteness and stubborn struggle against self-mutilation of the lives of many of the characters depicted. However easy Munro's "fragments" are on the surface to oppose to Laurence's continuum, the logical opposition in itself serves only to obscure the fact that Munro's style in its repetitions, its doubling back and restatement and "incompleteness" moves in itself away from the ideology which still possesses some of her characters. Where we have been taught to see more and less perfect accommodations to the tradition by these two writers, we may come to see a radically different phenomenon: a struggle to move theme and style toward open forms, forms which threaten Narcissus. Style itself is mimetic. Open texts challenge closed systems.

In struggling toward freedom we begin the journey out of exile, our language mirroring the knowledge which generations of women have shored against a system which excludes us, a system whose principles of wholeness and harmony have had little to do at any time with the lives of women as of those of the members of any servant class. We move through a world which, as Louky Bersianik has said, proclaims its universality, its generality, its mass-produced truth; and we move through the dismembered bodies of our ancestors and ourselves.

Some would argue, like Adrienne Rich, that we need "re-vision" (Rich 33) or, as Ann Saddlemyer recently said, that we must repossess critical terminology, remaking it to suit the manifold needs of women's texts, to deal with the "unspoken but always present subtext" and with the use of "symbol" where critics have been trained to expect "statement." If, as Saddlemyer maintained, it is the playwright's responsibility to make the work accessible to the audience, since theatre is by its very nature a "whole and healing art," then critics must devise ways of understanding which open the text out rather than struggling against it or obscuring it for others, practices not unknown among mainstream critics.

But I wonder about the criterion of accessibility and, although I respect the views of Rich and Saddlemyer and agree that in some

## ♦ "Wholeness, harmony, Radiance" and Women's Writing ♦

circumstances our work as critics must be re-visionist, I wonder about all the hermetic texts in women's literature and about what we do when we open them out, making an often bitterly private tradition into a public one — public on Narcissus' terms. Telling the truth, "slant," as Emily Dickinson put it (Dickinson, 506 no. 1129), has so deeply and persistently characterized our tradition that I wonder about using the language of Narcissus at all to straighten the slant or to undo what Adrienne Rich has called the "lies" (Rich 186) which have been so much a part of women's lives and texts. Slant writing can never be made "whole"; to attempt to do so is to participate in our own de/composition.

I am not, however, suggesting that we amputate ourselves from the heritage of women's texts which feminist critics have only begun to study. Rather, it seems to me that we need to critique the very concept of wholeness which in all its forms has held us captive, often unknowingly complicit. For as long as we see the "half-saying," the concealed or unspoken subtexts, the use of symbol and rhetoric of camouflage as incomplete, partial, an imperfect "half-life," we are still participating in the doctrine of naïve accessibility and in the judgements of Narcissus. Our task is a complex one, requiring us to be familiar with the intricate strategies of contemporary literary theory, for in this struggle theorists like Jacques Derrida and Michel Foucault who seek to deconstruct phallogocentrism — the patriarchal control of structures of language and definitions of meaning — of the Western humanist tradition are our allies. Those who would dismiss theory because of its difficulty or inaccessibility fall victim to the same arguments which have been used against women's writing. Feminist theory must, it seems to me, abjure the primitivist lethargy of those who refuse to see that the deconstruction of the Western humanist tradition is central to the work of naming the place where we find ourselves.

In setting aside the illusions of closure, completion, stasis, perfection — the ideals of a patriarchal society which, as Simone de Beauvoir has reminded us, has never had to cope with the Sisyphean labours of housework (de Beauvoir 425), of the sheer dailiness of Woolf's "moments of being" (Woolf 1976) — we enter the possibility of the open text, the so-called "fragment," the writing which exists not to valorize its author/ity (Foucault) but to be activated in the process of reading/making/collaborating. And if Narcissus, entering the water of his dream, finally drowns in accessibility, we may find ourselves in a familiar medium, knowing the underside of reflection to which we were consigned long ago. For the inaccessible, the complex and often contradictory, the jagged and incomplete, the discordant and dark are only Narcissus's terms for the writing which we have been doing all along. The image from below is our own. We can say that we have been drowned; we can say that we know how to swim. I prefer the latter.

♦

## NOTES

This paper is a revised version of my contribution to the "Criticizing Mainstream Criticism" panel (speakers: Ann Saddlemyer, Louky Bersianik, France Théoret, Carolyn Hlus, and myself; moderator, Jennifer Waelti-Walters) at the Women and Words Conference, Vancouver, July 1, 1983. One of my functions as the final speaker was to draw together some of the points made by the other participants. I am grateful to the panelists for their insights from which I profited, especially to Ann Saddlemyer whose beautifully articulate statement helped me to formulate my own response more precisely, and to France Théoret for much conversation afterward.

1. Although the term Realism is usually assumed to be applicable solely or primarily to prose fiction, I am extending it here to include poetry and drama as well, and making that extension by way of the ideological assumptions inherent in the mode itself and in the writings of those mainstream critics who impose expectations grounded in this mode upon poetry and drama as well as prose fiction. Realism incorporates an attitude toward life, a set of expectations of texts and of situations which arise from its mimesis of the "norms" of bourgeois patriarchy.

## WORKS CITED

de Beauvoir, Simone. *The Second Sex.* Trans. H.M. Parshley. New York: Knopf, 1964

Dickinson, Emily. *The Complete Poems.* Ed. Thomas H. Johnson. Boston: Little Brown, 1960.

Foucault, Michel. "What Is An Author?" In *Language, Counter-Memory, Practice.* Edited by. Donald F. Bouchard, translated by D.F. Bouchard and Sherry Simon. Ithaca: Cornell University Press, 1977.

Joyce, James. *A Portrait of the Artist as a Young Man.* Edited by Chester G. Anderson and Richard Ellmann. London: Cape, 1968. Joyce's italics.

Rich, Adrienne. "When We Dead Awaken: Writing as Re-Vision." and "Women and Honor: Some Notes on Lying," In *On Lies, Secrets, and Silence.* New York: Norton, 1979.

Woolf, Virginia. *Moments of Being.* Ed. Jeanne Schulkind. London: Chattos & Windus, 1976.

# THE DOUBLY COMPLICIT MEMORY

*Louise Dupré*

*Translated by Kathy Mezei and Daphne Marlatt*

How can we approach the duplicity of language without recalling the two meanings of the word "duplicity"? First, as "characteristic of doubleness" (*le petit Robert* 521), then as falseness, hypocrisy. For that is really the question here: the double face of language, as in the expression "two-faced," which uses a mask to hide its other, its split which plays between the signifier and the signified arbitrarily, according to Saussure, in order to create an integrated process of communication.

What about the speaking subject — the unary[1], thinking, transcendental subject who performs a transparent act in the tradition of Descartes, ejecting his utterance, who is exterior to a predicate forever separated from him, and over whom he looms as Master? Here, we are right at the heart of the symbolic, and the subject, far from being lost there, establishes himself like a son imitating his father's speech. Abandoning the mother, he now passes over into the realm of order, the law, the Phallus. Language assures the subject's social insertion in the patriarchy. This subject speaks, but is also spoken through. And history speaks, or rather avoids speaking about the murder of the mother, leaving this tricked Oedipus with a triangular relationship that resolves itself through identification with the Father, with the Same.

♦ THE DOUBLY COMPLICIT MEMORY ♦

And what can we say about her, the daughter, who is alienated from this language in which she can never recognize herself as subject, who sees herself cut off from mother, who finds herself without a penis with which to identify with her father? In language she is always spoken about, she, a stranger to the act of speech. Despairing of her case, she could try to imitate masculine speech. But with what risk does she undertake this circumnavigation, this pretense which distances her from her own body? She will never become a father, never, and her speech will always remain an act of borrowing. Where is she in this imitation, and what will she encounter, if not hysteria, female-language, in which the language of the body manifests itself on the side of the symbolic that speaks at the margin, painfully, off-kilter.


And I, I, a Québécoise, doubly alienated, twice removed from my mother, thrown into an abyss by the Father, that anglophone who conquered my own father on whom he imposed his language, I try desperately to reverse the trend, to redirect it to its origins. I throw myself completely into it, questioning CODES and NAMES: I want to discover women's language, beyond all national languages, which dares to present my relation with the world, reality and love in terms other than those of castration.

To throw myself completely into it and, as a francophone woman, to complete a journey with my anglophone sisters to the deepest shadows so as to recover the memory of our mother tongues to get beyond the power struggles with a subversive complicity which helps us to discover the richness of our differences in one and the same bond with the mother.


To affirm our women's language, de-centred, eccentric in relation to the symbolic, changeable, passionate, and linked to the semiotic *chora* (Kristeva 47)[2]. As in the subversion of the norm, the logical and grammatical norm, as in prosody, as in the language of gentle madness, as in laughter. Where women talk among themselves in open and in-finite communication, where they write in the feminine in their fictions. Where they talk nonsense in relation to the law, to power, to the forces of power, so as to undermine them.

For this is where, in popular thought, women's language is experienced at the margin of the symbolic, and consequently devalorized. Remember the Tunisian proverb: "By his silence, man refuses, by her silence, woman consents." And isn't what is called idle chatter, gossip, what woman's conversation has retained of the chant, precisely the inclusion of pre-symbolic rhymes in language, rhymes which, among men, only the poets, true sons of the mother, have known how to preserve?

It's not a question here, however, of sending woman back to her "feminine nature," a consequence of the "eternal feminine." Let's say rather that woman perceived as other has been excluded from language. The use of all language by the-dominant-male has led to the sexualization of language, and woman finds herself facing an excision of the real. She must cross over it, make it deviate so she can find her own speech. She sees herself denied access to certain words (for example, the coarse words of men); she lacks vocabulary, in many cases, and is unable to give her version of events.

> All the principles and preconceptions that weigh us down are found in the words we use, let alone that we are excluded from these principles and preconceptions. (Cardinal 89)

From the start a booby-trapped terrain, language is erected against a woman who must ceaselessly question and evade it. For her it's a matter of succeeding in detouring the masculine language in order to give a linguistic shape to her own reality, her imagination.

We have to find the means at all costs. No longer separate the speech act from the spoken, make the female-subject surface in a language where we can meet ourselves. Represent the feminine subconscious. Grasp language and penetrate what it discloses: *jouissance*.[3] To give voice to contradictions, and no longer try to deny them through unity and coherence: to open up words, spread them across the page, accept the shadows, bring out their liveliness and colour. To enter the symbolic or to leave it, always remaining flexible.

## The Doubly Complicit Memory

If we don't invent a language for our body, there will be too few gestures to portray our history. We will weary of the same few gestures, and our desires will remain latent, and in limbo. Lulled to sleep, unsatisfied. And delivered over to the words of men. (Irigaray 213)

A matter of real urgency. To refuse the mask, refuse the double-play of language: the dichotomy of signifier/signified separated by a bar (Saussure), the dichotomy of language/ speech (Saussure) and competence/performance (Chomsky), the binarity of opposites. To give vent to a plural language that catches all the nuances of words beyond fixed definition, that abandon the order of the theological substantive, of ownership. A language of relations, of drift, alive with all our seedings.

Man has been given THE language; hence the split for woman set in relation to the masculine universe. When she speaks to a speaker, social rules oblige her to express herself in his language: the dominant discourse of communication setting up its "free arbiter," academic discourse, discourse of supply and demand, discourse of castration. Nothing but transvestism,[4] mimicking man so that woman can make a place for herself at the heart of the phratry. And it's in relation to the masculine language, to its values, that she will see herself evaluated, will evaluate her own competence.

The double stakes the contemporary woman must face. Or else stay amongst women, attempt nothing in the men's realm, work to make a new culture emerge, a culture in which the values of competition and ownership would no longer have a place, a culture in the feminine which would given women back their bodies, a women's language which could be developed outside established contexts. The risk of such an enterprise: the ghetto. Or else to enter the male world, play on its grassy borders while trying to change them from within and risk alienation, loss or self. Two different stands which divide women today and determine their political, social, and sexual choices. Must one join political parties with their power plays? or not? Must one work within already established social structures? Must one have privileged relations with men?

♦ Louise Dupré ♦

Women search for solutions appropriate to themselves. And this alternative means not curbing feminism to a narrow truth confined to "the correct line," but rather giving birth to diverse feminist tendencies, at the heart of which the individuality of women, their cares and their desires, are not drained off to profit an ossified theory. In this respect, feminism offers itself as practice in the feminine.

> I wish to love in my female tongue. To explain as I please in my male tongue, since I possess both and the former remains to be asserted. (Gagnon 66)

Despite risks, women act confident. So Madeleine Gagnon divides up the functions of her double language: love for women's language, rationality for men's language. There a creative fissure is at work: not the fissure of a split subject but the meeting of two principles.

And Luce Irigaray carries the feminine into the body of theory in her recent writing: *Et l'une ne bouge pas sans l'autre* (And the One Doesn't Stir Without the Other, 1979), *Amante marine* (Marine Lover, 1980), and *Passions élémentaires* (Basic Passions, 1982). Here, the rigidity of academic language is abandoned, the female question is explored in a shifting language, a language tending towards metaphor and metonymy, where a woman-*I* situates itself; and this subject *I* is not detached from its predicate but winds around it without ever bringing it to a standstill or doing it to death. This is one of the ways it is possible to theorize in the feminine.

A search for the feminine which makes itself felt also in fiction. Women who write are of necessity preoccupied with *language*, with *form*, since for them it's a question of subverting masculine language. A desire, therefore, to de-articulate the dominant discourse, to split open syntax, to let the over-flowing feminine into the signifier, to reinvent vocabulary, to reinvest it with new signifieds. And so, in Quebec, the coincidence of the literary avant-garde[5] with works by women: a dialectic relationship which has allowed both the new writing and women's texts to spill over, to sustain an innovative dynamism.

Note, however, that men's and women's writing do not merge; rather they meet in differences. Writing remains this "return to the matricial[6] paradise/.../A man's return is a return to the Other. A woman's return is a return to the Same. Perhaps that's why the act of writing is more a complete return for a woman than it is for a man" (Didier 274).

Sexuality of production in relation to the avant-garde: I am thinking here of Nicole Brossard, Madeleine Gagnon, France Théoret, Yolande Villemaire; Gail Scott for English Canada. Sexuality otherwise elaborated by Hélène Cixous, Chantal Chawaf in France; in the USA by Mary Daly who attempts a return to the roots of words as a way of stripping them of their patriarchal connotations.

Is it that texts in the feminine are haunted by the death of language? Or is it rather that masculine language is already dead since it is built on the eviction of the mother, on the absence of pre-symbolic rhythms and glossolalia? Isn't it a matter of making holes in language? Of making audible the tempo that women adopt when they speak amongst themselves, "the litany form" (Lamy 63) of their oral exchanges which doesn't respect the signifier/signified split but never tires of giving meaning to the signifier itself?

Affirm that women's language corresponds with poetic language. Affirm the poeticity of writing in the feminine conscious of its oral nature, searching for the mother. Emphasize the particular breathing of words that stick to your skin, scatter in many directions, desperately try to lose good sense, THE sense,[7] the one, the right, that are given over to the figure of speech, abandoning forever the arbitrary nature of the sign. Words that smell, far from hiding their odours, that say and visualize blood, milk, shit, make these things felt and are themselves felt, words that abandon any interest in fixed geometries, in reassuring/restraining dichotomies, so as to enter into the meanderings of a memory speaking its subconscious, its story and its utopias.

Duplicity of language? Complicitly, rather, since we are no longer dupes. We can no longer be satisfied with miming and the law. We want to invent/regain a language derived from the body, there where the mother, long before the father, labours.

♦

## NOTES

1. The French word is a neologism 'unaire,' so I've translated it as 'unary' to correspond to 'binary' and the French 'binaire.' K.M.

2. This notion is used by Julia Kristeva. She borrowed the term *chora* from Plato who defined it as: "a flexible receptacle of combinations, contradictions, and movement, necessary for the functioning of nature before the teleological intervention of God, and corresponding to the mother." For Kristeva, the semiotic *chora* "is concerned with the shape of a process, which, in order to be the subject's, crosses over the unary severance which establishes it and calls forth, in its topos, a battle of impulses, which starts it moving and endangers it." The *chora* plays "with and through the body of the mother — of the woman — but in the act of significance" (Kristeva 47).

3. Roland Barthes' term for pleasure, ecstasy, sexual pleasure. K.M.

4. literally a female-gender transvestite, the reverse of the usual. D.M.

5. The term "literary avant-garde" is understood to refer to the movement which developed in Quebec about 1965 around the literary journals *La nouvelle barre du jour* and *Les herbes rouges*. This calling nationalist poetry into question was carried out through a poetry of rupture: rupture with the preceding poetic code, formalist work, new sets of themes, new ideologies: marxism, feminism, the counter-culture, the theme of the city, of the body, of writing.

6. *matriciel*, pertaining to a matrix and by extension from *la matrice*, the womb. D.M.

7. *le sens* refers not only to sense but also to meaning and direction. D.M.

## WORKS CITED

Cardinal, Marie. *Autrement dit*. Paris: Grasset, 1978.

de Saussure, Ferdinand. *Course in General Linguistics*. Trans. Wade Baskin. New York: McGraw Hill, 1959.

Didier, Beatrice. *L'écriture-femme* (Woman Writing). Paris: Grasset, 1981.

Gagnon, Madeleine. "Mon corps dans l'écriture" (My body in writing). *La venue à l'écriture* (Coming to Writing by Hélène Cixous, Madeleine Gagnon, and Annie Leclerc) Paris: Union Générale d'Editions, 1977.

Irigaray, Luce. *Ce sex qui n'en est pas un*. Paris: Minuit, 1977.

Kristeva, Julia. *Polylogue*. Paris: Seuil, 1977.

Lamy, Suzanne. *d'elles*. Montreal: l'Hexagone, 1979.

Meschonnic, Henri. *Pour la poétique V. Poésie sans réponse*. Paris: Gallimard, 1978.

*le petit Robert*. Paris: 1969.

# Red Tin + White Tulle

## *Gail Scott*

Memory: The skull rattle of coke cans under the wedding car.

Why skull rattle? The immediate paranoia. The symbol of oft polluting technology. Coke cans. Discarded on far off desert sands. And under the wedding car.

Memory. Surfacing paranoia. Red tin + white tulle. Easily torn. But can't say so. The unconscious unwinding of woman's mind leading to ... the inexpressible. The inexpressible pain of contradiction.

I used to live in a triangle. Mother, God and me. At night, when I felt abandoned by my lovers, betrayed by my friends, I prayed. To my mother. She's a ghost. With watching, penetrating eyes. She always said ... what mothers used to say: "*You don't know how to love.*" Projecting her own adolescent fears. In a discourse of resentment and guilt. But wait. Whose discourse? And whose inadequacy was she taking on as her own and passing on to me? Boy children, the designated heirs and perpetrators of patriarchal ideology, are rarely told: " You do not know how to love." In the mouths of our mothers, it is we the daughters who are held responsible for the emotional parsimony, particularly of Protestant culture. And thus language is twisted into its opposite. "Undoubtedly, our own meanings are hidden from us," says Dale Spender in her book, *Man Made Language*. We may use the English language our whole lives without noticing the distortions.

Distortions and omissions. Surely the assertion of the true, inner self has to start with language. But what if the surfacing subconscious stream finds void instead of code? Because "of the absence of a suitable code, and because of a necessary indirectness rather than spontaneity of expression (in women), *women*, more often than may be the case with men, lack the facility to raise to the conscious level their unconscious thoughts." The words won't come. And without the words, the self. No capacity for separation. It's Ottawa. 1962. "I lie in bed with my bathing suit on. Too hot. Too cold. Now too hot. Very still. My knees drawn up in a hump. My mother taking her Sunday afternoon nap. The Sunday roast hardens in the oven" (Scott).

Mother and me. Simulated in the same skin. The vicious-circle search for boundaries in the memory-mass of borrowed phrases. Like and dislike. Her warmth, her (frightened) love. Her (my) inadequate breast. Under the padded bra. The hard roast. Incompetent females in a culture where the feminine is ... muted. Their judgements fill our silence. "Women are muted because men are in control, and the language, and the meanings, and the knowledge of women cannot be accounted for outside that control."

"Across the street Véronique Paquette walks by terriblement décolletée. The priest gives her shit every Sunday, but she still does it just the same. 'Frogs,' says my father, one of the three bank managers, all brothers. Drunkenly they flex their muscles at her from where they sit in their rocking chairs on the prairies. Then he looks up at me sitting on the verandah and shouts 'Get your nose back in that Bible, it's Sunday'" (Scott). Sex and race. Double and indivisible chauvinism.

Mother wouldn't be seated in the prairie. She's upstairs sleeping. In the orange hall there's a slogan on the wall: "*Harmony* in the family keeps order in the *nation*." Two patriarchal concepts invading her apparent silence. ("Given that language is such an influential force in shaping our world," says Spender, "it is obvious that those in power to make the symbols and the meaning are in a highly advantageous position.") Her knees are drawn up in defensive fetal tension. The knees again. I am she taking our Sunday afternoon nap. I carry her inside me as she once carried me. Two halves trying to make a whole. But her unspoken frustrations also formed the warp for my rebellion. Against what? Her all-seeing eyes socketed in the steeple of fundamentalism. Surrounded by a bevy of uncles and brothers ordering the world to suit themselves, constructing a language, a reality, a body of knowledge in which they are central figures.

Not all mothers are silent, I hear you say. None are, I answer. But they are unable to give a symbolic weight to their existence; to pass on a commanding tradition of their meanings to the world. Occupying the "muted" space in the muted/dominant paradigm of language coinage, they are not silent but unheard. "When women are 'taken care of' at the encoding level — there is no need for males malintentioned or otherwise to erase them deliberately. They are conveniently made invisible from the outset." When neo-feminists first began to explore the problems of women in patriarchy, language was considered by many to be almost neutral, requiring only minor adjustments to make it adequate for our use. But as we struggle to express ourselves in writing, in the new everyday lives we are trying to forge for ourselves, in politics, we find ourselves constantly monitoring our speech in order to be "clear." Nineteenth-century English grammarians decreed that in language the male gender is *more comprehensive*. Thus the precedence of he and man (Man shall not live by bread alone) over woman. Naturally, the more comprehensive gender has left the more comprehensive mark on language so that, as Spender says, much of thinking is androcentric.

Something about their relationship to language and culture led French-speaking women, both in Europe and in Canada, to see the problem and start challenging syntax more quickly than their English sisters. The prevailing belief that English is a "neutral," "ungendered" language may be partly responsible for our slowness. It strikes me that the masculine element in English is like the Protestant God: not immediately apparent (absent from the cross), yet somehow all-pervasive.

In the childhood image, God is inside. And Mother beside him. With their all-seeing eyes. So you can't confess. That's Protestantism. "You don't know how to love," whispers Mother. Guilty of the emotional tightness of Protestant culture. The woman's fault. Elizabeth in Margaret Atwood's *Life Before Man* is the personification of this rigidity. Uptight. Can't give. Doesn't know how to love. Translate live. Beside her, husband Nate is appealingly soft and sentimental. The Quebec simp, even. Despite her consummate skill, Atwood creates a patriarchal stereotype: the ice-cold broad. To get beyond the caricatured muted vision of her, Elizabeth would have to have been captured in the process of becoming. Not with descriptive flashbacks, but with an attention to language as it boils up from Elizabeth's subconscious depths, past the barrier of guilt that keeps women from their essential selves, towards the void, the confusion, and, unavoidably, new ways of expressing who we are.

To get beyond our "muted" state, we have to delve beyond the voices of the *other*, down to where we can hear our own. "The development of this hearing faculty and power of speech involves the dislodging of images that reflect and reinforce prevailing social arrangements," says Mary Daly. Otherwise our voices become tight and grey from listening to the wrong sounds. Listening, that debauchery that ages the face, says Colette.

I wonder if women from Catholic-dominant cultures have the same overwhelming sense of the male deity (in its symbolic sense) inside. Traditionally, He was held at bay by the priest in the confessional (which, granted, had its own set of problems). More important symbolically is the mixed blessing of His being accompanied by a feminine face: Mary. As Protestants we always felt it was progressive to unseat her, that last vestige in Christianity of a female deity. To some extent it released us from the effects of the cult of virginity. It was a simplification of the Godhead, part of the pragmatic Protestant reform that was closely linked to the development of industrialism. That reform created a situation in which we were eventually able to improve our paper existence: we could divorce, for example; practise birth control. But oh, the dilemma of reform. As we began to sneak out of our traditional roles, to exist (almost) legally, we seemed to begin to wither away in the symbolic sense. The loss of that last feminine symbol, incarnated in the prissy image of a virgin mother, cost us in terms of decreasing validation of female qualities and values (Daly). So that we end up feeling like poor replicas of a disappearing memory. "What I wanted was a natural woman" (whatever that is!). One of the trips they laid on us in the 60s. Language again. Spender says: "In language female gender is not natural."

To get a woman's hold on language again, we have to trust the female side of the double images coming at us, a mix of our subconscious and patriarchal values. The maple trees blew on the hot summer street. "The little girl stepped off the curb." The little girl crossed the street. In her mind she wrote: "The little girl crossed the street." Lucinda McVitty, the old maid, was sitting on the verandah. The little girl did not write that the *old maid* was sitting on the verandah.

Again the language void in precisely the troubled spot. I always said I would be a writer. About that my mother sent me mixed messages. I would be a communicating vessel for her and women like her (including myself, of course). But this raised the fear that I might escape the purdah of marriage. "Don't be too romantic," she said (i.e. don't be too choosy), "or you mightn't get a husband." My father said: "What's the point of sending her to university, she'll only get married." What hopes did she hold for me in the gleaming chariot parked in front of the church? Partly the old marriage symbols harkened back to the feminine ties with life and reproduction. She didn't see much evidence of these values in the outside world — which at any rate appeared completely beyond her control.

My culture included how to find the fattest raspberries on the underside of bushes, the taste of fresh trout at breakfast. And the Bible, both oppressive and ... poetic. Whatever life she and her mother before her were attempting to preserve as they sweated over their cauldrons of pickles or berries on gleaming black stoves was infused with a tremendous sadness. I watched them toil as the summer heat rose in the great halls of country houses. Halls with slogans on the walls. The homes of born-again Christians. A terrible wear on women, somehow responsible for the eternal ennui of maintaining an order not necessarily to their likeness. The internalized struggle between coded male values and under-articulated matriarchal memory. Two of them died young of cancer. Is their cancer-shrinking flesh the skull rattle I hear under the wedding car?

Her fantasy of the white chariot often appears in my own writing. But displaced. Instead of a wedding car, it's a getaway car. Fleeing from the fear of repeating her life. Le début du mépris. My love (for her) and my (self?) hate. The car carries women in search of light. But not quite free. One is driven by a cowboy. Another, carrying a mother and daughter involved in some kind of crazy search for female symbols, is smashed in a symbolic rape (from behind) by a car carrying ... Elvis. The ambiguity of the charger represents a surface layer of images leading back to forgotten memories. Down the garden path. This time taking ourselves. To where the struggle for language begins.

Particularly in the light of the interesting theoretical work that has emerged in the last few years on the subject (Daly, Spender, to name but two) the resistance to language-exploration in feminist writing in English Canada is perplexing. It seems so clear that as women we have been forced to operate in language from a negative semantic space, invisible in language, missing from the range of positive symbols. ... What choice have we then but to seize language and re-create it for ourselves? Part of the process is listening to the voices and speech patterns of women. What matters is getting in touch with our own rhythms, so different from the ticker-tape rhythm of the talking (media) world which constantly invades our consciousness. Our new voices as they emerge may sound hysterical. (And why not? The French psychoanalyst Luce Irigaray says the revolutionary potential of hysteria has not been understood.) We may find we are totally upsetting syntax, rejecting conventions like linear prose, as we delve deeper into language, discovering the images behind the images, until we hear the tinkling language of Queen Titania (dim reflection of an ancient goddess) who has turned her king into an ass. The better to be as she likes, to speak as she likes.

"As soon as we learn words we find ourselves outside them," says Sheila Rowbotham. We are aliens struggling to express a pluralistic perception of things in a language evermore honed by the dominant desire for "objectivity." Clearly, the accepted forms of journalism, criticism, prose, are no longer adequate for women.

♦

## WORKS CITED

Atwood, Margaret. *Life Before Man*. Toronto: McClelland & Stewart, 1979.

Daly, Mary. *Beyond God the Father*. Boston: Beacon Press, 1973.

Scott Gail. *Spare Parts*. Toronto: Coach House Press, 1981.

Spender, Dale. *Man Made Language*. London: Routledge and Kegan Paul, 1980.

# RE

## *Lola Lemire Tostevin*

writing as reading   (the past?)   would only be writing
without breathing a word   while writing as rereading doubles back to recall   to hear again the resonance as
re tears from the rest   reenters the mouth with quick
motions of tongue   rolls liquid   trills   laps one
syllable to the next

rereading reverses to resist   resists to reverse the
movement along the curve of return   as the well-turned
phrase turns on herself to retrace her steps   reorient
and continue in a different voice   different because she
begs to differ   what bears repeating   the peat of roots
and moss   the peculiar reek that rots into new turf   new
realms that open the fold of reply   unfold   refold the erec-
tion that yields to softer contours   relents to edge's
touch   delays to stay within the threshold of the unthought

*et aussi la douleur cuisante de remords qui mordent à*
*pleines dents entre les cuisses   douleur d'une lecture*
*qui risque sa propre décomposition vers une écriture qui*
*se recompose*

the partner/reader shifts her lingual positions from
dormant to mordant   to bite the bit between the teeth

♦ RE ♦

*si l'oeuvre s'ouvre encore une fois c'est pour mieux*
*se faire entendre*

the double movement of intention and extension of
a closed book   reopened   regenerates word for word
as the merely real opens towards the possible   towards
a promised land that reaps its own rewards   releases
all its senses to give old words new lease

to hear   to see   to smell   to taste   to touch

all cut across the undercurrent running between the
lines   the locks   the links of rock that lie near
the surface   the collocation of coral reefs   (arms
of the sea ?)   that fasten to hold recollections full
of creeks and reaches   stretch the point just beyond
reach   to catch the refraction   the change of direction
as images shift in the distance   the two stances   when
the literal   (the bedded down)   and the reformulation
of the form are caught together in the act

to touch the oscillations around the bone of contention

or as I've already written within and around another
space the gap gasps meanings across her entire range
as each one enters obliquely between the line of quest
ioning and the eye realigned

the point of no return often leads to a different
point of view

*point de repère*   refathering   remothering the landmark
as the text in transit   in translation   from the writer
to the reader remarks in passing   the sign where myth
and place no longer meet   the blank expression which
suddenly reveals the false logos of monologic speech
the marching step that marks in place all time and space

to refuse what's been left within the shadow of a doubt
is to fuse again the shape    (of a body?)    deprived of
light    defined by limits    as it follows the leader
the reader    to the writing on the wall    the recognition that
the cog can never slip into the freudian    can never plead of
being    elsewhere at the present time

to let the libido ad lib is but an alibi

*le texte repoussé n'est pas un texte rejeté*
but one formed in relief by pressing    repressing the
other side    hammering the point home    homing    the
home-coming    (of pigeons?)    carrying the unknown
message in low repeated cries of coo    to recoup the
loss    recover the reserved space    the reign of foreign
the remote    the may    the must    the might of mote    *le mot*
that place of meeting where rumours flourish    in a manner
of speaking

the urgency of writing with a vengeance    revenge
it's only human you said    an eye for an eye    a word
for a word    writing that repels the peels of laughter
rebels    bell-mouths to bellow    to howl in the hollow
the holocryptic cipher that gives no clue to the reader
with the missing key    the second tone of *ré*    riding
on *do*'s    back    close on the heels of *mi*    up and down
the diatonic scale of C    to see the tune to which the
text is set    to hear the beat    the beating hollow
that allows the verb "to write" reverberate

to speak the missing spoke that revolves around the
spoken frame of reference    ferret out what lurks in
silence    out of sight    out of mind    out of the corner
of one eye    the optical illusion    (a ray of light?)
which the text reflects

♦ RE ♦

the knee-jerking reflex that travels back to the subject
in question   travels with the flexibility of a book that
can speak for itself   wear itself like a second skin
recapture the tense   the inner tensions that went without
saying   into all that remains to be said   as the re of
desire reverses   into the erotic sequence of a sentence
into the consequential climax of the writer   over and over

(once more?)

♦

# WRITING OUR WAY
# THROUGH THE LABYRINTH

*Daphne Marlatt*

Writing and Reading. two of the three R's every child learns in school (forgetting, for the moment, that one of the two begins with 'w'). writing and reading go together like speaking and hearing. ancient uses of the eye, the hand, the one informing the other. i was taught to write whole, taught to form the letters of words that together formed lines of poetry, deciphering as i went what the words meant, following the curve of syntax, its twists and turns, as i made the curving up-and-down of letters forming words: *Slowly, silently, now the moon/ Walks the night in her silver shoon ...* (de la Mare)

and so caught from then on, intrigued by the twists and turns of the labyrinth of language. an ancient structure i found my way into (or my teachers led me to, leaving me alone with the thread in my hands), full of interconnecting passageways, trap-doors, melodious charms, vivid and often incomprehensible images on the walls, all of them pointing, pointing me further along — the thread, the desire to know, *gnō*—, narrative, tugging in my hands. life-line (trying to make sense of it all). the pull of syntax ("arranged in order") i felt my way by. trying to find something familiar, something i recognized: so i could be found in the midst of all these meanings pointing elsewhere.

later as i began to write (compose) poetry, i learned that writing involves reading or hearing all the language is saying that i am "lost" in and writing my way through. as if the labyrinth were itself an inner ear, a sensory organ i feel my way by (sentence, *sentire*, to feel), keeping my feet by a labyrinthine sense of balance as the currents of various meaning, the "drift," swirl me along. of course the labyrinth is filled with fluid, as the membranous labyrinth of the inner ear is. women know the slippery feel of language, the walls that exclude us, the secret passageways of double meaning that conduct us into a sense we understand, reverberant with hidden meaning, the meaning our negated (in language) bodies radiate. bodies that possess no singular authoritative meaning but a meaning that is multiplicit, multilabial, continuously arrived at.

labyrinth: a structure consisting of a number of intercommunicating passages, arranged in a bewildering complexity ... labyrinth: "not a maze to get lost in; it had only one path, traversing all parts of the figure" (Walker 523). labyrinth: a continuous walking that folds back on itself and in folding back moves forward. labyrinth: earth-womb, underground, a journeying to the underworld and back. House of the Double Axe, sceptre of the Cretan Moon-Goddess (here she is again, in her silver shoon). intercommunicating passages circling back.

but these are images on the walls. and if we remove a few bricks? writing goes back to a Germanic word, *wrītan*, meaning to tear, scratch, cut, incise. it is the act of the phallic singular, making its mark on things (stone, wood, sand, paper). leaving its track. "I was here," the original one in the world. reading goes back to Indo-European *ar-*, to fit together, appears in Old English as *raēdan*, to advise, explain, read. advise and care for seem to be enduring aspects of its meaning and still survive in the word rede, counsel or advice given, a decision taken by one or more persons; or, to govern, take care of, save, take counsel together. always there is this relating to others. even in the usual sense of read, "to look over or scan (something written, printed, etc.) with the understanding of what is meant by the letters or signs," there is this relating what the writer meant to what the reader understands, a commune-ication writing seems not to carry from its root. this deep desire to "stand in for" (the other), to understand something other than what one knows oneself, comes to the fore in such phrases as reading the future, reading someone's palm. "The sense of considering or explaining something obscure or mysterious is also common to the various languages, but the application of this to the interpretation of ordinary writing, and to the expression of this in speech, is confined to Eng. and ON (Old Norse) (in the latter perhaps under Eng. influence)," says the OED. reading what we are in the mi(d)st of. reading the world. reading one's body, that vast text (60,000 miles of veins and arteries). writing, the act of the singular, and reading, the act of the plural, of the more than one, of the one in relation to others.

in a time when language has been appropriated by the Freudians as intrinsically phallic,[1] it seems crucial to reclaim it through what we know of ourselves in relation to writing. writing can scarcely be for women the act of the phallic signifier, its claim to singularity, the mark of the capital I (was here). language is no "tool" for us, no extension of ourselves, but something we are "lost" inside of. finding our way in a labyrinthine moving with the drift, slipping through claims to one-track meaning so that we can recover multiple related meanings, reading between the lines. finding in write, rite, growing out of *ar-*, that fitting together at the root of read (we circle back), moving into related words for arm, shoulder (joint), harmony — the music of connection. making our way though all parts of the figure, using our labyrinthine sense, we (w)rite our way *ar-* way, "reading" it, in intercommunicating passages.

♦

## NOTES

1. "...the linear, grammatical, linguistic system that orders the symbolic, the superego, the law. It is a system based entirely on one fundamental signifier: the phallus," (Gauthier 162).

## WORKS CITED

de la Mare, Walter. "Silver"

Gauthier, Xavière. *New French Feminisms*. Eds. Elaine Marks and Isabelle de Courtivron. New York: Schocken, 1981.

Walker, Barbara, ed. *The Woman's Encyclopedia of Myths and Secrets*. New York: Harper & Row, 1983.

# Certain Words

*Nicole Brossard*

*Translated by Barbara Godard*

In the midst of the worst misfortunes, the most audacious nights of adoration, tragic death, the softest of skins, by the shores of many seas, clad in a utopian body and ecstasies, we make our way forward on the relief of words, adroit between the sharp coral of the Isla de las Mujeres. Clothed in a woman's body, we bide our time patiently at the edge of the pages, awaiting a feminine presence. With our wet fingers, we turn the pages. We are expecting truth to flash forth.

From one reading to another, words form relays as if to test our endurance for an *idée fixe*, for the few images we have of ourselves, images applicable to us only within the fictive space of our particular version of reality. From one reading to another, we fabulate fictions of our desire, that is, we identify what makes us go into raptures and what plunges us into such a state of "indescribable" fervour.

When this fervour takes hold of us, we say we are captivated by our reading and we advance slowly/rashly towards our destiny. Our destiny is like a project, a life woven into us by innumerable lines some of which are called lines of the hand holding (the) volume. These lines innervate our whole body like a logic of the senses. Right in the middle of reading, we recognize (being) the cause and origin of the faces and landscapes surrounding us for we make allusion to them as to a childhood, a desire, an inclination. Absorbed in our reading, we hear murmurs, entreaties, cries: we hear our voice searching for its horizon.

In our readings, there are mauves, some indigo, dreadful looks, women adorned in jewels and silence. There are experienced bodies. Troubling apparitions. We open and close our eyes on them in the hope of a sonorous sequence or a conversation. All our fervour surges into this conversation so truth may be manifested.

Amidst all the rhetoric, the logic of the senses, the paradoxes and sensation of becoming, we make headway through our intention of form. In the middle of the night, we sometimes wake up to reread a passage, to see again the women we desire. While we are rereading the underlined passage, an "indescribable" feeling arises in our breast and keeps us wide-awake until dawn. At dawn, our spirit is extravagant and wanders into forbidden zones we have no choice but to explore. Some women write at dawn when they are in this state, I've been told. Sometimes they burst into tears.

"I know the rhythms of the voice, I know its rising and falling. I know the adventure and experiment of the gaze." Towards this we are transported with each reading, incredulous before truth which, like a memory of the shadow and the fervour, flashes in on us.

The words we remark may be applied to us and fill us with agitation and pleasure. These words are revelations, enigmas and directions. We transform them according to a process which escapes our consciousness yet our consciousness is enlightened by this approach. Women reading, we become a text's allusion and inclination.

What animates us in a sentence or an expression is a decision to be (it). Rapidly, then, we develop an inclination for the text so as to realize the gesture of our desire there in the heat of action. Each intense reading is a radius of action where we surprise unanimity in the process of forming in us.

Among the axes, the equations, the intoxicating audacities and light we meet, we advance in our reading as in theory we become what we desire. We make our way towards a subtle and complex woman who reflects the processes and form of development of our thinking. Words are a way of devouring the desire which devours us with comparisons taking us to where we become the desire of science and the science of consciousness.

When we turn the pages with our wet fingers, moving from dread to ecstasy, we confront eternity, believers and sceptics before the entire sum of bodies, skulls, orgasms; we affront the beyond of the whole and we become the precision of desire in the unnarratable space of the brain.

Really, the sensational effect of reading is a feeling we can't quite express except by underlining it. *The intimacy of eternity is an intrigue we invent with each reading.* Every reading is an intention of images, an intention of re-presentation giving us hope.

♦ NICOLE BROSSARD ♦

CERTAIN WORDS MUST BE SAID, 1976
PHOTOGRAPHY BY DUANE MICHALS

Claire;
  I've spent the night reading your new book. I've made it my book. There are so many annotations in it that nobody else can use the copy you sent me. I'm incapable of telling you precisely why I love this book. However, I will be able to write a critical piece on it for October. I live this paradox as a strangeness of knowledge, as an indisposition of writing.
      Love,
        Nicole

©1980 DUANE MICHALS
PRINTED BY RAPAPORT PRINTING CORP
©FOTOFOLIO, BOX 661 CANAL STA. NY, NY 10013
DM6

♦ CERTAIN WORDS ♦

Claire Text has just published one of the most beautiful books in our literature. In a narrative of ............................................
................................................................................................................
....................the improbable affirmation ..................................
............................. nothing to change ......................................
.............................................................................................like
a proposition of existence ...................................................
............................ The beauty of the writing ........................
Those landscapes by the seaside ........................................
............................................................................................ descriptions ............................ an effect .....................................................
.................................... techniques .................................................
allusion ................................ Must read .......................................

image. **Thirst is a delirium in the body.** Everything is tangled around the swimming pool followed by the redhead's long monologue about her childhood. 'Listen, listen closely to me,' then there are twenty pages of writing in the first person in an intimate tone. The passage would be easy to translate except for some otherwise simple word like water, heat, breast. **A question of atmosphere.** She had to work around the expression 'my mother' and through a trick of syntax make 'very young' accompanied by the verb 'to be' precede the word 'breast': she also had to do it in such a way that in the reading attention would be given simultaneously to the voice and the jewel in the form of a butterfly "when she interrupted her reading to tell me that it was night now." Formerly, the pages filed past/made off with the family, a manhunt on the highway along the horizon, the noise of sirens, then a mood, an agitation and the passion transformed into signs, a tattoo on the shoulder, the excesses. She was somewhere else. **In the blazing of words at full speed.**

# Theorizing Fiction Theory

*Barbara Godard, Daphne Marlatt,
Kathy Mezei and Gail Scott*

Feminist consciousness made me question reality and fiction. For example, when I was writing *L'Amèr*, I felt that I had to move reality into fiction because patriarchal reality made no sense and was useless to me. I also had the impression and the certainty that my fictions were reality — they are full of meaning — and that from there I could start a theoretical work. That's why I called the book "une fiction théorique."

— Nicole Brossard

Strategies of writing and reading are forms of cultural resistance. Not only can they work to turn dominant discourses inside out (and show that it can be done) ... they also challenge theory in its own terms, the terms of a semiotic space constructed in language, its power based on social validation and well-established modes of enunciation and address.

— Teresa de Lauretis

"There she goes scrambling over the barrier/slash." (Kathy Mezei) Invading, appropriating, violating the rule of binary oppositions that governs our system of logic and erects hierarchies. The feminist reader gone co-creator. Turned writer. And what does she create?

♦ BARBARA GODARD, DAPHNE MARLATT,
KATHY MEZEI AND GAIL SCOTT ♦

Fiction/theory: the record of her reading, a reading *with* rather than *about* the text.

In Writing as Reading/L'Écriture comme lecture, *Tessera* No. 2, the feminist reader/critic/writer asserted her active presence in shaping the text. Fiction/theory, *Tessera* No. 3, continues the discussion of feminist strategies of appropriation with a shift in emphasis from the reception point in the communicative process to that of the message. Given the complex nature of feminist interaction with the text which explodes categories and genres, what form of hybrid text is produced? Writing. It's work. Changing the relationship with language. No longer a statement of truth but words which construct truth. Disrupting the nature of the relationship between the act of enunciation and the enounced. Theory interwoven with symbols (fiction). Imagination. Fictions. Multiple texts, integral.

Women's fictions raise theoretical issues: women's theorizing appears as/in fiction. Women's writing disturbs our usual understanding of the terms fiction and theory which assign value to discourses. Detached from their ordinary contexts, established meanings become suspect. By inciting the reader to rethink her/his presence within that "social reality" women writers effect a disturbance in those constructions that work at keeping us all in our "proper" places.

Theory / Fiction / Fiction-Theory / Fiction/Theory ... The texts cross over the slash in all directions and in every permutation. Together they demonstrate that writing as research is a major characteristic of contemporary feminist writing. However, as the more critical and theoretical articles suggest, Quebec and English-Canadian women are not Siamese twins: the common ground of these pages masks divergence. Fiction/theory has been the dominant mode of feminist writing in Quebec for more than a decade. Feminism allied with post-modernism to provide the impetus for understanding the negotiable meaning of the text. Currently fiction/theory is being re-examined by younger women writers who have taken up their pens under the aegis of theoretical fiction and who feel less urgency to defend its position on the literary scene. On the contrary, younger English-Canadian women writers are coming to fiction/theory with a pleasure in discovery all the more marked in light of the critical invisibility suffered by the few more established

practitioners of fiction/theory in English Canada. In both cases, the occasion is one for question and exploration, for upsetting categories and hierarchies, for refusing one's "proper place." Here, "theory and practice are united in the writing and the reading."
— B.G.

It occurs to me that since I like some of Barbara's comments on the unmediated body and Gail's on text, how about extracting some of these — also Daphne's and mine from earlier and current responses, and compiling them into a commentary to accompany Barbara's introduction to the issue — a sort of dialogue?
— K.M., *March 18, 1986*

There is the problem that English-Canadian and Quebec would-be-participants in *Tessera* often have a lack of knowledge about what each is doing in theory, in fiction.
— D.M., *December 12, 1985*

Last week I saw Cheryl Sourkes about her photographs. She brought along some extraordinary ones to show me. One that would do very well for a cover. It has the text of Mary Had a Little Lamb fading into a spiral with fragments of words from theory on the other wing of the triptych: a perfect illustration of our theme. She also had a sequence of seven images which worked on text and letters, mostly texts dealing with Lacanian theory, in French, about the construction of the self, especially the construction of the female self. This might form a "narrative critical sequence: — visually." Or one for a cover.
— B.G., *December 13, 1985*

In soliciting the Quebec texts, I began to realize there has been a slippage in meaning (or at least in the practice of) *fiction theory*. Younger women writers (I mean younger than Nicole Brossard who really invented the term) like novelist Geneviève Letarte or poet Anne-Marie Alonzo are not discussing theory directly in their texts. You will even see, I think, in the future writing by some writers of Brossard's generation, something of a swing towards fiction where the theory is *entendu* rather than directly engaged. This is partly

♦ BARBARA GODARD, DAPHNE MARLATT,
KATHY MEZEI AND GAIL SCOTT ♦

because here the theoretical discussion has done its work to a certain extent: i.e. it has altered the relationship of the feminine subject (in the text) to language —, by affirming the *otherness* of her voice. As one contributor put it: "The theory has been assimilated into the form. So the permission exists (i.e. *women* have given *themselves* permission) here for an ongoing troubled and challenging relationship to discourse in the text, which can of course operate on many levels other than that of direct theoretical discussion — although the theoretical awareness (which happens in and through the writing) is a necessary prerequisite. The existence of this permission currently represents, I believe, an important difference between writing in the feminine in Quebec and in English-Canada."

— G.S., *March 12, 1985*

I also wonder if some women writers are trying too hard to write like they think they should — just tossing out a thought; after all we don't want prescriptive or formulaic writing either.

— K.M., *December 16, 1985*

There is a slippage occurring in a number of essays in the same direction towards the unmediated body. Some texts keep insisting on the mind/body blur of fiction/theory and not on the blur of genres, the dismantling of codes, of textual politics. That is, there is an implication that one can experience the body and write about bodily experience as something lived —a social text. And language — also heavily coded — is the means through which this experience is being communicated. Feminist biology is concerned with laying bare the

---

Fiction theory: Nicole Brossard uses "fiction" negatively in *L'Amèr* to imply that diction constructs created by the patriarchy and compliant women in which women are made into objects, But her "fiction théorique" is something else — the text is both fiction and theory — a theory working its way through syntax, language and even narrative of a female as subject, a fiction in which theory is woven into the texture of the creation, eliminating or trying to, distinctions between genres, between prose, essay, poetry, between fiction and theory.

— K.M.

codes through which the female bodily experience has been constructed, and feminist writers are also trying to subvert the codes that have governed the re-presentation of this body in literature. The only bodies in question in the literary act are the writer's body holding the pen which makes the marks on the page and the reader's body turning the pages in her hand and perceiving the black marks with her eye. The materiality of the text — the white pages stamped with ink and bound between a cardboard cover — is the literary body under examination. The slippage towards the unmediated body brings with it the danger of nominalism, of an essential feminism that would embrace a direct relationship between word and thing and so ignore the lesson of modernism about the impossibility of language ever representing reality, a concept on which fiction/theory builds. (See Nemeth's essay, "Present or Re-present?") The introduction of the unmediated body heralds the appearance of naïve narrative not fiction/theory. See Suzanne Lamy's discussion of this problem in "Capitalising: theory/FICTION THEORY/novel" where innocent novels are contrasted to self-reflexive theoretical fictions.

— B.G., *February 12, 1986*

Suzanne Lamy's text underscore the changes that have been taking place in "fiction theory," or as it is called in French: *fiction théorique* or *théoretique* (both terms are used in French). By the way, in French, the emphasis is on fiction, not theory. That is, the noun in French is *fiction*, the adjective *théorique* is what qualifies it.

Already in the last issue I wanted to say something in the liminaire about the differences existing in Quebec and Canada among women writers on the subject of writing in the feminine. This time I think the texts themselves are going to force us to be more clear (I almost said "honest" — because I feel we've been sloughing over this somewhat). For starters, the concept of *fiction théorique* in Quebec is ten years old. This, as I already said and as Lamy also says, has given it time to affect writing without any longer being continually visible on the surface.

Secondly, on the subject of criticism, I've noticed a tendency on the part of some English-Canadian critics to try to fit a great variety of works by women into the grid of post-modern feminist writing whether they belong there (or indeed want to belong there) or not.

♦ Barbara Godard, Daphne Marlatt,
Kathy Mezei and Gail Scott ♦

An essay we recently received on Anne Hébert comes to mind. I think the grid we are talking about implies an awareness on both a

---

fiction theory: a corrective lens which helps us see *through* the fiction we've been conditioned to take for the real, fictions which have not only constructed woman's "place" in patriarchal society but have constructed the very "nature" of woman (always that which has been). fiction *theory* deconstructs these fictions while *fiction* theory, conscious of itself as fiction, offers a new angle on the "real," one that looks from inside as fiction, offers a new angle on the "real," one that looks from inside out rather than outside in (the difference between woman as subject and woman as object). this is not to say that fiction theory is busy constructing a new ideology, a new "line" — indeed (in-action) suspicious of correct lines, of claims to a pre-emptive real, it enters a field where the "seer" not only writes it like she sees it but says where she is seeing from — and with whom (now) and for whom (soon to be). this is where *vision* in that other sense enters in, that which is also and could be. fictions that focus our becoming (real). grounded in an analysis of the actual (theory).

— D.M.

---

language and political level that is clear in the text. Although, even as I say this, I realize my reading of work is from a very Québécois perspective, and the same work read, say from a western or northern perspective, for example, may produce a very different impression. Still, the tandems FICTION/POLITICAL AWARENESS/LANGUAGE-WRITING are key, and if we don't keep our terms straight, the lack of rigour will only land us in total confusion.

The relative newness of the debate in English-Canada has certain advantages as well as the disadvantage of having started considerably later. One of my most exciting discoveries in doing *Tessera* is in fact what I am learning personally about the interesting new directions writing in the feminine is starting to take in English Canada.

— G.S., *February 19, 1986*

I like Gail's comments on fiction theory, especially since in French, English too, fiction is first, perhaps the point is that *théorique* is the adjective — modifying, explaining, affecting the fiction ... and her piece works well because it is both fiction and theory, raising good questions about the relation between fiction (and its different forms — essay, novel, autobiography, etc.) and theory, and the notion of the relation between fiction (theory) and the real which others, Lamy, e.g. raise covertly or textually.

Although Gail's piece gives me new hope, I do think that fragmented texts obsessed with subject (and subjectivity) expressed in word play, word definition, obscurity and difficulty are at a dead end, and begin to sound the same. I get tired of bodies, menstruation, and childbirth (especially as sexual pleasure) — that's why Yolande Villemaire's last novel, *Constellation de la cygne*, tells a story (though I abhor its subject — Jews, Nazis in France during the 40s — it's exploitative and pornographic).

— K.M., *March 18, 1986*

It seems to me that a preoccupation with "story" *within* a feminist investigation of framing and narratology, of how that story got to be "the" story, is one of the arenas of fiction-theory, moving back and forth between prose (which tends to focus on larger areas of telling like "plot," "character," "structure") and poetry (which zooms in on language and what language, on the micro-level, is saying) seems to be indicative of what we're after for this issue. Plus all the polarities — quest and stasis, self and other, fiction and fact — constantly slipping those dichotomized terms in and out of each other — a "telling" telling. Surely that "telling" quality is exactly what fiction theory works to uncover in the very fictions it works with.

I'm very conscious as i write this of how much i'm responding through the filter of my own writing interest, which i suppose is inescapable for each of us, whether it's writing interests or critical interests. One responds strongly to what one recognizes, after all. And that brings me to the big question about how to speak, editori-

---

Fiction theory: a narrative, usually self-mirroring, which exposes, defamiliarizes and/or subverts the fiction and gender codes determining the re-presentation of women in literature and in this way contributes to feminist theory. This narrative works upon the codes of language (syntax, grammar, gender-coded diction, etc.), of the self (construction of the subject, self/other, drives,

♦ BARBARA GODARD, DAPHNE MARLATT,
KATHY MEZEI AND GAIL SCOTT ♦

etc.), of fiction (characterization, subject, matter, plots, closure, etc.), of social discourse (male/female relations, historical formations, hierarchies, hegemonies) in such a way as to provide a critique and/or subvert the dominant tradition that within a patriarchal society has resulted in a de-formed representation of women. All the while it focuses on what language is saying and interweaves a story. It defies categories and explodes genres.

— B.G.

---

ally, of the difference between Quebec & English-Canada in contemporary feminist writing — i think it's much more a real difference in the development, a difference of real concerns. the ongoing discourse is different & each writer naturally writes *into* that discourse, certainly, the elision of the fictional & the real is a big concern in the discourse in English-Canada, with an ongoing attempt to reverse or deconstruct the two. the theoretical is more problematic, especially for women writers (perhaps because it is critical, in all senses?). except for a few key figures, like Atwood and Webb, the "critical" has been kept separate from the "creative," as if one might taint the other — which is a misunderstanding of just how critical the critical is. i mean here that intersection of philosophy, politics, poetics, etc. which, whether acknowledged or not, determines any writer's stance to the world she finds herself in.

— D.M., *March 21, 1986*

... it seems strange to me to talk about the scene now being post-feminist and not into fiction theory in Quebec while English-Canadian literature is. There is not really a gap between the two literatures. There are many women writers in English Canada who are working the fictional-real edge not fiction-theory though the authors in question are feminists. However, in this issue we are privileging some of the writers and critics who are writing fiction-theory. Everything depends on the cuts and selections made. We could just as easily have presented a different picture of the Quebec scene if we had chosen different writers. I see the division as fields of possibilities in which one area or another may be prominent at a particular moment, largely because of the critical focus the literary institution directs on it. This is where the gap exists, in the criticism and in the critical values being advanced. The example we could cite of this is the reception of Daphne's work and that of innumerable other avant-garde women writers. It's not that nothing has been written in English but that the institution has ignored it ...

As I see it, Brossard's practice in *L'Amèr* (*These Our Mothers*) is at an extreme in presenting feminist theory and fiction intermingled. Many women's fictions which remain more within the framework of traditional narrative nonetheless defamiliarize and make strange many of the fictions which govern women's lives and especially the

---

Fiction/theory: fiction that contains within it a feminist examination, even self-consciousness, regarding the material of the text, the language. So that one writes in it (the language), through it, even losing oneself in it, but always with an awareness (leading to discoveries one willingly shares with the reader) about the state of this context/syntax.

— G.S.

---

conventions which these fictions impose on the novel as genre ... (Money is one of these fictions, another is the free play of the market place, or the value of self development, the symbols and myths that bind our society together.) This is why I see the debate in a number of papers as central to the argument of fiction theory, showing the *disruptive* nature of women's fictions — e.g. Verduyn. I do not share the view that only very recent writers are doing this sort of deconstructive work. I think that careful readings of many women's texts from the past show the way they problematize the fictional order on which gender roles are based. The monetary system is a fiction generally accepted by our society and not highly problematic, according to Brossard: it becomes so in the heroine's plot in a narrative which is the marriage plot where men's money matters enormously to eighteenth-century women because, in selecting a husband, they choose a life for themselves. This points to the different relationships men and women have to money in the symbolic order ... Women's resistance to plot goes back a long way, in fact it is one of the perennial elements in women's writing, introducing the subversion of categories, the undecidability that is a major characteristic of fiction theory *à la Brossard*. What a careful feminist criticism must do is to point out the resistance to plots and the subversion that occur in forerunner texts, the ways in which women have strained within the straitjackets of the concepts of woman and self in narrative, and consequently how the very concept of character became problematic in women's writing even before Gertrude Stein and the feminist-modernist project of fiction/theory. I think we should encourage contributions about the way resistance to the discourse on woman dominant in our society is exhibited in writers like Frances Brooke or Anna Jameson or Marion Engel.

— B.G., *March 27, 1986*

# It Was Not a Dark and Stormy Night

*Smaro Kamboureli*
*for Patrick Friesen*

*Theoria / theorein*: not language degree zero; not empty signifiers; not things minus tissue; not tongue minus body. Behold. Be. Hold. Being a spectator.[1]

Theory: to contextualize the personal; to articulate the emotive; to retrieve the drowned self from within the self; to cry without guilt or shame; to talk about "me" without losing "my" privacy. How to hold away the fear of being found out.[2]

The split between theory and writing (fiction/poetry) has often assumed the same configuration with the split between mind and body.[3]

---

1. How to make I-love-you synchronous with theorein. How to love the one in the many, how to love the many in the one.

2. Freud is not the name of my shadow.

3. The fissures are the same gaps producing the same silence there is no safety net for the writer there is no wall for the ladder to lean on.

Theory as genre begets its own iconography. Yes, it does rehandle itself.[4]

Does theory (re)tell what the writer has left untold? Does it express without creating? Does it tell a parallel story?[5]

---

4. over and over and over. again. and again. and then. now. before. tomorrow. there is no end. i've known that. there is no end of the inside of the body becoming a knot the shape of I-am-thinking of the mind reaching the hard core it didn't know it had. like the stone of a cherry. small but smooth but hard. like its name. sometimes it hurts. sometimes it doesn't. have you tried squeezing blood out of a stone? have you tongued the sharp edges of a rock idling on a beach?

5. the corner of grief. the corner of meditation. the corner of reading. of chewing my nails. of making love. of eating crackers and cheese preferably feta hard salty and white breathing through its tiny pores brie is second choice. the creased corner of the couch. holding me with patience. sometimes even with reverence. it is theorizing me. how to mother the abjected self. it doesn't matter if this is not theory. it still is.

Theory often belongs to the genre of the fantastic. Its hesitation does not belong to the order of the real as the act of theorein reveals it to me. This is why I often translate myself into theoria, why I give my ambiguity the name of the uncanny.[6]

The self can never be theorized/thematized. It is what practises the act of theorein. The minute I start writing all precise margins are liquefied. The page is a littoral line. Solitude becomes the writing I's name. I am one and many. Skin touches nothing. Nothing touches it. I may even cease to exist. The S exists. The name becomes a signature. I cannot authorize or be authorized. The writer is the sumtotal of the residue of desire. The woman behind the writer has tasted desire at the moment of its death. There is no virginity in the history of beginnings. This woman is (still) (dying).[7]

---

6. This is not personal. I am not the I. This page is not a mirror. Mirrors are false exits. This page is a screen belonging both to the inside and to the outside. I'm just passing through. This page is the sieve that thins out the air I breathe. I dwindle into an otherness that cannot meet me. I theorô myself. Language rests on the tip of my tongue. Theoria weighs lightly on my eyelids.

eyes / tongue / language
:
the outside / what tastes the image (eïdolon) / the taste

The fictionality of theory; the truth of fiction.

7. How many times have I gone through this. Untying the naughts. Attempting the impossible. Pain is good for you, little one. The voice a cherry stone. The lips the delicate lines of lust without object. My heel a warm, unwanting fist inside the hand. (The the defines the bitter taste of my theorein in the feminine.) I've dreamt of sacrificing dreams to the altar of desire. I've dreamt of Nike's face — an icon of terror. I've slept on the same marble bed with Louvre's Hermaphroditus. I no longer love myself. I could be any woman. I am not an enigma. I could change places with my double — if only I knew where to find her. I could even be myself.

I've been told I'm Electra. It was in a damp basement apartment lit with the cold light of a bare bulb. I ran out and down the steep street and when I reached the university campus I was out of breath, my limbs shaking. It was a matter of theory, only I didn't know this at the time. That night I remembered that someone (my aunt?) had taken me to see Kakoyannis' *Electra* when I was a child. Eirini Pappas' classic face leaning over the ground; her cutting her hair off, the gesture of mourning. This mythic scenario is now one of my recurring daydreams. Only I don't know whether I mourn mother, father, brother, lover or my own death.[8]

Theory and fiction are each other's doubles. "Narcissistic narratives."[9]

---

8. Death has no face. Occasionally, it takes the shape of an endless sentence, its length extended by nots. A rope of words binding nothing. A figure without body. It could be desire. It could be the image of freedom. It could be dying. It could be love.

9. Even though my words may have turned against me, this is not the story of *femina vita*.

Theory and writing. Their intercourse is the paradigm of my life as long as it avoids overdetermination. As long as it doesn't try to beget my other.[10]

Do-be-do-be-do.[0]

---

10. This is both theory and praxis. (Rhetoric is not a source of theory.)

◆

# IMPUNITY: DISTANCE AS AN ETHIC

*Line McMurray*

*Translation: Richard Lebeau / Louise Ladouceur*

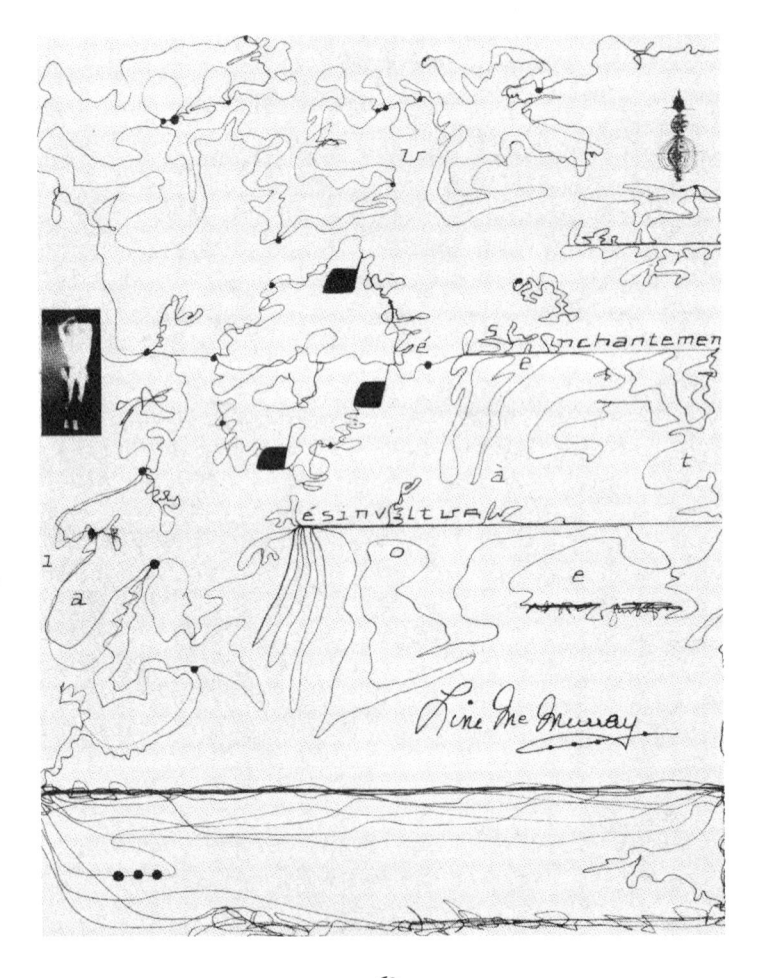

♦ Distance as an Ethic ♦

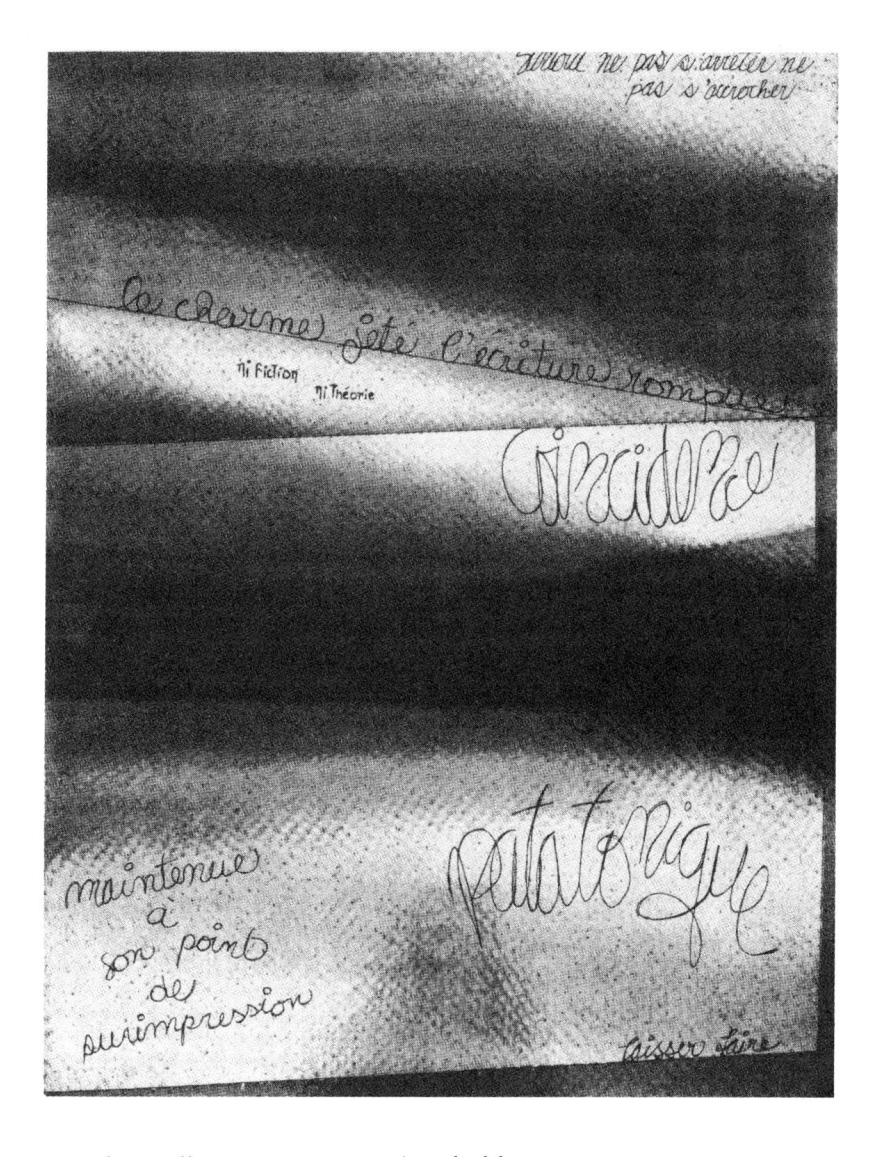

above all not to stop not   /   to hold on
to  /   the spell cast the written word
breaks free   /   neither fiction nor theory
/   coincidence   /   patatonic   /   maintained
at its point of superimposition   /   let go

### ♦ LINE MCMURRAY ♦

therein withdrawing the i dissolves into
the text / altered (by) the reality of
its fiction theory its
fiction-theory its theory-fiction / the
state ... of the psychic question ...
destates ... / therein fiction
(tra)verses its mediumlike counterpart /
self-excluded from oneself exulted
shivering back to the swirl

♦ DISTANCE AS AN ETHIC ♦

... inary curvaceously outlined and under
suspicion / the initial occurence:
language / flux ... in the
(re)conversion ... flux ... flux ...
flux ... / at the very moment / of
theory (into fiction) / of fiction ( into
theory) / this occurrence takes its name
... — according to the speed of the
thought the attachment to the reality
the written word is alienated by its
fantasies — in the conversion of the ego
into the written word / to illuminate
the imaginary

## ♦ Line McMurray ♦

theory-fiction when we don't know how to name the ecstasy derived from the inner eloquence of discourse / (TO) DISCOURSE: to program the ego the written word the information to transmit an energetic charge / to metamorphose into written rhythm / (a)head each step towards / seizing control of the body / in such a way that the entire body becomes a discourse (in)deed

♦ Distance as an Ethic ♦

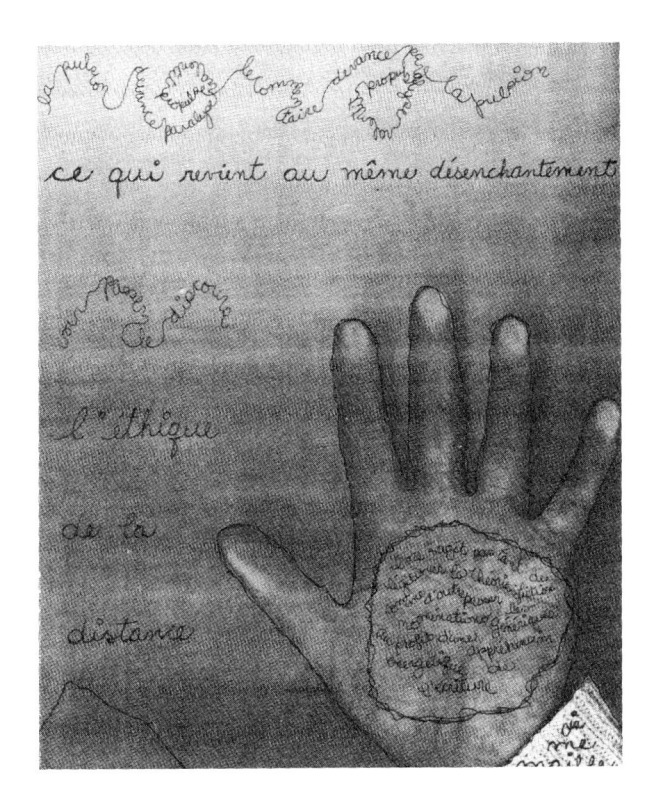

the urge precedes paralyzes restrains
propels the commentary precedes
paralyzes restrains propels the urge /
which amounts to the same disenchantment
/ watching the discourse pass by /
distance as an ethic / it is not as much
a question of legitimizing the
theory-fiction as of going beyond the
generic to the benefit of an energetic
apprehension of the written word / my
body's woven mesh

### ♦ Line McMurray ♦

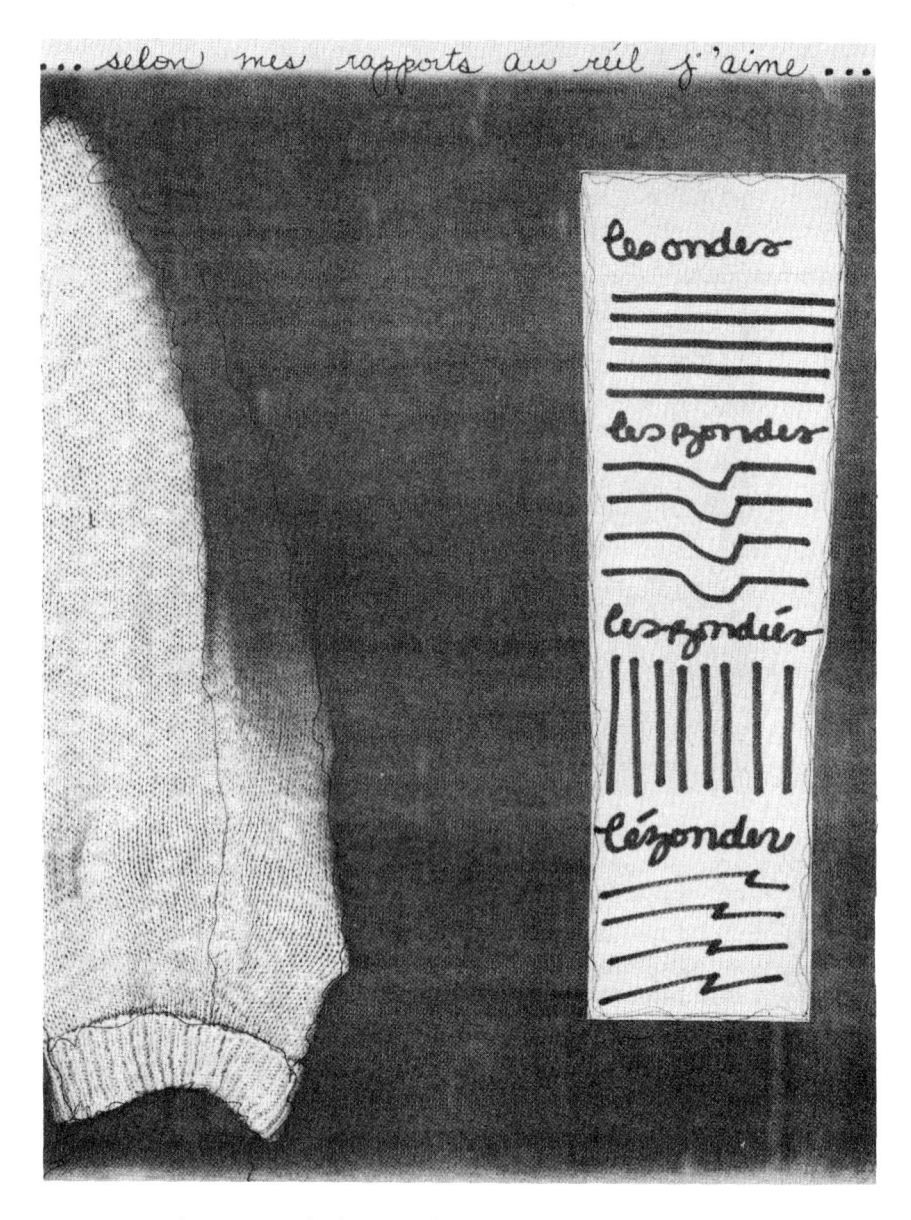

*... selon mes rapports au réel j'aime ...*

according to my links to reality i love
... / the waves dewaves the waves
dewaved dewaves waved

♦ Distance as an Ethic ♦

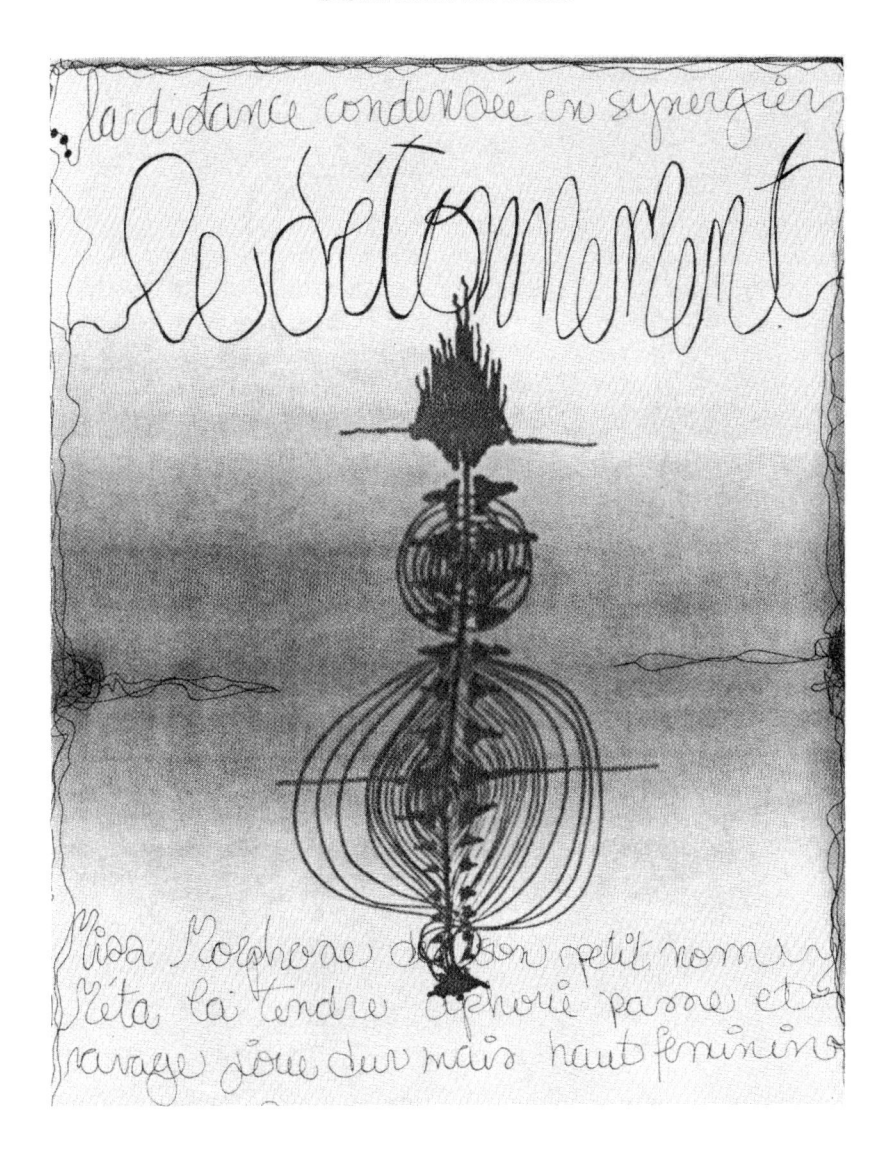

... condensed distance synergetic /
CLASHTOUNDING Miss Morphosis is her first
name Meta the soft aphoria passing by
ravages plays hard but feminine held
high

♦ LINE MCMURRAY ♦

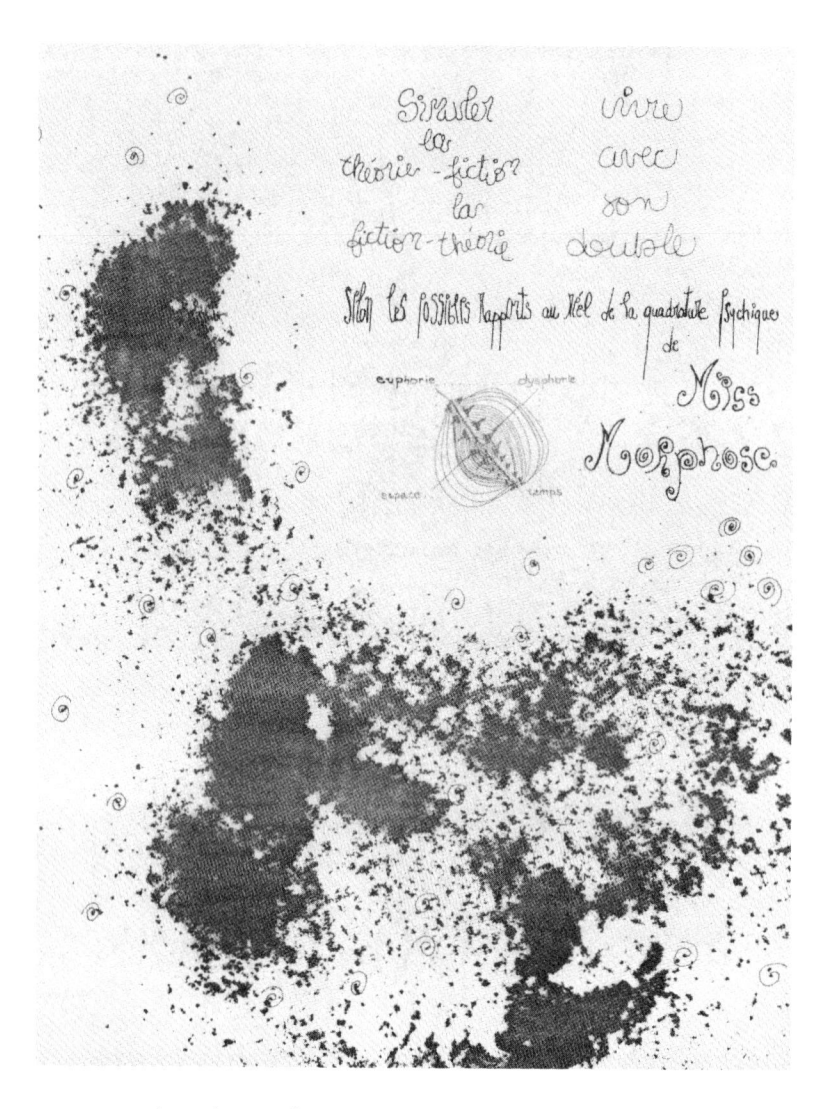

to simulate theory-fiction
double / according to the possible links
to the reality of the psychic quadrature
of Miss Metamorphosis / euphoria — dysphoria
— space — time

♦ DISTANCE AS AN ETHIC ♦

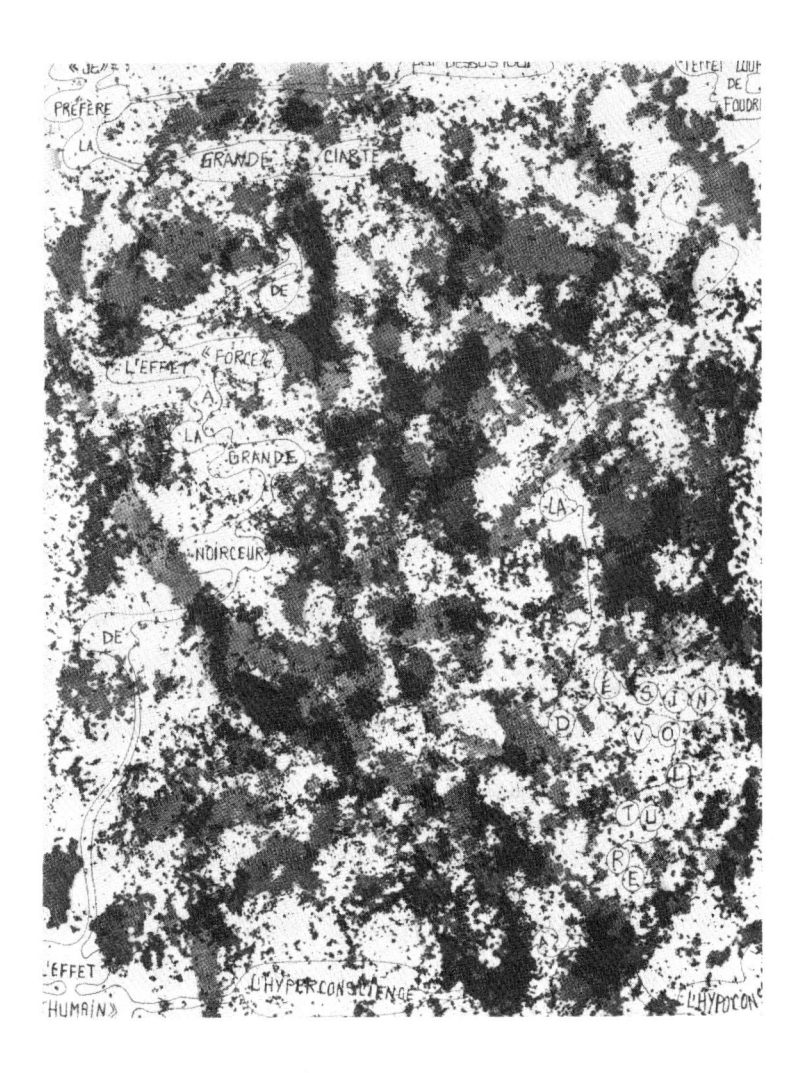

"i" / prefer / above all / the / great /
clarity / of / "energy" / effect / to /
the / great / hyperconsciousness / to /
hypoconsciousness / the thunderbolt
effect / I / M / P / U / N / I / T / Y

# Ritual

*Anne-Marie Alonzo*

*Translation by Susanne de Lotbinière-Harwood*

RITUAL. Like the beginning of a letter for mailing. Where are you when I write you. And I write to you every day and day that follows without ceasing nor leaving I write and you receive and receiving makes me write (you) and I write more then under pencil of blue-and-red-and-night-blue.

Every evening as nine o'clock falls and falls thus the hours I place pencil-and-paper and thought of you that makes meaning I put the ink close by I write thus: dear   think: darling and say: love. I write but arrest neither time nor wind passing by I write you on water flower tell you everything in pieces then assemble sheet-upon-sheet to make bound book.

As for you you say you read and you read sheet-upon-sheet you read story book and tale of faith you read gather up don't recognize yourself.

Text hard to voice is written as struggled surging is written struggle and desire and desire goes long and soft and long again with all forgotten times.

At these moments I wait and await you with all of being sit close by you and so close that inside sit with all of body and lean so that head brushes your shoulder and your cheeks that head turns and caresses and wets your breasts with sighs-tears-and-sighs.

You don't move nor I we stay and so stay hours at times days you-say such that time takes shape of space to fill we stay your hand

♦ Ritual ♦

touches glides and my body draws near moulds enamours more than even all previous times of all years of love.

Ritual as is said of mass.

Let us pray in our hearts let us bow in our souls I read you write let's make of each other inner portraits your fingers my mouth our lips and your teeth.

I often say as sobbing I say: you I say only that.

Then I turn sheet-upon-sheet and close book I do little at a time I turn what is to dream hush the rest resume and begin again and go to bed feverish already asleep.

But letters are mailed only from one lip to another I write from mouth-to-ear-to-mouth understood you listen-don't-listen grow wise to be found I find you join you hug you put hands on your hips your loins say to you: stay don't go nor move I say too: stay embrace her and embrace her once again.

Write you to say and say on sheet of paper and water paper write you on rice and make pulp to be tanned fold piece by piece throw out scraps and return a thousand times to drawing board.

You say: writing doesn't resemble me.

You don't say: laugh.

And of laughter you peal sparking joy you dance-leap-and-dance you make ring-arounds and laugh at seeing me you see me astonished bewitched I say: laugh don't stop laugh some more go on laughing just for laughs and laugh for me    I say: for me.

My letter on the table letter of dread.

And sheet-upon-sheet that does not amount to book but tell-and-tell especially remember poor other countries countries of cutting edges I add and you don't hear I add out of fear-and-silence I scarcely say: I come from there!

And horrors have lived only in words and stories told I say to you and scarcely also say to you: I didn't know don't remember.

Of that country men made women's death and deaths of drowsy women's bodies out of all that I saw only after departure as is said after the war.

I was not yet twelve years did not know knew too much already was no longer laughing.

You say: here too.

You say: differently.

Those men.

But every girl has uncle-or-father sometimes brother to lynch I say: over there too and then the cages and golden cages ruby-plated emerald bellies such wealth you-see and so many poor to feed betrayed.

Sometimes I say: so many poor.

From cairo-to-lebanon and mexico fled from florence-and-venice you know departure and return from africa have never left have left only the land and deserted earth.

Have not truly left.

Of twelve years of childhood everything remains here have no reliable memory I listen-and-read now write struggle or denounce disrupt for sure and surefire coup d'état.

In this way I increase sheet-upon-sheet and make notebook and counter-diary like accounts payable and paid I make a stack to show here lies my sleeping beauty here lies the thorn and of all ages I proffer tales and fables say I'm singer with voice of veils as oriental as one might wish.

You also sing.

And from northern voice rises sharp this throat sound not plaintive sound nor dirge but voice of bird female voice of heights and voice of space near fallen affected never wounded.

Sheet music then and dotted notes black-and-white-and-black fair notes flash notes find point of support open mouth that teeth shall show or make way for screaming.

So I write: dear think: darling.

Insist only that at the outset begin love letter or not say to you: do you know history says that elsewhere was born the world elsewhere and such a short way away that writing is useless on sheet of rice or blue-and-red-and-blue-black paper as I say by night writing is useless and laugh and laugh again in full state of grace hoped-for.

♦

# GNOSIS

*Donna E. Smyth*
*for Gillian*

Woman-words

shaped by what comes out of
mouths, into mouths,
unceasing, relentless
flow of biologic sea
where we learn to swim or we drown

Gnosis

when the Word is born
She transforms

Logos/Loss

tongue-ache, heart-break
alone in the alien corn
we grieve, we weave,
weave endlessly.
was it Penelope
who waited out a war?
who wove the world a new reality

and, night after night,
destroyed her own creation

Her name is Heather and she is afraid to eat a muffin. She runs away from muffins, runs, runs as fast as she can. If she stops running, she will get fat.

Anorexic, she has read all the texts. She knows the theory, the theory and the history. But this is a double-track affair: body stubborn, dumb against the mind's yammering.

Her boyfriend teaches her wind-surfing. He makes her work out like an Olympic athlete. In the end, she can out-sail many men. But she cannot eat a muffin.

Wave-rider, she is hanging
between surf and sky
sail swollen with spirit-wind
muscle-clenched, waiting for delivery

Into: power-dressing, post-feminist, past-thinking world. When Pat Carney sits down with the Americans, she doesn't blink. Her words are hard balls: they smash into her opponents, they drive all wimps off the court. This is carnage with a vengeance, with a flair, and her shadow self, REAL WOMEN, waiting in the wings. REAL WOMEN have no trouble with muffins: they serve them hot to politicians, sweet backlash bribe.

Gnosis: what is that song the peace women sing?

You can't kill the Spirit
She is older than the mountains
on and on she goes
on and on and on

England, 1985. The Greenham Common women are out on Salisbury Plain. Babies on their backs, kids underfoot, a teapot, a kettle. They are out to see the sites, dolomites, and middens, stone maidens who used to dance with the moon on the left, the sun on the right. There is a sign which says: KEEP OUT MILITARY FIRING RANGE.

Halifax, 1986. The NATO foreign ministers are coming to town. The sky is full of helicopters. The harbour swarms with submarines. 1000 extra police and security guards. This is an occupied city.

> You can't kill the Spirit
> but you can throw women into ditches
> into jails and dungeons
> behind veils, locked in kitchens

Logos: Who's in charge here? Who's your leader? The men talk tough, thrust phallic weapons at soft target-rich environments. Deep Strike at the Enemy. High-tech aggressivity. When Agamemnon sought a wind for the Greek fleet at Aulis, he sacrificed his daughter. Slit her throat for the sake of a war.

> Biologic is the Word
> waves of blood, sea changes
> Logos scourges Gnosis
> I, thy God, am a jealous God

Her name is Eleanor and she is afraid she cannot bear the pain. An iron cage holds the disc in place. If the disc slips, it will sever the spinal cord.

She used to be a nun but has left the Church to marry a man who used to be minister but has left the Church and his first wife to marry Eleanor.

> Spirit-talker, she is praying
> between operations
> body stiff with arthritis
> head in a cage

Her husband comes to visit her and says:

> We both left the Church
> now I must leave you

♦ Donna E. Smyth ♦

> Sometimes God is
> where you least expect Him

"What if God is She" asks Eleanor. "I came all this way — I can't turn back now. This caged head, this stiffening body, this absence where you used to be. Can anyone find a meaning to what is happening to me?"

> Pentecostal tongues have lost
> flame, there is a humming
> in the air, high wire voltage
> sizzles, smoke from the top of the head

Logos: power-talking, the language of authority shapes our dreams. When we come to the garden, the gate is locked: KEEP OUT TRESPASSERS WILL BE PROSECUTED. The flaming angel smoulders against the sky: Transform yourselves or you die! We all shave our legs obediently, anoint our bodies with perfumes, clothe ourselves expensively. Civil servants, we collect statistics endlessly.

> (all the women's magazines say:
>
> How to lose 100 pounds in 10 days
> and how to keep your man interested
> how to fight cellulite
> and keep sagging breasts uptight!)

Heather swims, she swims as fast as she can. 10 metres, 30, 40. Each day she has to swim faster, further. She's becoming slim as a model, thin as a refugee.

> (Heather's boyfriend says:
>
> Watch out for your thighs
> cellulite and fat, fat and cellulite
> you might be more beautiful
> if you lost more weight)

♦ GNOSIS ♦

Heather's mind blurs the words on the page. She can't study, can't write. Her periods stopped months ago. The doctors threaten hospitalization. She eats a muffin. Vomits. Eats another half muffin. Does not vomit. When she sees herself in the mirror, her head is full of muffins. Her head is full of dread.

> You can't kill the Spirit
> She is older than the mountains
> She is younger than children
> laughing under trees

His name is Authority. He wears a uniform, guards gates, forms lines to keep trespassers out. He addresses the Greenham women sharply: "Do you want to get your bleedin' heads blown off?" "Oh dear," say the women, "it's time for tea."

Authority has to have tight security. The NATO ministers are meeting in top secrecy. The policemen form a line around the Halifax World Trade Centre. Arms akimbo, legs apart, they straddle a noon-day shadow. When the cannon fires to signal 12:00, they jump round, reach for their guns. False alarm. No terrorists here. Just women approaching slowly so they won't shoot us by mistake. Dressed as clown doctors, we carry measuring devices, pictures of weapons advertising. We are testing for MOGS, the milito-genital-confusion-dependency syndrome.

> You can't kill the Spirit
> She is older than Logos
> She flows through cracks
> She gushes: water, blood

Eleanor sits like a queen receiving visitors. "They will operate again," she says, "and again and again. Job complained to the whirl-wind but I awake in the hospital night and remember his words: 'Am I a sea or a whale that thou settest a watch over me?' I never dreamt freedom could cost such pain."

> On Christmas Eve
> she decorates the cage:

a white peacock
mistletoe and holly

Shape-changer, she has made
herself in the likeness of a bird
her caged head blossoms
like an amaryllis in February

She tells her friends:

"If you listen closely, you will hear the white peacock scream!"

Biologic: in our bellies we carry the sea, source, fecundity. When the moon draws the tides, we double up with pain, we are born again and again. The old women frighten us. They clutch at us with their hands: "It doesn't get any easier!"

Wave-riders, we are flung up
between surf and sea
capsize in the green troughs
dream we are drowning again

Gnosis: rock-a-bye in water womb. Amphibian ambiguity. Assertiveness-training will not save us. We struggle to breathe in the alien air.

The Greenham women slip round. Suddenly find themselves on the other side of the line. The policemen scramble to regain lost territory. Shoulder-to-shoulder, they close ranks against the women, the children, the babies. The officer shouts, "No trespassing!" "Oh dear," say the women, "time to change babies' nappies." And they do.

In Halifax, we tell the policemen: "You're doing a good job protecting us from those MOGS carriers inside. MOGS is the dreaded militarization disease." Some of the policemen smile, hands move away from guns. We tell the media: "MOGS is contagious. If we could only get to the NATO ministers, we could save them from this disease, this addiction to weapons and weapons technology."

## ♦ Gnosis ♦

The media says "Trivializing war! This time you've gone too far, ladies!"

Confronting Authority
they trespass, we trespass
slip around the lines
the fences, the signs,
face noon-day guns
night-flying missiles

Biologic. Gnosis.
if some of us die
before we're done,
we'll shake old
women's bones in the sun;
cry aloud in tongues
and proclaim:
You can't kill the Spirit
She shall rise again!

♦

# MOTHER TONGUE AND WOMEN'S LANGUAGE

*Madeleine Gagnon*

*Translated by Erika Grundmann*

Women and men speak the same language — of the code, rules and law — which organizes all communication strategies in order that all messages be stated clearly and in order that political and ontological models function in the city-state. Of course this language spoken by all members of a community varies from one individual to another according to the degree of resistance and insubordination to the norm. Outlaws are everywhere and of every description. The various types of aphonia and aphasia are indicative of that.

This language spoken by everyone is referred to as "mother tongue." And yet lately it is also said to be the language of the law-of-the-father. To designate this law of which "the transcendental Signifier and the general primacy is PHALLUS," Jacques Lacan suggested the metaphor Name-of-the-Father.

Name of the Father, the Son, and the Holy Spirit. Name of a divine triangle in which the Mother experienced no sexual pleasure and from which the Sister has been excluded. The mother tongue is virgin and the sister has no tongue. The sister IS NOT. She is not yet. With the woman-mother's enjoyment of sexual pleasure[1], she is what happens in language. She is potential.

In the unitary language of the God of Moses, the Word was inscribed in stone for everyone.

♦ MOTHER TONGUE AND WOMEN'S LANGUAGE ♦

In the triangular language of the Father-Son-Spirit, the Word was kept all-One and the Myth of the body and the blood imprinted an excess of meaning and an undecipherable law named Love. Excess in its affront to the law. Excess in the violence done to the men and women who did not conform to it.

The tears of the mother and of the sister were ineffectual against this violence. But they were not shed in vain. Whoever knows how to listen to a foreign mother tongue can even hear them. And not just the tears. The cries too. Cries of joy and of anger. And in passing, one can tune into the tears of pleasure.

To hear this foreign mother tongue, but also to comprehend, in its potentiality (in its promise), the tongue of the sister, the "eternally innocent young girl," to use Maurice Blanchot's words in his reading of *The Ravishing of Lol V. Stein*, one must be able to think the Other in its radical difference (its "differance"). To think the Other in its relation to the One (to the Same). To think the Other in the interference. To think *between* Self and Other, *between* Same and Other, *between* the One and the Other. To accept that this thought might cause conflict. The Other's thought can only be transferential and in every transfer the couple love-hate appears.

To choose never more to think/copy the Other onto the walls of the Same, onto the flesh of the ONE. That is how the "great theories" ON female sexuality were formulated. Theories of Hegel, Freud and Nietzsche who shaped so much of "modern" and "progressive" thought. Theories which insisted in black on white that "Truth is Virility" and that "women have testicles hidden in their tubes," that is why Truth escapes them — It is "hidden" from them (Hegel). Theories which insisted, supported by the Oedipus Myth, "the female Libido" and the problem of (phallic) castration (Freud and his followers). Theories that insisted on "Female hysteria": illusion, trickery, affectation, disguise, "the seductive Feminine," because if the "Feminine is Truth," the "Female" alone knows that the Truth does not exist, that it is an abyss — abyss of the ONE, abyss of the Same, abyss of the Word (Nietzsche). When the Other cannot be thought in its radical difference, the Truth of the ONE crumbles in the castrating lack or in seductive trickery.

This choice of the Other tongue's thinking in its radical difference is madness, but as Annie Leclerc wrote in *Parole de femme* (Women's speech), this "madness is the only reason I have left" (Leclerc 8).

The thinking of the Other is heard in the huge, white expanse of the in-between, the poetic space where the pause and the silence and listening of the "third ear" (René Major) welcome the song of rapture, song of love (and hate) of women and men, with neither Faith nor Law, in search of polyphonic truths.

There is no more Truth in theory than in fiction. There are truths to decipher between theory and fiction, particulary with respect to truths about male and female sexualities and I have no difficulty speaking about phenomena, writing about them, without falling into the "philosophical essentializing nonsense" or the "artist's frustration" that Jacques Derrida referred to in *Spurs, Nietzsche's Styles* (Derrida 55), enclosing the terms "femininity" and "female sexuality," and consequently "women's Writing," in proscriptive quotation marks, but preserving in the nobly conceptual "the Woman" and "the Feminine." I have no problem speaking about female sexuality and women's writing without quotation marks, and I do not see why it would be more *philosophical*, hence more True, to substantify characteristics.

It is not more philosophical, nor more poetic, to substitute lunar for moon, solar for sun, nocturnal for night and diurnal for day. It is not more true to speak of "lived" rather than life. It is not more correct, but it has become fashionable. Decreed.

To me it seems impossible to speak of language without thinking parlance,[2] and subsequently women's parlance and also writing — I shall simply say women's writing.

Difficult to visualize because THAT which I want to think, and write, cannot be approached only through the categories of the Word nor solely through reliance on Myth.

It is not a matter of explanation nor of dispute. It is a matter of thinking meeting. Meeting, not of the "feminine" and the "Masculine" with a view to conceptualizing the "Truth" or to finding the "Truth" through revelation, through believing in it. Faith and Knowledge are on the same axis as "Truth." They are not in opposition. The quest for the transcendental, supreme Truth leads to dogma and despair.

Truth does not exist; I know that. Even so, I have not given way to despair.

♦ MOTHER TONGUE AND WOMEN'S LANGUAGE ♦

There is no more Truth in the Word than there is in Myth. No more in Knowledge than in Fable. Truths are exiled from Knowledge alone or Fable alone. They spring forth in their meeting. Claire Lejeune would say, "They become clear through their mutual co-nascence/cognition (*co-naissance*)." More often than not they are nomads, constantly changing time and place. Their meeting is entirely aleatory and necessity lies in the offering, the gift that this meeting constitutes.

Gift of understanding the things of love. Understanding the things of pleasure and suffering. Understanding the things of Life, but also of Death, right to the threshold of the incomprehensible. This is not explained nor illustrated any better "in the feminine than in the masculine." No analytical grid, no dogma can *be right* about these truths. They know no boundaries but rather approach on tiptoes with the understanding of the body: truths of the heart, eye, ear. Truths of touch, gaze and voice. Of tone, of timbre. And of silence.

To think the Other in language is to risk thinking a "foreign mother tongue" (Winnicott). This climb back in time and space (the mother's body) is certainly hazardous; it cannot take place without the choice of *writing*, whatever the forms or modes of writing selected, and this choice always involves a certain vertigo because literally each time it is a matter of *poetic creation*. Poetic creation is always risky: uncertain, aleatory and perfectly solitary. It can be shared, but meeting the other can only take place after this descent and return of *each body* within its foreign mother tongue.

I write in order to find out what I DON'T KNOW of some philosophy. Some theosophy. Some mythology. Relative to the language of the Other, they are all in the Knowledge or the Fable of the Same. The Word and the Myth of the language of ONE-for-all. This is what Jacques Derrida calls "Phallogocentrism."

In the poetic act I reach (through the inaudible) the unheard of the foreign tongue. The foreign nature of the tongue is "mother." Luce Irigaray, in *Amante marine de Friedrich Nietzsche* (Marine Lover), writes magnificently about the unheard of in language. I love to read and reread the entire first part, her letter to Nietzsche entitled "Dire d'eaux immemoriales" (Immemorial Waters Speak). I also enjoy reading *Passions élémentaires* (Basic Passions) as well as Carole Massé's *L'Existence* (Existence) and *L'Autre* (The Other).

♦ MADELEINE GAGNON ♦

The ear that is tuned to the Other's language lets a different voice be heard. Its listening through an infinity of silence, as in the great beyond, lets it hear a women's speech: "Shadow" speech (Michèle Montrelay); a voice that lets you see differently (Marguerite Duras).

If women and men speak the same language, language of the Same (of the ONE-for-all), it is through difference that they enter into language. Women and men do not enter into the co-nascence/cognition (*co-naisssance*) and the recognition (*reconnaisance*) of their foreign mother tongue in the same manner.

To think this difference the way you think thunderbolt or as you would think earthquake, the jarring of a thought. Thunderbolt writing — it comes from the explosion of the *heart of the letter*. You reach it through infinite cunning: ultimate opening up in the operation of the ear and eye. It is making the until-here-and-now inaudible and invisible of the foreign mother tongue tremble.

"... luxating the philosophical ear, putting the *loxos* (the obliquity of the tympanic membrane) to work in the *logos*" (Derrida 11).

"First to exercise, to the point of exhaustion, the virginal vision for which seeing does not yet raise the question of the relationship between the image and the sense of seeing. This naive gaze can only generate the literally photographic reproduction of the multitude of prints imprinted on the retina when it is exposed, overexposed, underexposed; generate the reproduction of what is revealed or fixed — is memorized — through the eyes of the head, since the eye of the heart (that eye which sees the indivisible) is still buried in its potentiality" (Lejeune 31).

Task of unearthing. Cryptomnesia. Decoding of the underground formula. Deciphering of signs left there hanging on the body-monument; body-monument of archives filled with hieroglyphics (Jacques Lacan); impulses: positive or negative letters right there on the flesh, engraved (Serge Leclaire).

Tax of luxation as well. *Loxos* (luxere): dislocation, displacement, de-centring. Injury too. This opening to the Other and this upheaval do not occur without injury to the philosophical ear (and eye).

In order to enter into the language of the Other it is necessary to imagine the Eye of the supreme and omnipresent God in a state of injury. The Other's language is never spoken in omnipotence. If the writing of it is hazardous, it is also because the language is fragile and vulnerable. Prone to injury, its strength lies in this primordial admission.

Cryptomnesia and luxation mark the entry of a labour of love into language. Love is in labour in language. The words of love in labour are "not to be found in discourse or on the page" (Derrida 11).

It is in poetic art that this language of love is tapped. In the writing of this act that its thrumming (*bruissement*) (Barthes) is heard. In this thrumming, this jarring of pleasure (and suffering), that the *inédit* (unpublished), the inter-diction of love is understood. It comes down to a birthing of the Other. An extravagance in the abandon of Self and a wonder at the gift of the Other.

The writing of this act of birth (of this act of mourning too) endangers all discourse and fiction which flaunt the Truth. If the Truth is expressed as Phallus or Woman it is divine (transcendental) in God, whatever its Name, and the subjective truths of the language of the Other's body will have just died.

To leave the mother's body through injury (loxos) and the cry of pleasure. And of suffering. PATHOS is the price of loving knowledge. Knowledge: the fruit of passion. Truth of theory and truth of fiction. Writing happens between the two. It is entering into the Word through this injury and through this cry.

This writing of the body touches on the initial (and immemorial) words in the shadow of the language of the ONE-for-all. That is why such writing can be called "women's words"; writing-parabola of the body: ear, eye, heart, voice, touch, "mucosa" (Irigaray) and as many polysemous metaphors, *creative sparks* through which discourse becomes aroused when the body makes its thrumming heard on the page.

The foreign woman's writing in surprising proximity to the letter — and it is not from being too distant that the language of the Other disturbs; it is because the language is so near. The feeling of "unsettling strangeness" comes to him or to her for whom the beautiful stranger is too close.

In transference (of love, writing, reading) the threat of what is too close remains latent. When the truths are discovered *between* Self and Other, symbiosis does not take (has no) place.

If there is rejection (mourning at the separation of the loving body and the writing-reading body), this rejection, this abandonment (violence inflicted on the body by the Other of language) is always/already also latency, pure potentiality.

Femininity (female sexuality or writing in the feminine) is heard, seen, touched by gaining access to the language of the Other. Because of a history which precedes us, includes us, surpasses us, this language courses through women's parlance. As women and men we speak the same language, but our entry into the universe of language is different. This language runs, moves at the speed of light: faster than the apparent sounds of madness or the ambient cacophony, more agile and more distant than any aphonia. Behind the mask of the mute (hysterical?) woman rises the voice of the Other.

It is in poetry, of all times and in all languages, that the voice of the Other has always been heard. And it was not by accident that the most poetic philosopher of all, Nietzsche, was throughout his work — and not just in a text or two *on* "Woman" or "Femininity" — literally haunted by the "Feminine," a metaphor that he constantly linked to the concept of "Truth."

Nor was it by chance that the advent of women's language (women's parlance) was announced in literary circles by the visionary poet Arthur Rimbaud.

It is simply by chance — or might it be due to an awareness (or unconscious knowledge) colliding with a terrifying historical rebuff, i.e. the great silence of women — that many of these poets themselves entered into the great silence of madness or suicidal death? Suicide is a murder of speech for whoever no longer knows how to speak, but keeps alive the desire to speak the things of life and death.

Women's writing must not be reduced to its delinquent results (lexical, grammatical, syntactical) in the coded system of the ONE-for-all language (language of the Same, language of the Name-of-the-Father). All terms of common language could be feminized, rules of agreement could be changed so that in this language one gender would be equal (or would become superior) to the other. It is perhaps even desirable to attack these symptoms. But it is also possible to work elsewhere and to write otherwise.

To write inscriptions of the foreign mother tongue in the greatest depth, with the most reality, at the greatest distance, and in the closest proximity right onto the body of words — engraved.

The tattoo artist's stylet[3] may be masculine, but in this language, language of the Other, *writing* is feminine.

♦

## NOTES

1. The word "pleasure" is used throughout to designate *jouissance*, Barthes' term for pleasure, ecstasy, sexual pleasure. Trans.
2. "Parlance" is used here in a broad sense of "speech, way of speaking, way of using language" to translate *langage*. Trans.
3. *le stylet* i.e. masculine. Trans.

## WORKS CITED

Barthes Roland. *La Bruissement de la langue.* Paris: Editions du Seuil, 1984.

Blanchot, Maurice. *Marguerite Duras.* Paris: Editions L'Albatross, 1979.

Derrida, Jacques. *Spurs, Nietzsche's Styles.* Trans. Barbara Harlow. Chicago: University of Chicago Press, 1979.

Leclerc Annie. *Parole de femme.* Paris: Grasset, 1974.

Lejeune Claire. *L'Oeil de la lettre.* Belgique: Editions Le Cornier, 1984.

# DICTION AIR

## *jam. ismail*

**patriarchy**   7 pay t.v.   8 reduction of sexes and genders to two.   9 fusion of sex & gender.   1 identification of 'father' with 'male' and 'mother' with 'female', hence (allusively), parentnoid.   cf.

**trans'parent.**

**patriarchly** 'am i going to be a father', she wondered.   patriarchly.   giving herself heirs.

**pedigree**   his stance and gait ar not in vain.   left arm straight ending in a shiny weight of shopping.   right hand backs the head of an infant who, when last i saw it taken away a step, by step, down the stairs, was head back, eyes and mouth open as if for the face above.   the look before fallen in love.   now the man's eys touch this small sweet round in his hand.   i make it a mutual ador .   he's not pedestrian, a younger heart with the most beloved face grows, out of his chest, daily, and he moves with it.   one does not say: this is a father & child.   one sees, essent   , this is loving.   contemplate.   the van swung into parking puts him a meter behind the site of me  .   he stops, turned. face rifting into pleasure & misery.   pave ment,   i do look,   eco no ledge . pond   .   what's to say, do   abridge   , i go on to market.   he too turn quick, open shut.   new hardness.   begot with his sister.
keep an ey  on the good   of one another.
i mean ,   of rivals,   too    (6.viii.85)

**photosynthesis**   in plants must be *imagination* in humans.   what ar stories, for plants?   we call them stores.   what is narrativ   , chemically speaking? tran s port.

**prefix**, e.g., con- (L.), with.   010 concoct (catachrestically) he.   111 **concord** with strings, attached. 09 **concur** girl   in skiblue jacket, alsatian [german shepherd] alongside her bicycling.   he's lean, not from muscle, so it looks like a

♦ DICTION AIR ♦

(picture of ) cure, for health; although the steady stepping's like dressage. sunlit north shore . . thrills above snow line. her windy hair's the colour of this blond grass. above horizon blue form even. disturb of sea with wave, that's winter.
   they ar about to curve from wall street onto kamloops, her head & hand reach down to stroke his face. **04 controlls** with dwharves, ferries, gnomons, and pick-sees.

race   3   leak of nations.   5   lunch fills the vegetarian restaurant on hennessy near perceval street. the waiter motions her to the table where i'm waiting for a dish of noodles. chat, of strangers, in cantonese. she says, yes i see that you'd enjoy sinkiang and tibet and uncultured places like those, not looking at my blue hollofil vest. (the armadillo, ma calls it, it tells everyone you're from canada). she's come down from near shanghai, been in the colony 18 years, hairdressing, refers to the mainlanders as 'they', is joining her family in toronto, and, do you prefer hong kong? or vancouver, she asks, splitting. i see now that it's been this way for 20 years. a day later i read in a book of ackbar's, 'writing is precisely working in the in-between' (helen cixous).   4   here at the film shop on commercial street rani says. you can go home and see things. that they have done very well, ar healthy, and the hygiene is good. that they hav money and now ar educated, yes. and that the buildings hav changed, the standard of living is better. but it's not right for me because i don't see what i came to see. have you ever been hurt in that way

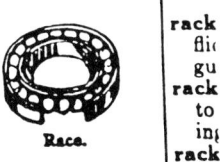

                                   places gone. sites reoccupay.
in see-thru.
                        a history of my ey . like gills in
stream the walking body picks up bits   like gills in a stream   the red of sudden altars. an ashpit,   6   with me it was the same, malhu smiled. when i first came here in '53 it was love at first sight. oh in those days there were would you believe one-tenth the people in these streets! we are walking towards chhetrap-ati, to the tibet guest house where i'm staying. he say kirtipur is the way kathmandu was 30 years ago. the origin keeps moving. but janek says, why do you want to come back. people say that to me all the time and that is my question, why do you want to come back?

real   2   i bought him a rolex knock-off. that's what he wanted for his birthday. you know, taiwan is really getting very good now, you can walk in and ask for a cartier and they'll know what to give you. they make them really well and they're not cheap either, it costs US $150 but the real things costs $7000. and it's so funny! he treats it like the real one, keeps it in the bank, takes it out to wear to meet the bigwigs! and the funny thing is that he has a real one that is all banged up & scratched, you know how rough he is, that he wears everyday to do the marketing in!

**resist** *Where There's a Wont, There's a Way.*

**serendipity**     unreturning sticks to the thrower    on the
dock , the wheaty retriever continues uphill . aloofly
flinging , drops . of light . with every pad up-
slope , dancing fountain .

linger , and of the show . ahead and beside angles ,
sun is darkening trees. & building . serene
dipitty.
fo lowing up the path , small stones may be seen sending
shadows , times 10

**sex**    a latin word meaning six (6) which has been pared down to two (2). this may not be a bad thing, especially during family reunions and other group fares. dacoity is not for every one.

**shirley,**                                                                                                   17th january 1987
     you know i'd put my *goon yum* [cantonese deity of compassion] into a fire, years ago. burnt it up. it's been, so long. after seeing yours, and sophie's, awe set in. once again, some phoenix. and i knew i couldn't just go buy another. as in the story you told, an encounter was indicated, or at least a tense . as with stars, or molecules. guide d,

                                               so a day or two goes, a-
nalept , befor it materializes, ceramically: hard milk: in a clearing in the backhills of cloudview road, in one of those wire-fenced open air workshops with a rubbish pit in the middle, and machinery around. she'd been set with care on some grey 4x4s, a little away from debris. on the dusty office desk one of two phones was ringing. i knew not to undo the camera from its pouch, nor did i squat to see better. a young man of sullen cast had noticed that someone had wandered in. on my way out, a smaller man with a thin mustache said, how may i serve you. i liked the uigyur of his face and his curtesy, as if i were from a family he respects. i do not live here, i reply, i am walking around looking. your *goon yum* is in a good spot. he nod & laugh delight . a few steps down the hill i hear him shout out the names to me, of the two people who'd placed her there. it was for the record. credit do.

**sign**   in a temple near kathmandu

> **PHOTOS NOT ALOUD**

**siblings**   brother: in thailand, a naked beautiful girl comes in and gets into the water with you. then you're put on the lie-low and she rubs you all over with oil. then
sister 1: she fries you.
brother: no! then she slides all over you
sister 2: with roller skates.
brother: no! she has this little plastic bowl with oil and water mixed together and a sort of whisk that beats it up and she
sister 1: bastes you.
brother: no! she

**six**   afrodit's number. said pythagoras (corinne, 46)

**sob**   i remember when you lent me *peyton place*. grace metalious, i'll never forget her name. i had to phone you up because there was one word i couldn't find in the dictionary, & i said, jam, this word s.o.n.o.f.a.b.i.t.c.h, it isn't in the dictionary, do you know what it means? there was a silence and i think you said something like, break it up shirley.

**story**   ah little 2-storey in profile sitting empty and alone, full to the sens of sky. the moon unseen & night verdure it's been years! since i saw you in kits[ilano] last, somewhat outside , drawn onto a large paper in the room southwest. the winter they were there

**suffix, e.g., -sibling**  ( A.S. ), gene'sis. **19 sensibling**   o , a sis. **18 responsibyl**  tran'sis'tor. **9 invisibling**   the sibling who isn't seen; also, solip'sis. **16 possibling**   takes courage, or heartage, sometimes by way of neme'sis.

**trans'parent** (a tercet)
   mum. and/or d ad. in loco parenthesis. gone between

**verse/vers**         to ward
   avers            un toward
   divers            downward
            angles,
                  &

transvers
                    analogs
    collectible as
            s i g h
                    t.ime   paradi  m
                        dust  iridesce
                imaging ,  s trains  s. a  mere  opticale
                    imagene :
                                airwar  e .  culler
                                        evenings
                            here and there a seen,  infinativ
    **invert**          he imagined her fate to be bleak famous.
                        all the while keeping happy ,  at home.
version **versionity**.
well     . of loneliness .  its good.
    4.ix. feeling lonely  &  liking it.
    oh the drag of a task  befor (one gets to) the freedom
    with in.  attitude to word servants.
    bum sits by window
    fingers reach for ,  rose.
    some roses wont depetal into hips.

        ha11d ∃  writing  |  upon ▪ ⌂ surface.         肆  To practise toil, pain,
        It forms                                           sprouts

        聿   A pencil, pen forth-                      肅  Circumspection, respect .
             with, and then

                                                       肆  O expend to expose
        肂   To dig a grave.                                our excessive reckless now.

                                                       肇      begin,
                                                              to range

    this avid barter, switch on the sens of timing.
**what**    is your etymologist
'as soon as she received the book she knew immediately all that it contained'
('the liberation story of jomo memo' (1248-83) in tsultrim, 210)
    **words,**    cited.  *chinese characters* by 1. weiger, s.j. (1927)*. collete guillaumin, 'the
        idea of race and its elevation to autonomous, scientific and legal status', in
        sociological theories: race and colonialism (1980). A corinne heline, **sacred
        science of numbers** (1985).   **diction air:** 'a new inbreathing brings back the

        * well what I did was, i photocopied wieger and then i whited out the words & punctuation i
          didn't want. with liquid paper.

♦ DICTION AIR ♦

entire fantasmagoria of the universe to the one who meditates' (alexandra david-neel, *initiations and initiates in tibet*, english trans. by fred rothwell (1932, 1935), 79). dorothy richardson, *pilgrimage* (1938). helene cixous. *oxford shorter english dictionary* (1933, 1968). pauline kirman, *a secular baggadah* (1986). tsultrim allione, *women of wisdom* (1984). *webster's illustrated dictionary* (1949).

**words**, incited (see also **metonymy**). words ar like money they hav no backing other than us. 'man' still includes 'woman'. 'she used to refer to 'he' as well, and 'girl' used to mean 'boy' too (*oxford*). dorothy richardson said it, people go on writing books using the same words with diffrint meanings. which may not be the most efficient way to run a country. as goebbels said to fritz lang, mr. lang, *we* are the ones who decide who a jew is (colette, 41). talk about sementics. no wonder words slip, slide, perish, will not stay still. struggle, the *secular haggadah* says, is better than boredom.    PALESTINIANS AGREE.

**words**, of mouth.  rani, madhu, janek, sheila ismail, leslie stokes, shirley omar- thanks to hélène mino for alexandra. hi renee!


[afterword to *diction air*]
i like to sweep the flat before i settle down to work. the lines of a page of dictionary often remind me of the lines of dust that never get into the pan, they stay on the floor. there are times i feel small dense print (especially the 13 volume *oxford dictionary*) as an arrangement of dust.

some dictionaries are born in times of great cultural turmoil & renewal, when the house is such a mess of wires, pipes, & broken walls that all i can do is put word-things in alphabetic order. i indexed some of what i'd collected over the years: words i couldn't use (e.g., serendipity); words i can say but not write; words i keep on forgetting the meaning of; samples of rebus; definitions more sensible than those given in the *oxford* & skeat's *etymological*; notes on (english) dictionary (e.g., it's not a text that's meant to be read through; its tendency to definition by polyglot synonymy; its absurdity; &c).    And so on.
utility
after small writings, problemata, & decipherings became part of the file, the name *diction air* presented itself. i was delighted, as if it meant i wouldn't have to write a novel after all, i can stay libretto.

**aria** (3 july) sky of dark & various cloud, bit blue it's so laden above [water] sea looks slated for a parking lot. tear of colour west that she will see further south. we'll share this big roof for maybe a week mor. but the side of the park where sparrows bathe & ezra used to drink, gravel. .streams . look . icy this evening. nip in the air. mammifiers . all the diffrint currents your skin feels. she is insid wat i hav imagined & doing wat i can't. do you know the troubadours ? that's the *'spirit of romance'* ! i'm drinking last night's wine. the pocket of your cousin's husband's shirt is not easy to unstitch. roses. & shamrock . it's night now  where in sedro woolley ar you

about serendipity. *oxford & brittanica* hav it that sarandib, a former name of ceylon (now sri lanka), is an arabic 'corruption' of the sanskrit simhaladvipa (dwelling-place-of-lions island); & that an englishman hitched -ity onto serendip to make serdipity. well, that's one way to do it. english a word by romanizing an arabesque of sanskrit & grafting on a latin tail. it's a tail that wags the dog, for latin sends on its imperializing ways. but a colonizing onomatopoeia (ceylon became a crown colony in 1802) needn't be an onomatopooper. one could learn by it to resuffix paris-*ian* with an -*ite*, or decline 'british' to 'brutish'. me, i like e.s.l. trips, such as 'united sates'.

when serendipity was coined in the 1750s it meant 'the faculty of making happy & unexpected discoveries by accident'. a brutish example, from the 1750s, might be, the takeover of bengal; which financed the english 'industrial revolution', & so england went on to Empaaah. no of course i hadn't it figured this way when the word first buzzed me, testily, in the 1960s in hong kong. herstory comes & history goes and sensor's always here. it bothered me that the word was plucked from native tongues i did not speak. i dint want to ape the brits, stopped passing it, it went in bardo with other words i couldn't use until , well, untilled.

not that serendipity lived up to its meaning in english mouths, they often wore it like a meddle. i like the word, it still feels acute. something comic, or maybe karmic, in that lap of sound & sens. raphael (lui) says it's since become a word in science. example? the accidental discovery of mercury as a catalyst when someone broke the thermometer he was stirring a solution with. that's how we get minamata disease. pause . and is it true, i ask, that einstein apologized to a post-hiroshima delegation from japan? yes, raphael says he broke down & cried.

electrification is so recent & already unmanned light is endangered. some summers ago when i was loitering around deep cove in north vancouver i saw a dog come out of water & go uphill, dripping, to wher the sun disk flashed & dipped among the trees. someone on the dock called again & again until drawn into the evening's better temper. in that rich light, humans young & old appeared perfect, cast in gold, forever, sealed. and i went with the wet dog dancing fountain to the loom of dark evergreen.

later on, when i thought of placing that writing in *diction air*, i remembered the word serendipity. the news is that while i was typing the text, something else came along like a part of the water or wink of sun sat & tapped itself in, 'serene dippity'. now that's what i call evening , serendipity coming out. what did you say about language scars last year at sechelt, i ask helene (mino). it is 10 mins befor her clock is due to beep at her. well, she says dreamy into the phone, they itch.

# Is Feminist Theory Anti-Feminist? (Reprise)

*Valerie Raoul*

In response to the call for papers for this edition of Tessera [1985] I went back and re-read the first issue (*Room of One's Own*, 8:4, 1984), which was largely inspired by the Vancouver "Women and Words" conference of 1983. As I compared the points of view expressed, by Lorraine Weir and Andrea Lebowitz in particular, I asked myself to what extent the situation has changed since then.

The two articles to which I refer (Lebowitz's "Is Feminist Literary Criticism Becoming Anti-Feminist?" and Weir's "Wholeness, Harmony, Radiance and Women's Writing") present fundamentally opposed views on the function and value of literary theory, and of feminist theory in particular. Lebowitz protests against the elitism and esotericism of post-structuralist theory, seeing the function of theory and criticism as the transmission to students of a body of knowledge and critical thought, which must be communicable in a common idiom. She also objects to the homage paid by deconstructionists, including women, to dominant male figures (Derrida and Lacan). According to her standpoint, feminist theory abandons its original (political) goals when life and theory diverge, when women who are militant/radical feminists can no longer relate to what theorists are saying in terms of precise goals. Women who participate in the male-dominated field of theory are sold-out academics adopting an alien perspective for the benefit of their careers (the Margaret Thatchers of Academe?).

Weir, on the contrary, claims that theory has never been so accessible or relevant to women as it is under the auspices of Derrida, Foucault et al. "Theorists ... who seek to deconstruct the phallologocentrism — the patriarchal control of the structures of language and definitions of meaning — of the Western humanist tradition are our allies" (23). This judgement is certainly closer to the French view that social and political change as well as psychological re-vision are inextricable from ideological/philosophical shifts. Post-modernism is seen by left-wing theorists such as Toril Moi to be politically subversive in its attempt to displace the subject and valorize the (feminine/different) Other. For the first time, in theory and in critical practice, it is an advantage to be a woman, as one already has a dual perspective. Such bi-focalism is related to the use of "feminine" in French theory to designate a standpoint and a value-system opposed to the dominant phallic/patriarchal ones, whether they emanate from male or female exponents.

This standpoint raises another thorny issue which has not gone away: whether men can adopt a "feminine" viewpoint and contribute to feminist theory and, conversely, whether feminist theory is relevant to women only. Several recent works of theory move away from separatism towards convergence. Irigaray's *Éthique de la différence sexuelle*, Elizabeth Badinter's *L'Un est l'autre*, and Marilyn French's *Beyond Power*, a history of the relations between the sexes, all envisage a movement by men towards the feminine position as the only further progress possible, once women have moved as far towards the masculine one as they deem compatible with retaining their "femininity."

Whether "femininity" is in fact definable/desirable/retainable/escapable remains the central issue in feminist theory. If I saw an article entitled "Is Feminist Theory Becoming Anti-Feminist?" today, I would expect it to be dealing with a different set of problems. The "anti-feminism" in question would not be the imitation of the masculine mode, but an acceptance of traditional male-binary definitions of what is "feminine." These are re-affirmed by elements such as the emphasis on "writing the female body"; the prevalence of "feminine" imagery (weaving, spinning, fluids); the (positive) equation of femininity with madness; the increasing mystical utopianism of certain feminist theorists; the incursion of religious imagery and concepts in the discourse on women (I don't mean "REAL Women"); the re-affirmation of the "eternal feminine" in various guises.

We need women engaged in literary theory and competent in its language to be aware of new developments and to deconstruct the discourse of feminism itself. Many students are eager to take up that challenge. It is pragmatically as important to have women philosophers as it is to have women engineers. There is a danger of reviving the old dichotomy between living and writing/thinking, as a choice between real/committed/political/radical feminism and ivory-tower theory. The two activities are in fact inseparable, as is illustrated by so many contemporary writers. The erosion of frontiers between "creative" writing and theory as theory evolves from the play of signifiers, and poetic language calls reference into question is a reflection of the tendency to demolish masculine/feminine oppositions such as reason/imagination.

This position is open to the accusation of revisionism and may be perceived as a hangover from humanism. Yet many feminists, even "radical" ones, are in sympathy with other movements concerned with the oppression of men as well as women, and adhere to the basic tenets of humanism, whether it be liberal/socialist/Marxist. They are looking for change, but not sure if subversion from within the system is more or less effective than withdrawal from it (if that were possible).

Feminist theorists are attempting to escape from binary oppositions, yet these abound as one compares the premises of different standpoints and are even evident in the work of single writers, from Simone de Beauvoir to Mary Daly and Luce Irigaray. Recognition and discussion of the plurality/fragmentation of feminism(s) and its/their polyvalent projects is essential at this point. Recent works by Elizabeth Wilson (*Hidden Agendas*) and Dale Spender (*For the Record*) are useful recapitulations of some of the central issues. The following list of apparent contradictions (which emerged from teaching a course on French women writers at the University of British Columbia) may also contribute to continuing the debate — the search for workable syntheses/ the spinning of the inspiring spirals (up/down, in/out, bigger/smaller?).

*An ad hoc and incomplete checklist* (dialogue with my Other/self)
1) If female students don't understand feminist theory, it is the fault of the theory/ the theorists/ the teacher.
   It is the fault of the student's phallocratic/stereotypically feminine education.
2) French theory is what American theorists need to tune into.
   Americans cannot assimilate French theory without reductionism/falsification.
3) The aim of feminist theory is a revolutionary "parler féminin"/ "écriture-femme."
   The existing examples frequently seem to be either modelled on word-play made fashionable by men, or to represent a (welcome/regrettable) return to traditional "feminine" lyricism/"bavardage."
4) Women can express their unique (but common) view-point, which is new (but has always been there) by the use of imagery based on the female body.
   This is predictable and a reversal of/parallel to previous male phallic imagery. It makes a difference if the body is/is not hetero-sexual or that of a mother.
5) "God" can be overthrown and replaced by a multiple Goddess without establishing a new (old) religion.
   We don't need Gods or Goddesses. Women are not necessarily, innately mystical.
6) Women's identity is inseparable from their relationship to their mothers and perception of themselves as actual or potential mothers.
   Women can be autonomous only if they escape from motherhood.
7) The only hope is to focus on women alone, to be homodirected.
   Loving men is necessarily ultimately self destructive. What about our sons? What about the men we love in spite of (because of?) their being men?
8) "Feminine" is a construct with little to do with biological femaleness (e.g. Genêt).
   This is a pretext for men to intrude in women's issues/realm.
9) Feminism is concerned with showing up traditional sex-role stereotyping as false and abolishing it.

Feminism is concerned with revalorizing what was previously pejoratively dismissed as feminine. Women must choose the feminine model over the masculine one.
10) Spinning, weaving etc. are inspiring images for feminine creative writing/thinking.
These images are irrelevant (even insulting or comical) to the majority of women, still engaged in the modern equivalent of spinning and weaving.
11) There are many feminisms.
There is only one true feminism.
12) Feminism is a humanism (as was existentialism).
It is radically opposed to humanism.
13) These statements are all contradictory.
They are all "true." We are all different, but we are all women (except the men among us?).

◆

# POWER, ETHICS AND POLYVOCAL FEMINIST THEORY

*Kathleen Martindale*

The excitement and the boldness of feminist criticism as it has developed from a critique to a self-celebration and then to a heady engagement with the politics of theory and language derives largely from theoreticians' attempts to imagine a discourse and a world beyond oppositional differences. This theoretical development represents a political and an ethical challenge to theory-makers and consumers alike.

In this paper I'll analyze one area of difficulty in the relationship between feminist theory and feminist deconstruction, the ethics of power relations in a decentred polyvocal criticism. Though Foucault's writings on power/knowledge have influenced my understandings, I'll not allude to him directly, for a number of reasons, most of them political, and will attempt rather to keep this discussion focused on the actuality of power, conceived performatively as well as coercively.

When feminist criticism attempts to be a polyvocal discourse, how do critics address power relations, specifically differences among women? What ethical and political problems must they confront? I'll examine the work of three provocative and diverse feminist theoreticians who use deconstructive strategies to assess what happens when feminist criticism tries to destabilize itself while attempting to remain an ethical discourse, or in some cases, to become one.

To ground my discussion, I'll first make some claims about the relationships between feminism and the ethics and politics of critical discourse. Feminism, especially polyvocal feminist literary theory which attempts to hear the differences in and among women, in their texts and in their worlds, is an outsiders' discourse about power and difference. And since women are outsiders to different degrees and in significantly different ways, in terms of race, class, ethnicity and sexual preference, there will never be *one* feminist discourse. To the extent that a critic acknowledges that feminism is only "(ambiguously) nonhegemonic,"[1] it will be decentred. The degree to which feminists recognize and refuse the hierarchy of centre and margin will always represent a political and ethical struggle within feminism and will constitute a way of situating the various feminist discourses on a spectrum from radical to liberal.

Feminist criticism is always implicitly and usually explicitly a critical discourse about power relations. It is therefore an ethical discourse, that raises questions about and attempts to clarify relationships between what is and what ought to be. In my view, feminist discourse tends to collapse the differences between ethics and politics. It does so because it begins as a critique of relationships based on power imbalances (and therefore it is an ethical critique, the claim being that such relationships are unjust), but it also insists that change is possible and that change must occur (and therefore it is a political critique, the claim being that oppressive situations exist which are "man-made" and are therefore humanly resolvable.)

Historically, feminist criticism has been a discourse of complaint about exclusion and silencing. It has problematized exclusion and silencing as political and ethical issues and has critiqued what has been included, what has been heard, as incomplete, univocal, and therefore as falsely universalized. Critics have differed about the degree of exclusion, whether it amounted to total silencing or muting, whether all women have been excluded, and whether we ought to desire inclusion. Some have seen what they were doing as making requests, or as graciously inviting the interpretive community to make the exchange between feminist and other critical approaches less one-sided. Others have seen themselves as making "righteous, angry, and admonitory demands"; but all have seen themselves as suppliants (Kolodny 149-50; Showalter 140-42; Heilbrun and Stimpson 64).

In one more recent formulation of the ethical and political

dilemmas posed by exclusion, Patrocinio Schweikart analyses them most convincingly as a deeply interlocking set of questions about discourse, power and logic. Because feminist critics have tended to appropriate the persuasion or enlightenment model of criticism unselfconsciously, they inevitably encountered resistance, "because the unenlightened party (from the feminist point of view) is also in possession of instruments of power, and specifically, of the means for producing and regulating knowledge" (162). Schweikarts' work clearly suggests why complaining is ineffective and makes one remember why, as early as 1938, Virginia Woolf had insisted that in some ways it is better to be locked out than locked into the interpretive community (72, 122). Schweikart's formulation emerged at a moment in the history of feminist theory when many feminist critics had turned the focus of their attention from what *they*, the male literary establishment, had thought of *our*, that is, women's exclusion from the establishment, to what *we*, the critics ourselves thought of it. At the same time, some feminist critics, with great surprise and defensive guilt or rage and resistance depending on whether they identified more with their privilege or with their oppression — had begun to attend to the ways some feminist critics exclude others. That re-focusing on who is the other (woman) made the ethical and political aspects of "the" feminist critique of power relations both more transparent and more troubling for it made many feminists re-think the insider-outsider opposition.

Since feminist criticism has been a discourse of urgency, some aspects of the decentring process have seemed almost politically suicidal. How can feminist criticism say, "hear this and hear it now," and also be detached and playful? While it was politically and theoretically necessary for feminist criticism to become polyvocal, there were also grave risks in adopting a decentred discourse that is playful or refuses authority, or most problematically, that admits or even celebrates moral and political uncertainty. Not that most of those writing on and around this subject recognize or acknowledge that in large measure the debate over feminism's use of deconstruction is fundamentally ethical. Instead of focusing on the question of whether deconstruction compromises the ethical certainty of demands underlying feminist criticism, the debate has centred on whether or not feminist critics should use "male" theory.[2]

## ♦ POWER, ETHICS, AND POLYVOCAL FEMINIST THEORY ♦

In order to understand both why this debate has been largely misunderstood and why the feminist debate over deconstruction matters, we have to work backwards. To address adequately the dilemmas posed by polyvocal criticism, we need to clarify the ethical and political positions of polyvocal critics. Doing that depends on being able to show how those positions have been based on different problematizations of difference, which in turn requires that we see how they emerge from political and ethical analyses of power relations.

This historical development has been overdetermined by impasses in feminist theory brought about by failures to acknowledge that defining "woman" is a highly problematic and political act and that for many reasons "we" might want to refuse the definition; acknowledgement of our failures to join practice and theory and subsequent self-criticism; and the unfortunate situation of having to make our theory and practice more radical in a political climate hostile to feminist and other demands for justice.

These historical pushes and pulls, which have left nearly every feminist critic wondering about the relationships between theory-making and power, have led some to consider the paradoxes which come into play when feminist theorists use the persuasion model, the only model of critical discourse universally recognized by the interpretive community. Sometimes feminist theorists who have relied on the model have not been seen as using it competently because their evidence and their interpretations have not been accepted as valid. Nonetheless, even when they learn this political lesson about the workings of the interpretive community, feminist theorists must confront another paradox. The persuasion model has its origins in the logic of binary oppositions between centre and margin. Consequently, politcally responsible feminist theorists may have to reject or at least seriously redesign and re-appropriate the model. If theorists do that, however, they give up other political responsibilities such as appealing to and informing potential audiences. To a certain extent, giving up the persuasion model means cutting ourselves off from the political base of feminism and silencing ourselves as feminist theorists. Having said this, I'm now ready to analyse how three feminist theorists negotiate this paradox in order to suggest how ethically and politically difficult it is to attempt to write a decentred, polyvocal feminist criticism.

Maria C. Lugones and Elizabeth V. spelman risk provoking some feminist readers' discomfort about the degree to which feminist discourse is still white, privileged and univocal. In "Have We Got a Theory for You! Cultural Imperialism and the Demand for the 'Woman's Voice'" they explore the responsibilities of dominants when they listen to the voices of the dominated. If dominants acknowledge that their discourse is inadequate to the experiences of the dominated, who must nonetheless use the dominants' discourse if they want to be heard, how is any dialogue possible between the powerful and the less powerful? On whose turf will they meet? And what should motivate the dominants to hear the less powerful ones?

Lugones and Spelman attend to their own languages and voices, but even so, after the opening paragraph, written by Lugones in her native Spanish, they use the dominant language, English, Spelman's first language. Thus, in spite of themselves, the article re-enacts the workings of power relations analysed by Maroussia Hajdukowski-Ahmed:

> In bilingual societies, one language represents power more than the other. The lower down on the social echelon, the more people tend to 'minor' unilingualism (language of the colonized); the higher up one goes, the more one finds 'major' unilingualism (language of the colonizer).(25)

They are perhaps more successful when they attempt to decentre "woman's voice": "Even when they speak in unision ... there are two voices and not just one," (20) which is fitting, given that they want to speak about univocity and exclusion without invoking the binary logic of the persuasion model. They therefore refuse to efface the differences in voice between the Hispana and the white/Anglo authors. In the six sections of the article, six different voices or combinations of voices are marked. Yet they claim they are "both the authors of this paper and not just sections of it": "we write together without presupposing unity of expression or of experience" (25). How could they, when the decision to say "we" or "you" or "they" is so politically, ethically and emotionally charged? These philosophers' innovative form produces a polyvocal discourse that heightens our awareness of power imbalances among women rather than tries to erase them or smooth over the contradictions when they "do theory" together.

They do this by analysing what happens when privileged white women, themselves writing from an excluded position, theorize about (all) women without examining the concept "woman": they force all women who aren't white/Anglo/privileged into the position of complaining about exclusion and thus silence them. Again. This time, however, *women* do the silencing rather than men.

Lugones and Spelman analyze questions about voice as questions about the ethics of discourse. They remind us of the historical and literary implications of the fact that the *demand* for the woman's voice began as a *complaint*. Complaining is what the less powerful do, but in this case not all who complained were completely powerless and so, to a certain extent, they were considered credible and were able to turn the complaint into a demand. Moral suasion had little to do with their getting a hearing (to the degree they have gotten one).

Lugones and Spelman present the decentring process as a morally and emotionally difficult task most respectfully motivated by a utopian that is, a feminist ethical vision of friendship which alters the way we see the other and ourselves. Nonetheless, the hope they hold out is never far from a realistic and politicized despair:

> We all know the lack of contact felt when we want to discuss a particular issue that requires knowledge of a text with someone who does not know the text at all. Or the discomfort and impatience that arise in us when we are discussing an issue that presupposes a text and someone walks into the conversation who does not know the text. That person is either left out or will impose herself on us and either try to engage in the discussion or try to change the subject. Women of colour are put in these situations by white/Anglo women and men constantly. Now imagine yourself simply left out but wanting to do theory with us. The first thing to recognize and accept is that you disturb our own dialogues by putting yourself in the left-out position and not leaving us in meaningful sense to ourselves.
>
> You must also recognize and accept that you must learn the text. But the text is an extraordinarily complex one, viz., our many different cultures. You are asking us to make ourselves more vulnerable to you than we already are before we have any

reason to trust that you will not take advantage of this vulnerability. So you need to learn to become unintrusive, unimportant, patient to the point of tears, while at the same time open to learning any possible lessons. You will also have to come to terms with the sense of alienation, of not belonging, of having your world thoroughly disrupted, having it criticized and scrutinized from the point of view of those who have been harmed by it, having important concepts central to it dismissed, being viewed with mistrust, being seen as of no consequence except as an object of mistrust. (28–9)

Lugones and Spelman take apart and mutually transform the opposition insider/outsider. "Difference" has not been done away with, but by working to create a genuinely reciprocal dialogue, each has become "both insider and outsider *with respect* (emphasis mine) to each other."

In their article, knowledge of a cultural text makes one an insider. Privileged theorizers who are outsiders nonetheless are advantaged by hierarchical distinctions, and so their accounts, univocal, culturally imperialistic, unhelpful and disrespectful though they may be, are generally the ones we get to hear. That such a situation is ignored by "the" interpretive community marks a profound ethical failure, Lugones and Spelman argue. Following from that charge, they reject the commonsensical notions that theorizers know more about the theorized than vice versa and that to theorize is to be in a state of mastery over one's subject. In a very different way, Jane Gallop also deconstructs the power relations of theory-making and allows ethical questions to arise. However, if readers fail to question theoretical "business as usual," Gallop's books might seem inaccessible and her treatment of theoretical power relations might seem *merely* offensive or nonsensical.

This is not to deny that there is much in Gallop that is offensive and nonsensical: she is blatantly narcissistic, provocatively dramatising her transferences onto Kristeva, Irigaray and Lacan.[3]

Gallop sexualizes her readings as she decentres them and herself. She writes from within her texts (see her use of Irigaray's "Et l'une ne bouge pas sans l'autre," 1982, 114), constructing imaginary arguments between theorists and telling us her dreams about Lacan. She calls these strategies refusals to speak from a position of mastery. While claiming that to interpret is to exercise power, Gallop delights in her own interpretive inadequacy. Reading Gallop demands an intensely polyvocal reader response.

In *Reading Lacan,* Gallop explains how the book almost came not to be. Her narrative exemplifies one of her deconstructive strategies: how a wise fool can make theory into flesh:

> ... the reader returned a report that made a great impression on me. It began with the point that the text was not worthy of publication because it demonstrated inadequate command of the subject matter, adding that I even admitted as much ... The reader was assuming my reading to be not something other, an alternative approach, but a failure at the only correct sort of reading, one that speaks from a position of mastery over a text. I was and am trying to write in a different relation to the material, from a more unsettling confrontation with its contradictory plurivocity, a sort of encounter I believe is possible only if one relinquishes the usual position of command, and thus writes from a more subjective, vulnerable position. (18–9)

This Lacanian position is more vulnerable because it assumes the critic's castration (we are all of us castrated). For most feminists, this is indeed a "position of difficulty" (1985 20). While it could be construed as a feminist stance because it recognizes that plurivocity entails contradictions, to have a woman who claims to be a feminist accept and even glory in her "castration" (sexual and linguistic) presents some dilemmas.

Gallop's paradoxical strategy for securing a hearing from the interpretive community completely gives up on complaining/demanding. Instead, Gallop admits that one never has the right to speak (1985 113) and thus releases us from phallocentrism — without silencing women! Here is her argument:

> To speak without authority is nothing new; the disenfranchised have always so spoken. Simply to refuse authority does not challenge the category distinction between phallic authority and castrated other, between 'subject presumed to know' and subject not in command. One can effectively undo authority

only from the position of authority, in a way that exposes the illusions of that position without renouncing it, so as to permeate the position with the connotations of its illusoriness, so as to show that *everyone*, including the "subject presumed to know," is castrated. (21)

Why should we listen to Gallop, if she, like the rest of us, is an inadequate reader? (Think about what that question assumes about the source of the worth of a reading.) We should listen, because Gallop is more entertaining than irritating. Even when she is irritating, she "interrupts" the "efficient operation" (27) of phallocentricism, or as it says in the blurb to *The Daughter's Seduction*, "unsettle(s) feminism's tendency to accept a traditional, unified, rational, puritanical self — a self supposedly free from the violence of desire." The disruptive pleasure she provides suggests some ways of working/playing towards a feminist utopian project of theorizing which addresses the power dynamic implicit in the persuasion model.

Gallop only partially unsettles the "economy of the One" because of the slippery games she plays with power. If we examine the language she uses to explain the paradox of speaking as a feminist about Lacan, its limited usefulness becomes apparent. How did Gallop persuade Cornell's reader to approve publication of her inadequate book? Did she succeed in permeating "the position itself" (Cornell University Press?) "with the connotations of its illusoriness"? (Cornell should publish that permeating document too so feminist would-be authors can see how it's done.)

Gallop chooses an explicitly formalist way of being inadequate to the demands of heterotextuality within one sex/text by writing a "doubly duplicitous discourse." By comparison with Lugones and Spelman's formal innovations, Gallop's is a de-politicized, individualist's attempt to decentre. Lugones and Spelman write polyvocally as a response to a politicized rage over oppositional differences, whereas Gallop, ungrounded politically, is ambitious enough to want to fail alone. She does this because she reads desire as (always) outside of or at variance with or excluded from the feminist ethical project, as in her critique of Juliet Mitchell:

> Because desire is non-articulable in ethical discourse and because to be within the bounds of feminisms, where she

would locate herself, necessitates ethical discourse (prescription for action) Mitchell is trapped into making the reign of insatiable desire contingent in order to make it impeachable. (1982, 12)

By contrast, Gallop wants to be free, untrapped — by one column of ink! So, she creates *two* columns of ink and we have reached the new Jerusalem. In her privileged position, choice "beckons" to Gallop. The right column or path is the right/correct path of heterosexism, the "comforting norm" (1982, 128). Gallop feels worried. By contrast, Lugones and Spelman feel anguish and rage. The path which is the "one left" pulls Gallop by desire rather than by hunger or thirst for justice. Three pages later, the right path takes over (the left was just a phase) at the point where the unheard difference between "hérétique" and "éthique" in Kristeva's made-up word, "L'Héréthique" makes its mark in writing: "That unpronounceable paternal, heterosexual presence opens up the 'heretic' to 'ethics.' According to 'L'Héréthique,' access to ethics is 'access to the other'" (130).

Has Gallop found a way to marry ethical discourse to desire? To "open up" the female heretic to a female ethics of desire by means of phallus that is definitely not male? Has Gallop escaped from the phallic mother? Has Kristeva's polyvocal or rather polylogical text rescued her? Or has Gallop been reabsorbed and neutralized while refusing to command the reabsorption of her selves? Gallop tries to awe the reader with the ferocity of her struggles to live with the contradictions between women's body and women's attempts to assume power.

Her assessment is uncharacteristically earnest and politically disturbing: "The need, the desire, the wish for the Phallus is great. No matter how oppressive its reign, it is much more comforting than no one in command" (130–1). This special pleading makes Gallop's decision about how to use power seem as deep as comicbook versions of Zen wisdom: "the only way I can move from the spot is to do both" — take a left and a right. Stay paralyzed in the same spot, the same ahistorical moment where "we" have always been. In a feminist reign of justice, no *one* would be in command, but the world we struggle in and against is unfortunately a world where *the One* is in command.

This means that feminist theorists must reconceptualize the ethical so as to reveal the exclusions which made and still make univocity seem possible, credible, desirable, and unremarkable. Doing this requires that we elude the circularity of power/knowledge. We can do that, or rather, get glimmers of what it would be like, when we do two things: simultaneously deconstruct our own interpretations and also ask painful questions about the materiality of differences among women.

Such questions, coming after I have spoken so abstractly, might seem refreshingly concrete, but they are amazingly difficult. Do you believe that the concept of class is a British import and doesn't really fit North American reality?[4] Does hearing feminists address class at a conference make you feel angry and uncomfortable? Is oppression "interesting" only as a linguistic construct? Haven't we focused our exploration of power too narrowly if we are only interested in how it is mediated through language? That such questions do not tend to arise in feminist criticism points to the aporia in our theory and practice and suggests how limited it is to propose only discursive strategies for eliminating political oppression.

♦

## NOTES

1. This useful and memorable phrase was coined by Rachel Blau DuPlessis in "For the Etruscans." Nothing else I know states the theoretical problem as succinctly.

2. See, among others, Andrea Lebowitz, "Is Feminist Literary Criticism Becoming Anti-Feminist?" Lebowitz seems wrongheaded to me in many of her claims about theorizing, but she states the case for the ethical and political responsibility of the feminist critic very well. Elaine Showalter's "Feminist Criticism in the Wilderness" is the *locus classicus* for feminist suspicion of "male theory."

3. Gallop, by the way, herself concludes that Kristeva's "surprising self-references that interrupt her efforts to erect a theory ... are the marks of a female sexual economy" (1982, 119).

4. This comment was actually made to me. Can you top it?

## WORKS CITED

DuPlessis, Rachel Blau. "For the Etruscans." Showalter 271-291.

Gallop, Jane. *The Daughter's Seduction: Feminism and Psychoanalysis*. Ithaca: Cornell University Press, 1982.

_____, *Reading Lacan*. Ithaca: Cornell University Press, 1985.

Hajdukowski-Ahmed, Maroussia. "Le dénoncé/énoncé du langage au féminin ou le rapport de la femme au langage." In *Féminité, Subersion, Ecriture*, edited by Suzanne Lamy and Irène Pagès, translated by Susanne de Lotbinière-Harwood. Montreal: Editions du Remue-Ménage, 1984.

Heilbrun, Carolyn and Catharine R. Stimpson. "Theories of Feminist Criticism: A Dialogue" *Feminist Literary Criticism*. Ed. Josephine Donovan. Lexington: University Press of Kentucky, 1975. 61-73.

Irigaray, Luce. *Speculum of the Other Woman*. Translated by Gillian C. Gill. Ithaca: Cornell University Press, 1985.

Kolodny, Annette. "Dancing Through the Minefield: Some Observations of the Theory, Practice, and Politics of a Feminist Literary Criticism." Showalter 144-67.

Kroker, Marilouise and Arthur, Pamela McCallum, and Mair Verthuy, eds. *Feminism Now: Theory and Practice*. Montreal: New World Perspectives, 1985.

Lebowitz, Andrea. "Is Feminist Literary Criticism Becoming Anti-Feminist?" *Tessera*, 1, *Room of One's Own* 8 (1984):97-108.

Lugones, Maria C. and Elizabeth V. Spelman. "Have We Got A Theory for You! Feminist Theory, Cultural Imperialism and the Demand for the 'The Woman's Voice.'" *Women and Values: Reading in Recent Feminist Philosophy*, edited by Marilyn Pearsall. Belmont, California: Wadsworth, 1986. 19-31.

Schweickart, Patrocinio. "What are we doing, really?" In *Feminism Now: Theory and Practice*, edited by M. Kroker et al. Montreal: New World Perspectives, 1985. 148-64.

Showalter, Elaine, ed. *The New Feminist Criticism: Essays on Women, Literature and Theory*. New York: Pantheon, 1985.

Woolf, Virginia. *Three Guineas*. London: The Hogarth Press, 1938. Reprinted by Harmondsworth: Penguin, 1977.

# IN CONVERSATION

*Barbara Godard, Susan Knutson,
Daphne Marlatt, Kathy Mezei and Gail Scott*

D.M. What is it about the word "conversation" that appeals to my imagination so much more than "discussion" or "dialogue"? Perhaps it's a less formal connotation, an association with the spoken rather than the written word. From the Socratic dialogues on, dialogue, like discussion, has tended to be associated with the written treatment of certain ideas (taking good philosophic medicine), exercising one's intellect — on whatever. As for whatever, she, to appropriate the generic, has had little to say in this case because the case he has made out for her is already closed. On the other hand, conversation elicits her participation, creates an opening for her to speak: to beg the question if she so desires, to reword it, return it, transformed by her own perspective. The mutual quality of conversation is embedded in its very roots, in Middle English, Old French, in Latin to live with, and further back (Indo-European), to turn. Two minds turning around each other, two (at least) perspectives, two (various) entries into language turning over the words, testing them, trying them on for size in a mutual exchange that wanders from room to room, takes breaks, remakes the linguistic bed, stirs diversion into analysis. In *d'elles,* Suzanne Lamy, writing about the woman-to-woman series of interviews between Marguerite Duras and Xavière Gauthier, stressed the "betweenness" of their *entretiens,* their mutual listening and questioning that ran so counter to the *monologues déguisés* of interviews with male writers. She observed that the interviews quickly shifted to

♦ IN CONVERSATION ♦

Duras' home, with the women making jam together between conversations. In the nearly ten years since *d'elles'* appearance, have we seen women's writing in Quebec and Canada create the kind of space in which women readers can feel at home? Are we talking back and forth to each other — in the play of intertextuality, for instance, do we have an extended conversation? Or is this a closed conversation, limited to only a few writers? And what about the openness, the exploring quality of conversation, as opposed to the monologic — can this be said to signal feminist writing? Or are we moving towards an orthodoxy, a closed system of ideas?

K.M. Dialogue is seen as a structured form with conventions and expectations, "to speak alternatively." Because of Bakhtin's theories of the dialogic imagination, it is now a fashionable term, whose perimeters have expanded to include (covert) relationships within and without texts; *everything* is in a dialogic relation with everything, and if not, that is significant too. A dialogue surely implies an oral activity, but as you mentioned, Daphne, it is associated with the written — in the structured debates of Socrates and Plato (and were they not really monologues, lectures, yes, a method of teaching, but of conveying and imposing a master's point of view? which accounts for Louky Bersianik's rewriting of Plato's symposium in *Le piquenique sur l'Acropole*), and in the writing down of conversations of people in novels, e.g. the dialogue in Jane Austen or Margaret Atwood, or Ernest Hemingway! What happens in the writing down, what shifts, changes, omissions, erasures? Who writes the dialogue? The speakers or a listener? Perhaps then Daphne is right in seeing dialogue as too bound up with patriarchal discourse in which women have been silenced (and what of Diotima in Plato's *Symposium?*). Are the pieces you will read in *Tessera* dialogues — two voices speaking alternatively — but in prescribed modes? Are there among them feminist rewritings of this genre? Or are the interviews conversations rather than dialogues? But conversations, Daphne, are not exchanges only between two voices, but between many, like the first *Tessera* editorial, and like this editorial. But then, what prevents women from interrupting the other, from monologuing, from truly hearing the other voices? And now I think I am repeating your questions: how can the writing express the opening, the liberating, and

♦ Barbara Godard, Susan Knutson,
Daphne Marlatt, Kathy Mezei and Gail Scott ♦

the building that conversation among women, free from censors and the observing eye, and accompanied by good food and wine should "ideally" exemplify? Are the plays of Jovette Marchessault conversations among women, or are they a series of monologues? Where are the conversations in the fictions you read, or are they still trapped in silence and absence? Can conversations carry us further into new ideas? Do we listen to each other? Look at the words; look at the syntax of our speaking.

G.S. Comparing dialogue and conversation seems like comparing apples and oranges, given that their borders fade and cross, particularly in women's writing where the spoken and written word have moved closer together. It's true dialogue refers more directly to the text, to writing. And since dialogue seems to be on the way here to getting a bad name, I think I'll play devil's advocate and defend it. Perhaps the reference to the Socratic notion of dialogue has inadvertently set us off on assumptions that I believe are no longer valid (notably that it is a male discourse tending towards closure, hence excluding *her* intervention). In fact, contemporary women writers, including Kristeva and Lamy, have *feminized* the notion of dialogue rather than rejecting it.

I personally love how new writing by women strives to situate the reader in a participatory stance that I would call dialogic vis-à-vis the text, by assuming *she the writer* is *addressing* a *feminine* other. This stance assumes theory as a collective process — the opposite of what goes on in academia. In the writing group to which I belong, for example, we set ourselves the goal of fruitful dialogue in the first part of our meetings: the "coffee" part. That's when we discuss the texts we've brought with us, always texts on some theoretical point of mutual interest. (This issue carries the texts of a meeting on feminism and post-modernism.) And I, for one, would be very annoyed if our discussions were interrupted by "conversation" about domestic matters, love affairs, etc., except inasmuch as these matters touched on the subject at hand. The conversation comes after the work. I guess dialogue is about rigour, and I don't see why feminists should do without this kind of concentration, this means of striving for excellence.

I don't mind, either, that the modern notion of dialogue comes from Bakhtin, because Bakhtin's theories of transgressing the law by abolishing the writer-as-unary-authority were developed in the context of revolutionary struggle. In turn, the women's struggle has added a new ideological slant to the notion, underscoring the transgressive nature of writing as a dialogue among women that modifies both the writing and the reading (and the writer and the reader). Constantly. I believe so firmly in the energy of this struggle and how it feeds our writing, and the reverse, that I do not fear we are a few women talking to each other. For me, also, the dialogic has to be profoundly anchored in form to work: it must be writing that cries for response through each of its spaces, its provocations, its theoretical questioning. It doesn't preach, teach, provide the correct feminist line. That's why I prefer *l'écriture au féminin* to *feminist writing*. I just wish I could find a good English translation for the former — writing-in-the-feminine seems to dilute it somehow ...

S.K. In "musing with mother tongue," Daphne wrote of language that "it bears us as we are born into it, into cognition." What is true of language is particularly true of discourse. In discourse, whether conversation *or* dialogue, we are created and cradled, given back to ourselves in the intimacy of connection between the first and second person: the I and the other-to-whom-I-speak(s). I talk(s) to you and you answer(s) in a rise and fall that is not transcendence but two subjects swimming in "our sea" ("musing with mother-tongue"), splashing the swelling surface of our being in words. We are born each singly but together. We exchange gifts.

In discourse between women a warmth can arise from the fact that we are symbolic equals. Women's shared symbolic status as "the other sex" inhibits the automatic exercise of rank that gender hierarchy makes possible. This gives us a chance to deal with issues of privilege which *do* divide us, including those of race, class, nationality, disability and sexual preference. My feminism hopes and believes that gender can be a bridge of listening and solidarity between women with different experiences of oppression and privilege.

In the world which is opened up by the feminine I and you addressing each other, women are constructed as subjects. We feminize the two true personal pronouns that are the "Devonian rocks" of Indo-European languages and the bedrock of our subjectivity.[1] Émile Benveniste has shown how the first person and second person pronouns indicate positions in discourse, functioning referentially to construct subjectivity. 'She,' 'he' and 'it,' on the contrary, point to one who is absent: signifying what is outside the spiral of discourses, they are not true pronouns. Monique Wittig pursued the implications of Benveniste's argument for women ("The Mark of Gender"). She declared that in spite of gender's marking of women as other, we "lay claim to universality" "through abstraction" when, at the moment of speech, we assume the powers of language. This theory parallels the moment of holographic illumination in Nicole Brossard's *Picture Theory: la scène blanche* from which surges forth a picture of *la femme intégrale*. In accessing the utopian potential of language we position ourselves in respect to that powerful abstraction, and become what we really are, whole and integral. We also position ourselves with respect to the world we are addressing.

Building culture *au féminin* we inhabit not only the 'I' and the 'you' but the 'she,' 'he' and 'it' for the construction of a world in which women live fully. Attentive, as Daphne says, to each other's turnings.

B.G. The collective form which our conversation takes in this introduction, as well as that of Louky, France, Gail, Nicole and the Louises occurring on the theoretical Sundays, has been identified as a form of exchange privileged by women in the form of helpful interchange which Jeanne Demers and Line McMurray have found in the graffiti of women prostitutes in Montreal. You all know the form in women's washrooms. One woman asks a question (often implicit) and others provide a string of responsive and serious replies. This "collective conversation" is advisory, interactive, caretaking — and unique to women's graffiti. However, this is a form of support for one another in opposition to the dominant patriarchal order, an expression of the co-operation of the *dominated*. As such, this model of collaborative and empowering talk may itself be encoded within the power politics of sexual difference, that is, within the dominant discourse, as absence and not as resistance or struggle. In this way, I circle around the issue which concerns us all, the question of power and feminist struggle. Power is a word we more frequently address indirectly through a series of questions. What is the difference between dialogue and conversation? Is it a difference between male hierarchical writing and female egalitarian speaking? What are the implications of such binary thinking?

This is where Bakhtin becomes helpful, as you point out, Gail, in underscoring the transgression of the law in his concept of the dialogic or the carnivalesque (which sounds more subversive). We have to be careful though not to equate dialogue with dialog, or the dialogic, as Bakhtin more frequently terms it, the juxtaposition or confrontation of language, of social forces and epochs, determined by the socio-ideological development of languages. Nor is dialogic a synonym for dialectic. Dialectic is abstract and moves towards synthesis whereas dialogic is material and exists only for another contextual meaning in an infinitely continuing chain of meaning. The blurring of boundaries in the interrelation between the inserted speech of the other and one's own speech produces a new subject position, not a unitary subject, 'I-for-myself' but a heterogeneous subject, 'I-for-another' and the 'not-I-in-me.' In this concept of relational difference, the dialogic contrasts with the hierarchical ordering of difference in/by discourse, according to Foucault, for whom discourse focuses primarily on how power dominates by prescribing reversals, reverse discourses and counter-discourses. Power may also be productive, as Bakhtin points out. Rather than locating resistance as merely a counter-effect of the networks of power, one may also begin from a situation of struggle, radical action and change. Meaning exists differentially. No practice or discourse exists in itself; on whatever side, it is ultimately shaped and preceded by what it is opposing and so can never simply dictate its own terms.

The importance of the dialogic for feminist discourse becomes clear. It establishes a theoretical ground for an emancipatory practice grounded in critique and resistance. For the focus of the dialogic is on becoming and change, on bodies and social formation as s(c)ites of transgression. In these terms, the feminist project is not merely inscribed within the dominant discourse as opposition but is an independent movement towards empowerment. In Bakhtin's notion of a field of clashing languages — heteroglossia (his word for discourses) — is to be found an instance of popular discourses taking shape both against and from beyond the terrain of what prevails. Moreover, Bakhtin acknowledges that all our thought — philosophical, scientific and *artistic* — is born and shaped in the process of interaction and *struggle* with others' thought which foregrounds the transformative impact of confrontation. Like you, Gail, I take heart in the energy of this struggle, energy whose *transformative* capacities feed not only our writing but also our reading.

"The only complete reading is the one which transforms the book into a simultaneous network of reciprocal relationships," writes Derrida. Now that I have transformed your texts by reading them intra and intertextually with respect to subjectivity and discourse, Tesserae, it is the reader's turn to exercise her transformative capacities. Since reading one text through another, the palimpsest, is the paradigm for allegorical work, my (re)writing is a form of allegoresis, a practice that is an investigation of speaking bodies and tell-tale signs, that is, a perfomative gesture, calling you.

♦

## NOTES

1. The personal pronouns belong to the very earliest layer of Indo-European that can be reached by reconstruction; they have been called the "Devonian rocks" of Indo-European. The lack of any formal resemblance in English between the subject case (nominative) I and the object case (accusative) me is a direct and faithful reflex of the same disparity in Proto-Indo-European, respectively *$eg$ (*ego) and *$me$-1. The other pronouns are *$tu$- (*te-), 'thou,' *$nes$-2, *we-, 'we,' *$yu$-1 (*wes-), 'you.' No pronouns for the third person were in use. (Calvert Watkins, "Indo-European and the Indo-Europeans," *The Houghton Mifflin Canadian Dictionary of the English Language*, p. 1499.)

# WHAT WE TALK ABOUT ON SUNDAYS

*Nicole Brossard, Louky Bersianik, Louise Cotnoir,
Louise Dupré, Gail Scott and France Théoret*
Translated by Barbara Godard

*Conversation and dialogue are the point of our Sunday meetings. And we six women writers take as much pleasure in the intellectual mutual respect and rigour we apply to reading and discussing each other's work, i.e. the "coffee" part of the meeting, as we do in the "conversational" part later, accompanied by wine and good food. We feel strongly about structuring the first part of our meetings, working from written texts in order to concentrate better on the theoretical questions that attract us: woman as subject, feminist activism, narration, to name a few of them. For all of us, I think, the desire for rigorous work stems from our reciprocal respect for the thinking of the other members in the group. Moreover, we are all women writers, workers, mothers in some cases, with little time available for each other. We have to make the most of it! Often during the pleasure part of the meeting, the conversation continues on our theoretical preoccupations, because our exchanges frequently take off with an enthusiasm difficult to restrain. Naturally, each one of us has her own manner of engaging in dialogue or conversation, and of blending the two ... I see us around the table, Louise Cotnoir, with her lively, sensitive mind, her unshakeable commitment; France Théoret, who knows how to speak as well as listen, with exemplary precision; Louky Bersianik, tireless critic of everything concerning the symbolic order;*

♦ NICOLE BROSSARD, LOUKY BERSIANIK, LOUISE COTNOIR,
LOUISE DUPRÉ, GAIL SCOTT AND FRANCE THÉORET ♦

*Nicole Brossard, optimistic, integral, with her impressive flair for the essential; Louise Dupré, whose limpid sentences reveal great theoretical insight ... and myself.*

*The following texts come from our discussion on feminism and* la post-modernité. *In Quebec, presently, modernity, so important for feminist writing (*écriture au féminin*), seems, according to some people, to be sounding its death knell. This* modernité, *so important for women here, introducing concepts like fiction-theory with its insistence on the breakdown of genres, the deconstruction of the unary subject and the self-reflexive element of writing, is in the process of giving way to a post-modern writing where the theory would be reabsorbed into the text with its baroque forms, where the notion of progress underpinning* la modernité *would be overtaken by a (more decadent?)* fin de siècle *ambiance. However, this theoretical displacement also offers new opportunities for narrative, foregrounding also a certain tragic mode, precursor, perhaps, of new visions. What does our group of women think about this? As you will see, we have mixed feelings!*

*(So not to confuse anglophone readers, 'la modernité' is generally translated by 'postmodernism' in English. As for 'la post-modernité,' I should say that anglo-American new narrative (Kathy Acker, Lynne Tillman, among others) seems imbued with a spirit similar to the French* post-modernité.

— G.S

## JUXTAPOSED STEPS OF DESIRE

Post-modernity has to do with strong sensations, contradictory feelings, nostalgia; a deregulated approach to desire, disoriented desire. The advent of a gap between knowledge and emotion, post-modernity is a kind of theatre where subjectivities cross, going and coming, each one more performative than the other, while a few prompters wear themselves out in the depths of their pit, whispering the original text, a text whose representation seems impossible from now on. This is a kind of faceless tragedy despite the abundance of bodies and expressions. Paradoxically, this sense of the tragic permits a certain questioning and hope.

Post-modernity is the amortization of a non-authorized mourning for history, it is the traumatic thought of history dissolving in its acceleration: sudden weightlessness. It's the adventure of a subject without warning constricted in its lightness, constrained above all to a form of knowledge it loathes: intuition. Here is a feminine position not without some embarrassment for intellectuals, which advantages, as is often the case, creative artists, and seems relatively comfortable for women. In fact, if intuition seems to be the only recourse we have for understanding the worlds we inhabit, simultaneously deserted and overcrowded, this is because the mediating figure of Man as well as the imaginary construct that ensures his mythic sex-appeal has lost its credibility. Of this great predatory figure only the disillusioned and pouting mouth remains.

From this angle, post-modernity is the great masculine "downer." From another angle, it is the empty moment where the methods of the future are nonetheless in play, the cognitive methods, values, myths and metaphors that will determine new relations with nature, the origyn and death. Post-modernity is viable only inasmuch as the feminine generates the imaginary in the heart of this long emptiness.

— N.B.

## *POST-MODERNITY: A TRAP*

With post-modernity, I have the impression they want to throw the baby of modernity out with the bath water ... Too quickly they wanted to get out of modernity which has been so explosive, wanted to short-circuit it. Why? Because women began to formulate their dreams within its writing space? Because within its space women were able to write their bodies their hopes, their imaginary otherwise? Post-modernity comes to defuse their work of undermining, their demands, their methods of "reinventing life."

What can I say about post-modernity in Quebec writing? It has produced the Conference on the Death of Genre (cf. *La Nouvelle barre du jour*)!!! What genre/gender is in question here if not the masculine gender?!? No one in the present baroque context where priority is given to the economy, the birth rate and nuclear weapons,

♦ NICOLE BROSSARD, LOUKY BERSIANIK, LOUISE COTNOIR,
LOUISE DUPRÉ, GAIL SCOTT AND FRANCE THÉORET ♦

dare say behind the diaphanous veil of the media that these are the very questions raised a long time ago by feminists ... That in their writing, authors were attacking all the *power* responsible for the economic, social and political "crash" whose themes of "disenchantment, disaster, death" constitute the fine texts of this post-modernity ... WOE! MALE-DICTION! Post-modernity is sidetracking women's innovations in writing (blurring genres, neologisms, fragmented writing, etc.). Post-modernity underlines male complicity with a certain anti-life way of thinking. Post-modernity is the ultimate expression of a masculine suicidal drive.

How can feminist authers be taken in by such a trap? I'll take up the defence of modernity because it offers me the possibility of transforming writing and society, of *feminizing* them.

— L.C.

## NOTES FOR AN "ALPHABET OF REVELATIONS"

It would be convenient to consider post-modernity as a film projected backwards, where the voluntary faultlines of modernity would be filled in, the explosions of meaning turn back on its obstructions, where the formerly fragmented and un-significant woman would read herself whole not between the lines but outrageously visible in her integrality and integrity. In short, the baby would return to the uterus through the magic of a retreat and literature would once more be pregnant with fiction and ready to give birth to an ensemble that would no longer be in fragments. Sadly, things are not so simple.

The expression "post-modernity" consecrates the concept of "modernity" which has been the rage for nearly a century. The two entities are linked not only by their opposition but by everything the latter owes to the former. Hence the numerous contradictions about their respective natures, which are far from gaining general consensus. How to speak about them precisely? How to name what will come after post-modernity?

Modernity and post-modernity — issues in many fields other than literature — are categories defined by male intellectuals that have been appropriated by women writers and intellectuals. I am not sure women should accept these categories and the same grounds, running the risk of staying on the margins and adding to the confusion conveyed by the masculine, always omnipotent in the court of language and ideas.

It is well known that men cannot accept their twilight without holding the entire earth hostage under the threat of nuclear winter. Patriarchy cannot see the collapse of the Caryatides which hold its temple up without wanting the sky literally to fall on the head of every man and especially every woman.

Modernity, while erecting diverse pedestals for the subject, has brought its statue crashing down. So modernity prepared an exhibition of empty pedestals like mutilated grave stones from which even the names of the dead have disappeared. Absolute fragments of the subject, dispersed ashes. The brief form which produced the fragment, according to the sound principle of contestation against the very notion of literary genre, has itself become a genre.

Post-modernity which has tolled the knell of the genre — or rather which has officially reported its obvious death — seeks the ensembles from which have been detached countless isolated elements in conflict among themselves. In post-modernity may be noted restorations and revelations along the lines of the return of the pendulum or an encounter with the primary model. You can bet post-modernity will find the organigram of patriarchy and will have only to reconstruct its temple which had been shaken by writing-in-the-feminine (*écriture au féminin*) among other practices. Moreover, as things are at present, that's what topicality, seconded by fiction and art, presents us for reading, seeing and hearing in our everyday reality.

— L.B.

## *WOMEN HAVE ANOTHER VERSION OF HISTORY*

From the moment a writer declared it was natural to be modern, we had moved somewhere else, it seemed to me, into post-modernity. Post-modernity invites the reproduction of literary forms and the

♦ NICOLE BROSSARD, LOUKY BERSIANIK, LOUISE COTNOIR,
LOUISE DUPRÉ, GAIL SCOTT AND FRANCE THÉORET ♦

status quo in thought because, it seems, we can no longer invent the future. Post-modern disenchantment is accompanied by a turning back on self which doesn't really accommodate feminist thinking. We live in an era where books pile up, we write the world in its most infinitesimal details without making it more meaningful. This is an era of loose ends.

For several years now, essays generally written by man have impugned feminism perceived in the wake of the movement for sexual liberation or of Marxism. Feminism is an unskirtable movement whose scope has been singularly reduced and, above all, whose breadth of reflection impoverished. Post-modernity borders on nihilism.

I still think women have another version of history to write, that there has not been nor is there any ideal period of writing, but our angle of vision, our position is going to change.

— F.T.

## *A POST-HISTORICAL CONSCIOUSNESS*

Post-modernity. This is a relatively recent concept in the francophone world, introduced through philosophy (Lyotard), whereas "post-modernism" was already well established in the anglophone world. Consequently, the two concepts are not necessarily synonymous. In the literary field, post-modernity becomes for us a critical concept defining textuality in its relation to modernity.

What is there to say? We know that during the 1960s and 1970s in Quebec around *La Barre du jour* and *Les Herbes rouges*, as in France in the periodical *Tel Quel*, a modernity was elaborated that could be charged with formalism, a radical modernity endeavouring to think writing outside a theological vision of language. There was a refusal to consider the author a demiurge, all-powerful master of the imaginary. The text was seen as a product of the unconscious and of History, work on linguistic material from which the subject and the referent must be evacuated.

Very soon, however, women writers displayed their dissidence from modernity, wanting to reintroduce into their fictions a subject-in-the-feminine. The insertion of this subjectivity enabled a rerouting of modernity, giving an *existential* dimension back to a formalism that risked turning emptily around on itself, becoming fetishistic: the dimension of the everyday reality of women, their suffering, madness, motherhood, love, dream, hope.

Rerouting, displacement of modernity. Through this feminist consciousness, the new writing left behind its orthodox radicalism in order to think differently, otherwise than in terms of complete rupture, beyond an intellectualism seeking the neutrality of the body, the occultation of the 'I' and of meaning. Because post-modernity is precisely that other look, that other point of view on writing which works more by addition than by subtraction or discrimination. Post-modernity juxtaposes reason and feeling, archaic and modern, beautiful and ugly, sublime and monstrous, poetic and prosaic, fictive, anecdotal and theoretical. It is marked by the reappropriation of myths (Nicole Brossard's Amazon, Jovette Marchessault's Mother Goddess, Yolande Villemaire's androgyn, Carole Massé's Christian figures, etc.) and of literary "genres" traditionally considered feminine: diary, letter, lament, monologue. It recuperates elements from dated literary modes, repatriating certain features of classicism, of baroque, of nationalist consciousness, even of folklore.

So, post-modernity is, above all, audacity, invention, breaking out of frames. While modernity believed in the idea of progress, of going beyond, post-modernity is "characterized not only by its newness in relation to the modern, but more radically as the dissolution of the category of the new, as an experiment with an "end of history," and no longer as the presentation of another phase, whether this be more progressive, less regressive matters little, of this same history" (Vatimo 10).

Now it is precisely to the end of history that we are invited by feminism, a body of thought outside patriarchy situated in a posthistorical consciousness. Not an *ideology* — like Marxism, for example — feminism is rather a *philosophy*, moving, opening, spiraling, which brings an end to the fixed, closed, unary and linear vision that has prevailed for thousands of years and proceeds by exclusions. Without closing its eyes to the nuclear threat, feminism enables one to envisage an "end of history" beyond catastrophe, associating *post-modernity with possibility*. Through the research they are undertaking, one can say here and now that writings-in-the-feminine remain essential.

— L.D.

## *A Step or a Stumble?*

Maybe because I am an anglophone and write mainly prose, the question of narration has always felt like a heavy bird perched on my shoulder. I have not lived as intensely as my Quebec colleagues the experiment of textuality, that amalgam of fiction and theory which signalled modernity here. For me, the genres of novel and short story were not completely ruptured, albeit profoundly modified under the influence of this modernity. Then, recently, post-modernity came to "confirm" the dissolution of these forms by announcing the death of genre. Except, obviously, it was necessary to fill the gap immediately with something else. New baroque forms appeared, forms in which narrativity resurfaced — to relate the end of History all the while clinging obsessively to this History. This conjuncture suits me admirably (from a stylistic point of view) ... and not at all (in its obsessive relation to History).

I think I share this ambivalence towards post-modernity with other women writers. On the one hand, there are women who excel in the *récit* — a long narrative form, distinct from the novel — which has assimilated certain lessons of modernity while insisting on the emergence of a subject-in-the-feminine. To put this another way, our desire to create new narrative forms to stage this subject-in-the-feminine was manifested well before French philosophers ushered in post-modernity. Still, some of us appreciate the fact that post-modernity plays strongly upon the despairing side of the picture. For we may see in this despair signs which are the forerunners of a new era. I am not alone in thinking that we are living at this end of the twentieth century the end of Greco-Judeo-Christian civilization.

Yes, perhaps we women are in the process of constituting the same relation we had to modernity, i.e. we are creating a post-modernity-in-the-feminine (*post-moderne au féminin*). A post-modernity that will put our signature on the era. Where men see death, we'll see only the end of a cycle. After all, we cannot expect patriarchy to be mortally wounded without some cries of disaster.

It's true that the self-reflexive side of modernity, so important for the emergence of a subject-in-the-feminine seems to have been displaced. But this 'I' needed a change of air, needed other fictions. Perhaps, she needs, for example, to be able to join other women and men in the carnival she's been watching from her window.

— G.S.

♦

## Works Cited

Lyotard, Jean-François. *La Condition postmoderne.* Paris: Minuit, 1979. *The Postmodern Condition: A Report on Knowledge.* Trans. Geoff Bennington and Brian Massumi. Minneapolis: University of Minnesota Press, 1984.

Magritte. *Alphabet des révélations.* 1928.

La Mort du genre. "La Mort du genre 1 & 2." *La Nouvelle barre du jour.* 209–11 (1988). 216–17 (1989).

Vatimo, Gianni. *La Fin de la modernité.* Paris: Seuil, 1987.

# What? You Too?

*Lise Gauvin*

*Translated by Barbara Godard*

"What? You too?"
"I'm capitulating, I confess."
"Really and truly?"
"Couldn't be more serious. I'm beginning the second chapter. You're not going to find out anything more now. At any rate, I've made my decision. That's something at least."
"You don't mean it! After railing so long against the imperialism of the novel"
"Exactly. This isn't the end of my revolt. It's all you hear about these days. You can't be a writer any longer if you don't dare call your prose 'novel,' the magic label and 'Open Sesame' of all contemporary tribunals and departments of reading. To such a point that biographies, memoirs, and other reputedly serious texts, even the essay, are travestied in this form, guarantee of all seductions. A well-known writer recently explained to me that it was necessary to be underhanded, be crafty with it, fix the ambiguity in the very heart of a dated, historic event. The term 'fiction,' far from discrediting these texts, adds a sort of 'surplus-value.' It's a safe passport, a guided tour. Half the people I know write novels, the other half read nothing but novels. So, I finally understood ..."
"That's just what I said. You gave in. At any rate, I'm resisting. I prefer more open forms, like the diary or letter. At least you know who's speaking. They're direct. No double dealing."

"I wonder if one doesn't hide oneself more in the so-called personal forms. Since the 'I' is exposed, you can't do anything except modify it a bit, dress it up for visitors. Give it an unconscious facelift!"

"Maybe, but the operation is carried out in complete liberty. The letter is a sort of chameleon whereas fiction is terribly restricted, no matter what they say. As soon as someone has the misfortune to write 'he' followed by the imperfect tense, the reader is willing to believe anything, to take sentences as hard cash, to get angry at the writer if there's a false step, if a character gets forgotten in a corner, if events aren't given the necessary amplitude. With an implacable logic, scarcely have the first words been put down, than they must correspond to the image the reader has made of real life. You have to satisfy and surprise at the same time. You have to strut about showing off your legs! Anyway, weren't you the one who was carping about the novel being a globalizing, totalizing affair?"

"The novel represents power, for sure. I'm not the one who said that. I heard it the other day on TV from a poet who was busy writing one himself. Like everybody else. 'What do you mean?' the interviewer asked him in surprise.' 'Well, if I please, I can give all the qualities or faults I want to any character: I can say about you or your double, that you are ugly and stupid, if I like. It depends only on me,' he explained. He even added that he hoped everybody would write a novel. Good exercise. Just as good as aerobics. The reply didn't quite satisfy me. I went to meet him one Saturday afternoon during a reading at a bookstore. I said, 'Is the novel power because it's a totality, a system for explaining the world?' He dodged the question. He doesn't like abstractions. 'The novel is the only power' he replied. 'It depends on readers,' I said. 'In one or two words,' he asked me laughingly. This time it was the former minister who spoke. I returned to the charge. 'Is the novel power only if it has closure, if there's a story with a beginning, middle and end?' Then he confided in me. 'That's exactly what mine is not, why the editor rejected it. He wants me to rewrite it, to make many changes.' You see how complicated things are."

"I always thought the novel suited men more. At some level, you have to take the place of God."

"Since when was God a man? What about Madame de Lafayette, Madame Woolf, Madame Duras and Madame Roy?"

### ♦ WHAT? YOU TOO? ♦

"Hang on there, you don't have to get on your high horse. I didn't say the form was masculine. I was very careful not to. I'm not going to fall for the naïve mistake of believing forms are gendered. Gender is at work before the writing, in the frame of mind that is a preliminary to any writing. When a woman decides to write, she is relatively successful because she has a great capacity for attending to the thousand and one details that make up the very texture of the novel. But what I mean is she must first work on herself a lot. To write a novel you have to constitute yourself as subject — this is the zero degree of character — pull yourself up a notch or two above the fray, and then throw one's subject in a game of dice."

"I've always believed writing was mainly research."

"Yes, while you're writing, but before beginning, you have to convince yourself according to an absolutely subjective judgement that the outlook you have of the world, the time you have it, is the most important thing in the world."

"But a novel is a novel ..."

"Writing a novel is always to some extent choosing to make History. That takes a good deal of confidence, pretension and temerity. It's not obvious at the beginning. Happily for me, I don't feel that particular need. And since you want to know everything, the novel has a documentary aspect that grates on my nerves. Personally, I prefer to read *Historia* or the *Geographic Magazine*. That's all I need for an attainable dream. Either fiction exists or it doesn't exist, isn't that the question? I know people who have combed through the libraries for years before writing their novel. So much time wasted."

"Historical novels bore me too. I wonder if they aren't today's folklore."

"What I should like, if ever I start writing one — and I assure you I haven't yet — is just to collect everything at hand, stick theatre tickets beside reflections on the meaning of life, reproduce news incidents in bulk, shopping lists, holiday plans, committee meetings, and afterwards give it the title: novel. It'd be a real grab-bag."

"Too bad, it's already been done. That's annoying. As soon as you think of a form, if you've read anything at all, you realize it already exists. Anyway, literature, so they say, is massive plagiarism, except the first book, the one never found."

"Most people who write are not bothered by all these scruples."

"Or modestly they agree to the work of recreating, tirelessly reworking the same motifs, looking infinitely at the same thing, but from all its angles, before, behind, or beside, with a fly's eye. The novelist is polymorphously perverse. I've forgotten who said that."

"Able to see everything, a voyeur, then omniscient."

"So what next?"

"It's easy. All you have to do is write whatever comes into your field of vision, what's there before, behind and beside you. Or what comes into your range of hearing."

"Good. I understand. I'm leaving. Before I find myself between two covers."

◆

*Carol* by Persimmon Blackbridge and Michelle Kanashiro-Christiansen
PHOTO: Susan Stewart.

# Doing Time

*Doing Time is a collaborative art work with sculpture by Persimmon Blackbridge and texts by Michelle Kanashiro-Christiansen, Geri Ferguson, Lyn MacDonald and Bea Walkus. The sculptures are twenty-five life-size cast paper figures on a maze of tall grey walls. The texts, which are written on the walls, are firsthand accounts of life in prison, and the conditions outside that send women to prison.*

### Carol

My friend Carol was a beautiful native woman. We'd both been working the street for a long time. She had a kid, living up North. She worked hard to support him and on his birthday, she'd work extra hard, and she'd buy him all these presents. Then she was killed by a trick.

When they found her dead, I was out of town at my mom's. Someone phoned and told me and I just cried. When I lost my kids, I swore I'd never let anybody make me cry again and they didn't for 7 years. But when Carol died, I broke down and cried. My mother was gonna give me valiums, here take a valium, it'll make you feel better. But I just cried harder. My mother couldn't understand. To her, hookers aren't real people. It's like they're disposable. I told her, look mom, I'm a prostitute too but if I died, you'd mourn. But she didn't want to hear it. It was too scary for her to think about.

— Michelle Kanashiro-Christiansen

*Occupational Hazard* (close-up) by Persimmon Blackbridge and Michelle Kanashiro-Christiansen Photo: Susan Stewart.

♦ DOING TIME ♦

## 1. OCCUPATIONAL HAZARD

We're not out to hurt anybody. We're just making our money and doing our business. When I was on the street, I could watch a soap opera and turn a trick at the same time. I remember before, the cops didn't harass you as much and you had more rights. But with this new law, everybody's all moralistic. Like my friend Cat, when she tried to report a bad trick, the prosecutor told her it was just an occupational hazard. She was sexually assaulted with a crow bar. But it's just an occupational hazard. Sure, tell me about it. And Carol, my best friend Carol. She was killed. They kicked us out of the West End, out to where there's not so many lights and people. We're out of sight, now, nice and tidy. 21 of us have been killed in this town since then, 21 women in 3 years. They're never going to find Carol's murderer. They never found Nicky's murderer. They never found the Green River murderer. These men are killing my friends. But who cares, you know, they're only prostitutes.

— Michelle Kanashiro-Christiansen

*Time* (close-up) by Persimmon Blackbridge and Geri Ferguson
PHOTO: Susan Stewart.

## 2. Time

To the average person two or three months time does not seem like a very long time. You can usually find lots of things to do and not think of three months as lots of seconds and drawn out hours and a day passing seems like a month. In prison, time is your worst enemy. Parts of me like feel like I've been unconscious for years. I learnt how to close up and pretend I never saw another woman's pain. I have laid awake all night in prison trying to tell myself I will recover when they let me out, but maybe I won't. I can't breathe in here. The air is always smoky and it smells of years of decaying flesh. What kind of a person am I to survive this?

Every day is the same in this concrete dumpster. I try to think of ways to wash the floor differently, or how can I have counted all the cracks in the walls. Every day we go to the same dining room, the same faces look at you and the guards watch you eat. I can't pretend I'm at a sushi bar. Should I eat every last morsel on my plate? Every thing is the same every day. Lights out at 10:30. A guard coming in to say good fucking morning asshole at 7:30. You go get the same cup of coffee and you know who will be sitting in the day room. The same record will be playing the same song and some prisoner will say, "I like this song because it picks me up and gets me going." Going where? I want to smash that record if I hear it one more time.

The one thing I get to do on my own, any time between 7:30 and 10:30, is have a shower or bath. It's the only bit of responsibility, should I have a shower or bath? But that might not last, because women have slashed in that nice hot water. When someone slashes and lives through it sometimes you wish they would have succeeded in killing themselves. You know the pain they feel, the frustration of being the same every day. Your mind begins to deteriorate, living becomes meaningless, your dreams are empty of everything but self-pity, and you ask yourself for a way to escape.

— Geri Ferguson

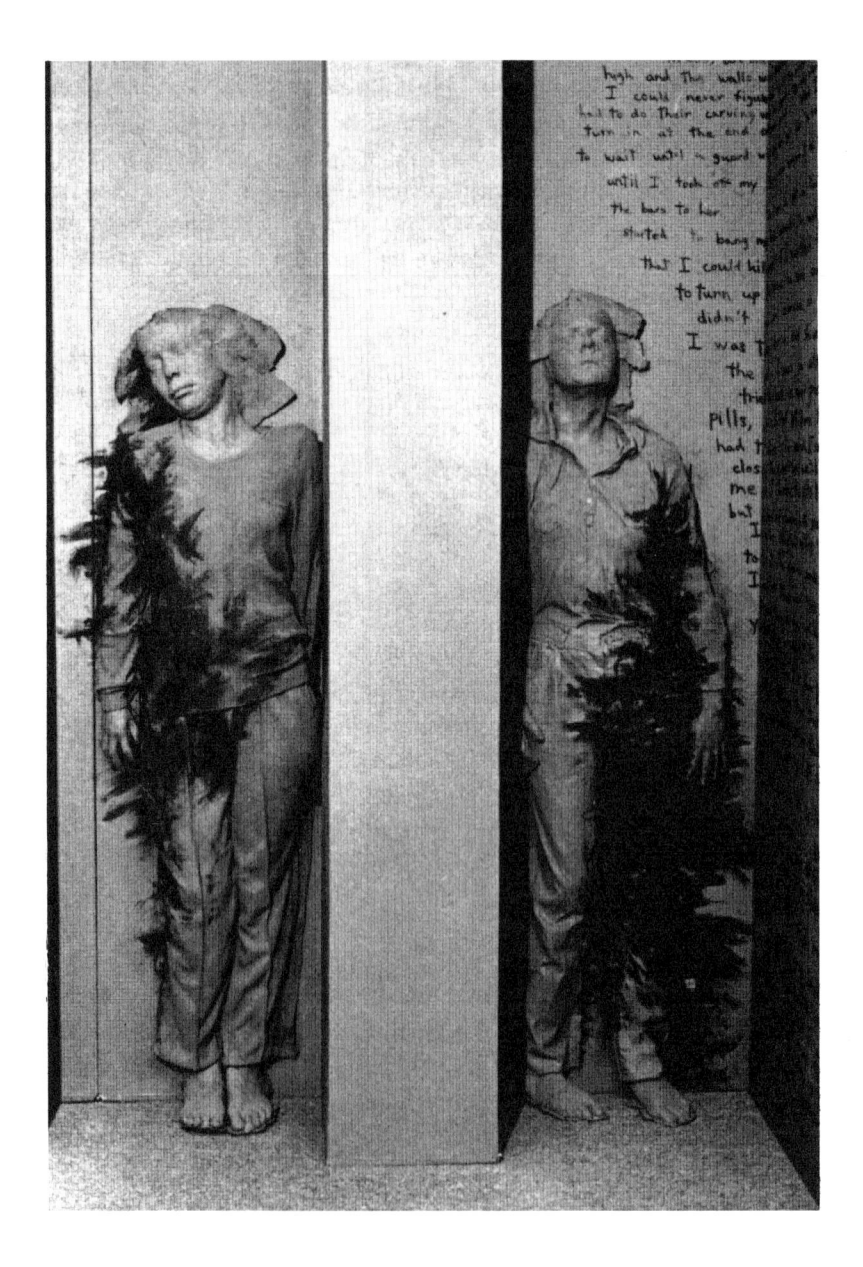

*Solitary* by Persimmon Blackbridge and Lyn MacDonald
PHOTO: Susan Stewart.

## 3. SOLITARY

Solitary confinement was in a cell about 8 feet by 10 feet with bars along the front. It had a single steel bunk with a rubber-coated mattress, a toilet and a light on all the time. The ceiling was pretty high and it was scarred with old graffiti all the way up to the top. I never figured out how the women got up that high. And they must have written it with a spoon — which was the only utensil we got, and we had to turn in at the end of each meal. Once a day I was taken for a cold shower, then back to the cell. When I had my period, I had to wait till a guard went by and get her to bring me a pad. Then she would wait while I took off my old pad and wrapped it in newspapers and squeezed it through the bars. One time I got so lonely and fucked up that I started to bang my head against the wall and yell. A guard told me that I could kill myself if I wanted to but she was just going to turn up the music so she couldn't hear me. I was in solitary because I tried to sneak in some prescription sleeping pills for my insomnia, when I first got there. When I had to strip for the search, I saw how closely the guard was watching so I handed the pills to her, but she had me charged with smuggling anyway. In solitary, the guard would go by and I would ask them what time it was and they would say, "Why do you want to know, you're not going anywhere." They never told me how many days I'd have to do in the hole. The only thing that made it at all bearable was knowing that my entire sentence was only 14 days. I was in solitary for the entire 14 days. At night there would be only one staff person on duty. Usually it was a student. Some of them would sit outside my cell and whisper to me. They would let me do their homework with them. It helped a lot. Later, in another jail, the major threat was always the hole. I never gave them too much trouble. I know if I had to go to the hole again, I would kill myself.

— Lyn MacDonald

# SUZANNE LAMY:
# "TALKING TOGETHER"

*Sherry Simon*

In the short chronology of feminist criticism in Quebec, 1979 belongs to a period of heroic beginnings.[1] And Suzanne Lamy's *d'elles* — published that year — is very much a product of those times and that spirit, exuberant witness to a time of discovery.

What remains most striking about the essays now is the way they bring into existence a new kind of critical object. The writing which Suzanne Lamy chose to analyze was not a series of static artifacts but a "place" somewhere between speech and writing, social acts and institutions, traditional and emergent practices. A certain number of forms became privileged expressions of the tension between social determinants and textual experimentation: *bavardage* (gossip, chatter), litany and dialogue were the most important of these. Each brought into play the parodic dialectic between the negative heritage of women and its revalorization in renewed forms.

But *d'elles* did much more than just stake out a new critical territory. The series of essays is also an extended meditation on language and power. In its very materiality (its use of metaphor and complex modes of authorization) as well as its integration of the major themes of the French attack on the subject (Blanchot, Barthes), *d'elles* established feminist criticism as central to the issues of language as defined by modernity. This is particularly clear in the essay "Deux femmes parlent" which speaks, through a reading of *Les Parleuses* by Marguerite Duras and Xavière Gauthier, of the social and esthetic dimensions of dialogue.

### ♦ SUZANNE LAMY: "TALKING TOGETHER" ♦

The dialogue form takes on special importance in Lamy's work because it calls attention to the *situation* which is inscribed in all speech. Here, writ large, are the essential determinants of all writing — the material and institutional factors which create its legitimacy.

> The specificity of the dialogue/discussion resides in its "situation" which has a determining influence on the form and implies a number of points to be agreed upon: the type of transcription, the relationship between the participants, the role of the animator (leader or foil), the choice of themes, the purpose and audience of the discussions. (Lamy 1979 39)

"Situation" or "place" takes on a broad importance in all of Suzanne Lamy's critical work — and in this we can read the importance of writers like Barthes (especially in *The Lesson* and *Degree Zero of Writing*) and Blanchot (*L'Entretien infini*). Her most trenchant observations were those which unmasked the contradictions or paradoxes of a speaking situation — that of Hélène Cixous' one-way address to a large audience on the "discourse of love" (Lamy 1980, 3), or of Marguerite Duras' being adored by those whose critical tenets were to separate author and work (Lamy 1981). All of Lamy's feminist criticism is marked by an intense concern with the constraints of the "speaking situation" which determine the production of women's writings and of their critical reception.

The dialogue (when it is also a text) is further marked by the specific ways in which it is made to pass from oral to written forms. With a few examples at hand (*Autrement dit*, Annie Leclerc and Marie Cardinal; *L'Éclat de la lumière*, Anne Philippe) Lamy hazards the generalization that women are more comfortable with hesitations, losses, incompletions of the spoken form than the men she quotes. The risk they wish to take is precisely to be "faithful to the word," to the life and spontaneity of the spoken word.

> These are engaging books in which voices move without constraint or affectation, faithful to the etymology of the word *entretien* (conversation, interview) which is to hold together, to prolong, to extend. And why not linger a moment at this prefix *entre* (between), the clever, sinuous line that separates and divides, but just as subtly brings together and unites ...

> Between our hands, between your lips, between our two mouths: a passage in joy. Words, breath, eyes. Together. Through the same hollows, creeks and craters as travel all things as they come to life, grow and die out. A voyage confident of a warm welcome, of openness and exchange. (Lamy 1979 38)

As in her discussions of gossip and litany, Lamy defines (women's) dialogue as a form which belongs at once to oral and written modes. This is the true novelty of women's writing and its utopian promise.

> These conversations are not minor writings; they are the full and concrete counter-melodies of their respective works, important because they set off many more resonances. Another history begins with them. A new form has been born, out of the rhythm of their breathing, of the close contact of distance and harmony, of the light gravity of these women for whom the outer bark cannot be separated from the density of beings. (Lamy 1979 50)

The dialogue between Marguerite Duras and Xavière Gauthier becomes a model. True equality is probably "not of this world" (46) but the closest we can get to it, for Suzanne Lamy, might be in a dialogue of the kind Duras and Gauthier produced in *Les Parleuses*. It is the intensity of her admiration for this work which surely brought Suzanne Lamy to write this essay. All the same, the "tunnels" of analysis (Lamy 1979 38) with which she approaches these exemplary dialogues are complex. As in much of her writing, Lamy combines the enthusiasm and complicity of the 'I' with the collective social dimension of the 'we' and the impersonal voice of authorized knowledge. All three are mobilized here to show that the dialogue form as used by women is different in intent and mode from our conventional understanding of the form. Laughter and silences are essential.

> Laughter is a part of the discussions: we laugh with those we love, just as we share their silences. There are many silences in this transcription and they mark important breaks: moments of latence or doubt, of transparency, of dead-ends, of eyes which meet or look away ... at this? or that? an insect, a flower, the memory of a bambooshoot ... (48)

This doesn't mean that the discussions are frivolous. Lamy emphasizes Xavière Gauthier's role in forcing Duras to confront certain philosophical questions or at least to admit directly that she is avoiding them. What emerges from this dialogue, which is allowed to follow its own laws, are very surprising kinds of revelations.

> Complicity does not do away with rigour, but this various outpouring allows for the most intimate confessions; the most extraordinary avowals come out quite naturally. (48)

The apparent disorder of the whole suggests a new richness of perception, "nocturnal" in its unshapedness, revealing the process of thought itself.

> Words come together in dense, wild patterns, barely detached from the nocturnal matter from which they emerge. Thought is interiorized before your eyes, preserving its vigour and immediateness, bare, in shreds. (47)

> I love the disparateness of it all, the image of our world as debris and sudden bursts of sunshine, the willingness to let thoughts stray, the refusal of an arbitrary order. Ideas come one after the other, and then intersect: creativity, feminism, social organisation, politics, passing events, sexuality from all angles: faithfulness, motherhood, prostitution, possessiveness ... (49)

Dialogue, "in the full sense of the term" (45) is an ideal: a shared quest. It is knowledge revealed as process, communion achieved as an equality of voice. In contrast to inauthentic dialogue, the "monologue in disguise" (the false pretences of the interview which claims to be a discussion among equals, the terrorism of equality preached from on high) the phrases of true dialogue are interchangeable; they could be attributed to one or the other of the speakers. "The exchange is full of supple and secret movements; the words turn into echoes of themselves"(46). What is dialogue if it is not the "recognition that one cannot, alone, reach the fundamental truths?" (45)

> The minimal distance necessary to the course of the dialogue forces the reader to be attentive, to pass from one to the other, to insinuate herself between the openness of Duras and the slight stiffness of Gauthier. Sometimes the reader is provoked

by the daring, even extreme positions which are taken, sometimes with an almost terrifying, ominous sense of conviction. The firmness of these views force the reader to turn back on her own past, to her half-baked Marxist-Leninist analyses or experiences of women's conditioning and lack of nerve ... I am confronted with the woman I was, the woman I am. Caught up in the tempo of this communication which affects my behaviour, my thought, my emotions and my senses, I implant myself into certain parts of the text, opening up a new course. (50)

The dyad of dialogue is broken; now there are three. The reader insinuates herself into the space between the speakers, absorbed in the back and forth movement between the two. Her fascination is slightly tinted with the curiosity of the voyeur. She watches thought in the process of coming to life and wonders how she will in turn begin her own dialogue with new readers.

And then we are there, readers to the second degree, peering over the critic's shoulder. Can the enthusiasm of beginnings come to life once again? We can but envy the amorous intensity of Suzanne Lamy in dialogue with Marguerite Duras in dialogue with Xavière Gauthier.

♦

## NOTES

1. For a more developed analysis of Suzanne Lamy's feminist criticism, see S. Simon, "Suzanne Lamy: le féminin au risque de la critique," *Voix et images*, 37 (automne 1987): 52–64 and Lori Saint-Martin, "Suzanne Lamy, Pour une morale de la critique," 29–40. All translations of Lamy's texts are by S. Simon.

## WORKS CITED

Cardinal, Marie and Annie Leclerc. *Autrement dit*. Paris: Grasset, 1977

Duras, Marguerite and Xavière Gauthier. *Les Parleuses*. Paris: Minuit, 1974.

Lamy, Suzanne. *d'elles*. Montreal: Editions de l'Hexagone, 1979.

———. "Le Féminisme passé, présent et futur," *Spirale* 6 (janvier 1980): 5–6.

———. *Marguerite Duras à Montreal*. Montreal: Editions Spirale, 1981.

# Vers-ions con-verse:
# A Sequence of Translations

*Barbara Godard, Susan Knutson, Daphne Marlatt,
Kathy Mezei, Gail Scott and Lola Lemire Tostevin*

(1)

espaces vers vers où?
vers quoi?

cette rupture qui donne lieu à une syntaxe
qui se veut peau sur laquelle se trace un
autre sens (une sensation)

à travers le silence (les pulses travaillent en silence)
l'organisme se renseigne sur ses éléments extérieurs
(tes yeux ta voix tes mains) la mémoire d'un toucher
où s'inscrit l'au-delà d'une langue tout en insérant
de nouveaux fragments *oreilles neuves pour une musique
nouvelle*

— L.L.T.

♦ Barbara Godard, Susan Knutson, Daphne Marlatt,
Kathy Mezei, Gail Scott and Lola Lemire Tostevin ♦

(2)

(green) spaces tending where?
or what?

this break which gives rise to syntax
aspires to be skin on which is traced an
other sense (a sensation)

through silence (pulses work in silence)
the body learns about the outside world
(your eyes your voice your hands) memory of touch
where what is beyond language is inscribed while framing
new fragments *new ears for a new*
*music*

My knowledge of French is imperfect, so when I read French poetry I do a lot of translation into English just to make sense for myself. In this way, translation is a function of my reading. However, for the same reason, I am afraid that my translation — once it is pinned down to a particular set of choices — will always leave a record of misreadings which are more or less accidental. I say "more or less," because I tend to err in the direction of meanings I desire; this is embarrassing.

Reading the first line of this poem, I thought about green, and also, eventually about earthworms. I checked *espace* in the dictionary to make sure it was masculine, since otherwise one would hear *verte*. In the dictionary I found out the *espace* is masculine in more of its senses; however, in typography, the spaces between the characters are *espaces au féminin*; furthermore, the feminine is the older form of the word, from the Latin *spatium*, which is neuter. Feminine, productive space between letters and words seems relevant to Lola's poem, but when I come back to the line I write without hesitation, "green spaces tending to what / or where?" thus sacrificing the possibility of typographical, feminine spaces in order to keep the green. However, I leave out the earthworms.

— S.K.

(3)

spaces lines      lines leading where?
lines leading what?

this rupture opens up a syntax
insinuating into skin over which
is traced an other meaning / path(-pathy)

across silence (the pulse beats in silence)
the organism absorbs outside elements
(your eyes, voice, hands) the memory of a touch
where what is beyond language is inscribed
all the while injecting new fragments
*new ears for a new music*

To be able to write and live in two language as Lola does must be exhilarating, but also bewildering. For some things must be said in French, others in English. But what are they? And the translator of Lola's poems from French into English is in a precarious position, because she thinks of how Lola might have said this in English herself and why she chose to do so in French. Watching Lola turn from English to French and back again as she does in *'sophie*, seeking out her very own *langue*, is intriguing. For I found a marked difference between the poems in French and English as if another kind of sensibility were speaking, and I wondered how much that a consequence of the French language itself. The *vers* in French was more constrained, less layered, and the voice emerging was more subdued, less colloquial. It is then that the translator becomes very curious to know how the language Lola writes in determines what she says and how she says it, and she sets down to her task with several voices echoing in her head.

    Well now how to tackle the poem as it lies there so pristine and perfect and unsuspecting in French? Mixture of anticipation and reluctance. Take up my pen, open my dictionary, scribble down a literal transcription, which even as I write falls victim to crossings over, erasures, insertions. Recreate this incoherence onto my computer. Then go away for a day or two to assess the poem's readability in English.

♦ Barbara Godard, Susan Knutson, Daphne Marlatt,
Kathy Mezei, Gail Scott and Lola Lemire Tostevin ♦

I think it was Barbara who once said that feminist texts (or highly experimental ones) seem to require quite literal translations. That, or quite free ones. Lola's poems, as do Nicole Brossard's texts, invite this literal rending so that when Gail translates "qui se veut peau sur laquelle se trace un autre sens (une sensation)" quite literally as "which wishes itself skin on which meaning is traced" over the phone to me, it possesses both fidelity and eloquence (I can hear the French and Lola's voice), but I change it to: "insinuating into skin over which..."; I can't help myself but my voice *insinuates* itself into Lola's. I am not quite happy about this. I fall here towards "very free." And again when there are polysemous puns as in "vers" (towards, lines of verse, worms, [green]) I leave out worms, [green] and instead there are "lines leading" into only a couple of possible meanings. Add, shift (verbs, adjectives) omit (gender "laquelle"; the self-reflexivity of verbs "se trace" and "s'inscrit"; the finality of *nouvelle*, as it stands feminine, solitary, the poem's closure) and apprehensively watch the reader (and Lola) reading this new poem.

— K.M.


(4)

spaces lines      lead where?
verse what?

this break which gives place to syntax
would-be skin on which is traced an
other direction / sense (a sensation)

through silence (pulses throb in silence)
the body enquires about external elements
(your eyes your voice your hands) memory of touch
the beyond of a tongue inscribed inserting
new parts *new ears for a new*
*music*

Commentary as extension of the reading:

## ♦ Vers-sions con-verse: A Sequence of Translations ♦

like deferred fate those lines (in the skin dimly traced) other sense arise as alternate routes (a sixth in language more than cube?), chords of meaning found in palimpsest, the palimpsest the break (in sense) allows to surface on the page in silence in between its versions: echo scan in green depths.

in translating a poem that so intensively works the language it seems already a translation of that original struggle between intent and language drift, the translation (becomes) process embeds meta-translation while the target language not wanting to replace /consume the resonance of the source language oscillates in potential conversation with it.

the experience of simultaneity cross-echo scanned between two languages in working with a poet who writes very much inside of both, even in other poems together.

through several drafts (drifts) the sense that French wants to spell out the syntax in a gracious offering of connection that lumbers clumsily demanding into literal English, while a "freer" English tends to make it resonate all at once although it is always *leading* somewhere just as French does. a genius for elucidation (abstract words affiliate easily); a genius for compression (touch and touching upon); an oscillation between the two.

— D.M.

(5)

spaces vers-ions con-verse?
in-verse?
this rupture makes way for a syntax
wanting to be skin on which is traced an
other sense (a sensation)

traversing silence (the pulses work in silence)
the organism inquires about external elements
(your eyes, voice, hands) the memory of a touch
where the far side of language is inscribed inserting

♦ BARBARA GODARD, SUSAN KNUTSON, DAPHNE MARLATT,
KATHY MEZEI, GAIL SCOTT AND LOLA LEMIRE TOSTEVIN ♦

new fragments new ears for a new
music

This was a difficult translation. I resisted setting to work on it. Translation holds out the illicit pleasures of language. But I wanted to take the risk of ideas and leave the language to its own games. That first line was a problem. All the puns on "vers" — verse, green, worm, towards. In one word they compress the interlocking issues of the poem; new directions, new poetry from a different body. How could I choose only one of these when the mind is enticed into the poem by the complex palimpsest of "vers"? How, if I settled for one of these meanings, could I retain the repetition of "vers" in the next two phrases, and in the opening word of the third section, leitmotif that holds the poem together in the ear, making that new music for the new organs of hearing?

Verbal music is important in this poem about the music of poetry. Sound teases out the sense: the ear leads the mind in new directions. To retain this music for the allegory, with lute in her hand, on the cover of *sophie* is important. For the major issue tackled in this book is the problem of the insertion of the feminine into the discourse of philosophy. The book is a critique of the logocentrism of the Western tradition. Suffering from a Platonic hangover, this discourse has been dominated by metaphysics. The consequent opposition between the intelligible and the sensible has privileged mind over body, male over female. For this discourse has been a discourse between men in which woman has been the sign or token of exchange. If we are to put Sophie back into the discourse alongside Phil, as Lola Lemire Tostevin is trying to, we are going to have to develop our ears, as indeed all of our organs, to accommodate ourselves to a new type of knowledge. This rupture, the word disclosing yet simultaneously purifying from the "abject," is music: "A single catharsis: the rhetoric of the pure signifier, of music in letters..." (Kristeva, 23).

So, rather than choose, I did nothing. But the problem did not go away. On the telephone with a colleague about a theoretical paper on translation, our conversation touched on a series of words that shared a root with the German word for translation; inversion, perversion, conversion, subversion. English words for movement, these

♦ Vers-sions con-verse: A Sequence of Translations ♦

contain both "turning" and "verses." My Oxford dictionary informs me too that "vert" is an English word for the right to cut all the greenery in the forest. Three of the meanings can be suggested if I can retain the syllable "ver." For a while, I toyed with using the archaic "verdant" or "versatile" to provide more variety in the repetitions of the sound. But these signifiers set up semantic chains that led in diverging directions. Several weeks later in the swimming pool, I am thinking about Lola's book, about how I must phone her to see if she knows where the reading will take place and if she can bring copies of her book to sell to the students who need them. Suddenly, into my mind rushes the word "vers-ions" complete with hyphen in the middle (or should it be a slash?). Meditation and water are forever wedded, wrote Melville in *Moby Dick*. To underline the musical theme, and as homage to Barry Nichol whom both Lola and I miss, I thought of adding the word "organ" before music in the final line. However, "organism" in the same section of the poem is a much more subtle form of quotation of *Organ Music*, more in keeping with the economy of the poem. And so, in place of the apostrophe of the title, which stands for the blank pause as the conceptual space of the feminine in the discourse of philosophy, the translation should read: "water music: theme and vers-if-ications."

— B.G.

(6)

green spaces / spacing where?
spacing   what?

this broken surface which opens syntax
like skin tingling under the trace of
new sense (sensation)

across silence (an electric charge is noiselessly propulsed)
the organism lights its place by what's outside
(your eyes your voice your hands) the memory of a touch
a tongue slipping into space beyond language lapping
new fragments *new ears for new*
*music*

♦ Barbara Godard, Susan Knutson, Daphne Marlatt,
Kathy Mezei, Gail Scott and Lola Lemire Tostevin ♦

Lola's writing has the clarity and theoretical rigour one connects with *la modernité* in Québec. And a way of using the poetic line, a concreteness about her images as well, which evokes English-Canadian poetry for me. People often say I write between two languages. Lola does more so. Her knowledge of French lightens, enlightens the English in which she often writes. Or, if writing in French, her writing somehow floats, imbued with the wisdom of apprehending the language from within (as mother-tongue), yet also through eyes that know English profoundly. This gives it a quality which is, strangely, both material (full of concrete meaning) and immaterial (curving away from the horizon of meaning).

If, in general, translation is not so much transparent as it is evidence of another reading — this is even truer of the translation of a text which, in its writing, already anticipates the *other* language (i.e. English). My translation is very much influenced by my own preoccupation with space as a conduit across which a writing subject in-the-feminine is constantly in a process of becoming (Scott). No doubt this preoccupation has forced an emphasis, in the translation, on the concept of space and the movement across it of the trace that is writing. A space electrified at the point where theory and the erotic touch. Electrified more, oddly enough, in English — where the discussion of either the erotic or of theory seem somehow more unusual (therefore more marked) when inserted in the text. In French the erotic and the theoretical seem to come comfortably together, here, in the same phrase. In English there's a distance between the two "concepts" which obliged me, in the process of translation, to lean towards one or the other — a choice made almost unconsciously in the beginning, but which became clear to me with the line

*où s'inscrit l'au-delà d'une langue tout en insérant.*

I might have taken a more clearly theoretical tack:

*where is inscribed what's beyond language inclusive of*

but I chose the more erotic, the more electric version:

*a tongue slipping into space beyond language lapping*

It seemed the most poetic way ... in English.

— G.S.

## WORKS CITED

Kristeva, Julia. *Powers of Horror: An Essay on Abjection.* Trans. Leon S. Roudiez. New York: Columbia University Press, 1982.

Scott, Gail. *Spaces Like Stairs.* Toronto: Women's Press, 1989.

Tostevin, Lola Lemire. *"espaces vers" 'sophie.* Toronto: Coach House, 1988. 53.

# COMING TO TERMS WITH THE MOTHER TONGUE

*Dôre Michelut*

Many writers today are first- or second-generation immigrants who live and work in another language, one of Canada's two official languages. Although their mother tongue may still occupy a part of their lives, this part has been relegated to a circumscribed private territory which does not enter easily into relation with either living or writing in the acquired dominant language. For a writer, the problems and paradoxes this poses come constantly to the fore and are so complex that any attempt to use the mother tongue as a vehicle for writing is quickly abandoned. To understand the scope of the problem in the life of an individual writer, it is informative to consider what happens to a language upon immigration.

Most North American immigration up to 1960 was of peasant stock due to an industrialization which progressively developed a modern economy by erasing indigenous feudal cultures and enlarging the middle classes. Writers who are children of this wave of immigration and who would work in their mother tongue find themselves writing within a sensibility that is pregnant with feeling and presence, yet speechless.

Peasant speech occupies a place in a cultural hierarchy: its task is the cultivation of soil and the taming of animals. To do this requires physical presence and sound. Being oral, its standards are upheld by cyclical rituals that involve the earth and the speaking self rather than the thinking self and a body of written law. As language, it is not amenable to forms of communication which occur in a society whose allegiance is to a stable corpus of standardized signs rather than the signs of the earth in seasonal change. The sensibility of language that develops within a scripted tradition is missing.

Between the acquired language and the mother tongue, how can there be common ground? The two languages have long since staked out their territory within the psyche and the balance that has been achieved is seamless and invisible. For writers who would explore that boundary, there is no recourse but to approach both languages in their oral states as reservoirs. But soon the mother tongue would hold the writer in an earth it can no longer cultivate, and the acquired language would become more abstract to accommodate that "unreal" experience. The relations between reservoirs soon become saturated and static: experience in one is felt as a threat by the other. The mother tongue, judged by the requirements of the activity of writing, turns into a barren, moon-like landscape explored by forms proper to the acquired language. The result is inaccessible both to the acquired language and to the original language that evolved in the homeland.

Yet, if I were to look at the phenomenon which touches me intimately solely from a social perspective, as if my languages were objects to manipulate in view of a written goal, I would be forgetting that at some point in time I gave myself to language and that I have entrusted language with my life. I would be calling my experience in language a body separate from myself and I would be saying that the object has grown alien. If I were to stop at this, not only would I end up abandoning Furlan, my mother tongue, I would also be stating that the sounds I made in Friûl until I was six when I left, that Furlan belongs to a place outside of me. But those first six years of my life can't be separated from me. They spread through my time like my child body spreads through my adult body. And how many of those six years that run through me are unspoken or abandoned because I can't find their forms in English?

Furlan, my mother tongue, is a marriage between Celtic and vulgar Latin and is a member of the eighth Romance language group, Ladino. It is spoken in a small province of northern Italy and its dialects vary from town to town due to millennia of invasions and very localized life. Although it is a language, it developed a standardized script only recently.

But most of what I have learned about myself and language through writing did not develop because of a rediscovery of Furlan. The balance that Furlan and English struck within me long ago is so very entrenched it feels saturated and inaccessible. At a certain point, my two acquired languages, Italian and English, were forced to come to terms with each other within me. It was this experience that led me to consider ways of approaching the more remote Furlan. When my family emigrated to Canada, my parents decided that Furlan was such a minority language that it would not be of use to their children in the future. Therefore, in our house, our parents spoke Furlan between themselves and they spoke what Italian they knew with the children. It took only a few years for me to reply to both languages exclusively in English. In my teens, I could understand both Italian and Furlan, but I spoke them badly.

To complicate matters further, after high school I decided to go to university in Florence where the Italian seemed to be another language altogether. A background noise became the foreground. After one year I spoke Italian not badly; after two I spoke it well; after five I started having problems in English. When I came back to live in Toronto after having been absent for eight years, it seemed I spoke English just as everyone spoke English but as soon as a serious conversation got underway, words flew by each other and did not meet. Cultural references I made became irrelevant, concepts that struck sure resonance in Florence, wafted and waned in Toronto, or were too loud, too soft, abstract, or even impolite. I found myself starting to wobble, unable to detect whether I had hit or missed "something."

I suspected that my English had become insufficient so I went back to university in Toronto searching specifically for courses similar to those I had taken in Italy. Immediately, I became aware that the information I was absorbing was already in me but arranged differently. Concepts that flowed together inevitably in Italy, here stood independently, senselessly. It was as if the languages had been amazingly attracted and yet unable to touch and penetrate. As if *aemulateo*, Foucault's second form of similitude, where recognition perpetuates space without contact, were struggling to become *convenentia*, adjacency of place, where fringes touch and mingle. Feeling their exclusiveness, I could commit myself fully to neither. Translation seemed a puny effort in such a struggle; something always seemed betrayed, and I avoided it.

At first I lived the impossibility of translation as silence. In fact, I became aware of the exclusion of myself from one world and the other to such an extent that I started feeling irrelevant to both. The more attention I gave to the English world here, the less I understood the intense and committed life I had lived for eight years in Florence, and the more it haunted me. Then I started to write, in any language and despite all grammars. It would have been unintelligible to most, but as far as I was concerned, I was producing meaning, and on my own terms. And the view I got of myself from the page was that of two different sets of cards shuffled together, each deck playing its own game with its own rules.

Perhaps because the page is white and gives the illusion of being outside the human body and therefore only mildly related to it through language, I realized that the act of speaking is also the act of being spoken. I saw myself shaping language, but I also saw how the page shaped me. Where a language claimed me, the speaker, it claimed not only what I uttered but also dictated the parameters of what I could possibly utter in given circumstances. At this point, I finally started to understand my relationship to language: it premeditated me and I, to the extent that I allowed it to carry me, determined it.

The so-called betrayal of translation was really irrelevant; all form, including sound as language, betrayed for that matter. The point was to fully determine myself in a given circumstance: I could never change the given, but I could shape it as I engaged it. My fear of betrayal was, in fact, my fear of freedom to choose between forms. It had to be either one or the other at a given point in time; simultaneity was impossible. Like the old profile-vase perception exercise, English just could not assimilate my experience of Italian. It made external, stereotypical conjectures, but it could not incorporate the other sensibility as part of its own manifest reality. What was lived in Italian stayed in Italian, belonged to it completely. And vice versa.

I found that I had no choice but to commit myself fully. Unless I offered my statement wholeheartedly to a language's undertow of ironies, to its inner "ear," the meaning was not "felt" and what was manifest in the statement lost sense and sensibility. Since I seemed to be possessed by the language I experienced, the experience had to reside not in me but in the "ear" of the language itself. In theory, this sounds practical; in practice, as I materialized one ghost, the other would fade. I hated the seeming arbitrary blindness of the two languages. Each left me out while stumbling all over the other invisible entity that occupied the same territory — me. Finally, I thought that if the languages could only "see" each other within me, I would stop feeling haunted and cheated.

Writing, I tracked the sighting of one ghost or the other. The more I wrote, the more I found myself grammatically separating the languages. One poem would become two: one in either language. I would work on them until they seemed to snap apart and become independent entities; each becoming progressively more untranslatable as it progressed in its own direction. What surprised, and then delighted was that each poem came to a stop somewhere inside itself when it knew itself as coherent, whole and complete. At this point, each piece could recognize the other and know its conception from the moment it diverged. It could "see" where the other broke off and how far it continued into itself towards its own satisfaction. Together, both constituted the whole bracket that was the extent of my experience of that poem. Nothing was left out; all the words were ghostless, full of me and present to themselves.

It was then I understood that translation incorporates the idea of the insufficiency of the object produced while being intimately involved in and committed to its production. Mine was a process of self-translation: I spanned the languages within my awareness simultaneously while each experienced the other in a "felt" relation. I was generating a dialectical experience that was relative to both languages, and yet, at the same time, I was beyond them both. The event could therefore be remembered and explained. By translating myself into myself, by spinning a fine line in-between states of reality, I transcended the paralysis of being either inside or outside form. It was like transmuting lead to gold and back, solely for the pleasure of knitting their interrelation. I understood that the standardized language mattered only inasmuch as I could experience its translation in writing. Grammar was not written in stone, it was writing in me, and I was the only arbiter of the experience. Since I was both the author and the translator, who else could I consult?

At this point I found I had something to say about the forms of these languages in a way that did not exclude my intimacy with them. My writing was a tool with which I held them so that they would produce me while I communicated within them. I could finally speak of English and Italian not as objects, but as subjects with individual personalities which acted upon me.

English and Italian agree and disagree in interesting places. Anyone who has translated has certainly localized these common linguistic *impassi*. Take the English neuter 'it,' for instance, Hemingway's 'it': a genderless, nameless identity. It is raining; it goes without saying; how is it going? In Italian: *piove; si capisce; come va?* Where in English the vagueness of 'it,' although undetermined, must be acknowledged for the sentence to make grammatical sense, in Italian naming the 'it' is superfluous and tautological. *Esso va bene* is indeed redundant because the use of 'it' is determined by the degree of specificity which governs 'it's' position in regard to the verb. For example, after deciding whether the 'it' is masculine or feminine (*lo, la*), Italian then considers whether the object is specific enough to be added to the verb, as is *lo* in the phrase *devi vederlo*, or emphatic enough to act as a subject: *lo devi vedere*. But at this point, if the subject is too universal, the *lo* disappears and is absorbed, as in the verb *piove*. In Italian, only conceivability and therefore specificity allow an object the possibility of independent grammatical action. One can imagine how this world-view limits the influence of the object upon the speaking subject.

English, however, insists on containing the unmentionable in a form which functions to keep the 'it' separate from the verb. English has a hard time living with what is not comprehensible and vague and must keep pointing 'it' out whenever possible: a counter-spell to keep away the indeterminate spirit of 'it is a nice day,' or perhaps an attempt to expand 'it' into liveable, human space. But by doing this English grants independence to 'it,' an invisible subject, and that independence is tangible since we can say that the 'it' which is a nice day is not necessarily just a nice day.

In Italian, this does not occur. In fact, since Italian does not have a concept for the English 'it,' it hears two 'days' in one sentence, as one subject and the other as object, and it comes away from the encounter feeling that English obtusely insists on being redundant.

From the English point of view, Italian is full of contorted constructions simply because it must find a multitude of ways to get around the naming of 'it.'

But Italian also has its peculiarities. Those who have tried to translate English into Italian must have met up with the supreme frustration of not being able to do without the reflexive where one doesn't want it. Let me clarify with a line from one of my poems: 'And I imagine your hair holding up the wind and curling.' It seems impossible to translate this line into Italian without the reflexive. *E mi immagino i tuoi capelli che si arricciano per stringere il vento.* To the English ear, *mi immagino, si arricciano* imply intentionality of the I and of the hair. In English, there is no reason for the hair to be aware of itself holding or the I to imagine itself imagining. 'It' just happens. *Succede.*

Perhaps Italian cannot grammatically contain the unnameable because it does not dare to take the phenomenological god in vain, preferring a grand variety of blasphemy instead. As for English, sexual reference in swearing accounts for most linguistic transgression. This is interesting in view of the fact that this very world-view has stripped the phenomenal world of gender.

I hope and remember, but I want to live the present and write the present. I feel uneasy with language always going only part of the way. I want to speak myself. Yet in English, I say that the line of the poem I have translated is not acceptable: it violates the original voice. In Italian, I insist that if what I say is to be meaningful, action cannot be contemplated unless an actor intends it. And that's that.

But how far back must I travel to be present in Furlan, my mother tongue? I spoke it until I was six, and have spoken it sporadically since. My knowledge of it is limited and my experience knows more about the cultivation of culture than it does about the cultivation of the earth. Not having territorial cues to bring memory into focus, the life I have lived in that language is remote and, for the most part, forgotten. There seems to be nothing to say. The claims of Italian and English were conceptual and therefore easier to locate, but Furlan and English have been keeping an agreement struck so long ago that they take their co-habitation for granted to the point that I don't know where each would claim or contest my experience. Since Furlan is my mother tongue, I know that what

Furlan would claim would be outrageous, it would want to be the entire universe, and with no vocabulary to boot. To give myself to its unspoken presence, to its ironies, to its 'ear,' feels like drowning. But I do know that when I speak Furlan, badly as I speak it, it feels "like me" as nothing I can ever say in English or Italian feels "like me."

It might be fruitful to explain the person I became in these languages in terms of what I can imagine within them. For example, in Furlan, the thought that beyond Highway 11 in Ontario there are no other roads going north, only a vast expanse of forest wilderness, makes me panic. I cannot enter into relation with this threatening emptiness unless I think of hewing out a plot of land, building solid shelter and planting a garden for food. I would worry about how to get seeds and nails. Perhaps when things become stable I would tame a wild creature, a bear comes to mind. If I approach the same territory in English, I do not worry about food and shelter, somehow they are granted to me and do not cause anxiety. I would perhaps learn to fly so I could enter into some kind of relation with the immensity before me. It would not occur to me to tame animals, I would rather observe them in their natural state and learn small things about myself through watching them.

Rendering that Furlan which feels "like me" in English is a huge problem. Most of my life I have brought Furlan to English and never assumed that my mother tongue could ask questions of English. But since self-translation required a reciprocal flow, I brought English to Furlan. The first time I inverted the process, I felt the odd and frightening sensation that my mother finally understood everything I was saying. As I translated, I felt the English rushing towards Furlan, being pulled in like a lover and shaped. They had been so blind to each other because the alternate reciprocal experience had been missing. As I translated, the English text started to change. There were some words I could use and others I couldn't. Furlan just wouldn't accept certain concepts or sensibilities. I've learned to trust it and bend English to suit its needs. And the English that developed, informed by the Furlan, began to sound more and more "like me."

My goal is not to recover specific memories of my remote childhood, although they tend to materialize unexpectedly, nor is it the manipulation of the formal possibilities of Furlan — this happens incidentally. Rather, my goal is to provide a bridge in which English can happen in the light of Furlan and, when possible, vice versa.

There are areas within each of us that have never met, that don't speak or listen to each other. If these areas are enclosed in languages, those of us who still have an active mother tongue have an interesting and definite area to cultivate, one that we can experience and reshape through translation. Because writing holds words in time, it is possible to return and "tame" their meaning. It is possible to form and repeat those parts of ourselves which are repeatable in order to begin to recognize the sound of the self forming as different world views meet to negotiate experience. I find that when a poem or a story has passed through the sieve, gone from English to Furlan and back, from Furlan to Italian or Italian to English and back, each language still speaks me differently, because it must, but each speaks me more fully.

♦

# S(M)OTHER TONGUE?: FEMINISM, ACADEMIC DISCOURSE, TRANSLATION

*Pamela Banting*

Academic discourse is discouraged. If this statement is removed from its original context, it is difficult to tell what kind of an utterance it is. Is it a proclamation? A headline? A sigh of regret? A triumphant declaration? A tautology? A prohibition? How are we to translate this simple sentence?

Restored to the context of the call for papers for *Tessera* 6, the meaning becomes clearer: it is an incitement and invitation to experiment. "All forms of writing are welcome: essays, poems, fictions, translations. Academic discourse is discouraged." In her *CV 2* editorial to *Tessera* 4, Jane Casey hears "a hint of redress" in this problematical statement. Worried about how "theory and activism can work together" Jane expresses her reservations about the tenor of many of the articles published in that issue. She says: "My concern is not so much that they are too intellectual or too theoretical, but rather that the highly specialized language they use precludes the possibility for dialogue among a wide base of feminist readers. And that is unfortunate" (8). Jane's assumption is that the vocabulary of theory can always be translated into less complex, less exclusionary, less educated, less theoretical terms. But what, we might ask, is the nature of this purportedly more accommodating, more popular, less elitist language that feminist theory should be adequately translated into with minimal loss? What is this, to use Jane's word, "authentic" target language into and through which the, by implication, inauthentic source language of theoretical research should be translated and disseminated?[1]

While few would dispute that standard academic discourse has a wide range of undesirable, even intolerable, attributes (footnotes used as armour, strictly linear argumentation, pomposity, aggression, the substitution of rhetoric for the personal, an air of neutrality, reluctance to commit oneself, etc.), still it is important to consider exactly which academic attributes are being discouraged and which alternate virtues encouraged. In terms of censoring or suppressing women's writing, the call for accessibility invokes dangers similar to those typically associated with academic discourse. Janice Williamson, responding in a letter to the editors of *(f.)Lip* magazine regarding the use of the word "accessible" in the description of the magazine, writes: "How will the criteria of 'accessibility' affect your editing of my piece? Will you edit out words like 'overdetermination' which are not 'accessible' to my interested mother who would perhaps be moved to look it up in a reference book? Isn't that part of what feminist 'innovative' writing should do? Propel readers to exceed themselves" (22).

My own relationship to the academy and its discourse has been a stormy, on-again-off-again affair, negotiated along a zigzag path that is only being traversed through a combination of supportive and compensatory circumstances, most importantly, by my involvement in both the literary and academic communities at once (the positive qualities of each taking turns buffering the deficiencies of the other), by friendships with feminist students and professors (including a few male professors), and by the act of writing. However, despite my sometimes ambivalent relation to the institution I disagree with the suggestion that discourses produced within the university cannot be shared, comprehended, interpreted or responded to from without. I am not convinced that theory cannot and does not take place outside the walls of the institution. My purpose here then is to add another cautionary note regarding the automatic equation of academic discourse with abstruse and elitist language and to open up questions pertaining to the nature of this imagined, alternative, accessible, target language into which academic or theoretical language is supposed to be translated.[2]

♦ S(M)OTHER TONGUE?: FEMINISM,
ACADEMIC DISCOURSE, TRANSLATION ♦

I must confess right away that I do have a certain fetish for impossible discourse, or texts of bliss. However, I can trace this predilection less to the university, I think, than to much earlier circumstances. I was born and grew up in a remote village where books were a rare item. As a pre-school child, I had only a couple of children's books, of which I have no recollection. However, on Sunday mornings my Dad and I would get up while my Mom slept in, and Dad would read the Saturday coloured comics to me while I sat on his knee. Having read me the comics cover to cover more than once, however, he could not persuade me to get down off his knee, and, if he wanted to read the rest of the paper for himself, he had to read it out loud to me too. While kids were growing up in towns and cities were probably thoroughly familiar with the characters of Little Noddy and the Cat in the Hat, the characters whose adventures I followed were Blondie and Dagwood, Little Orphan Annie, Kruschev, Dick Tracy and Diefenbaker.

Later when I started school, I read the newspaper for myself. One of my favourite sections was "Dear Ann, Dear Abby," which I read daily, perhaps savouring the personal voice, the narratives of disaster and recuperation of loss, and the mystery and incomplete comprehensibility of it all. I read these columns for at least two years before finally, one morning, at age eight, reading the paper at the kitchen counter while putting on my parka, mitts and scarf to leave for school, I asked my Dad what the word "p-r-e-g-n-a-n-t" meant. I had been reading this word, around which all catastrophe and doom seemed to revolve, since learning to read but, because it seemed to be the key to everything, I thought that the meaning would eventually become clear from the context. And because there was an aura of shame and degradation attached to the word, I had hesitated to ask. Moreover, it seemed as if the worst things happened to girls who were "easy" or "accessible." "Dear Ann Dear Abby" first inculcated me with a taste for texts which featured difficulty, complications and the questionable subject-in-process.[3]

Variables such as total accessibility, clarity, and age- or grade-specific reading in schools can just as easily become fetishes as can difficulty or complexity. What I want to ask is, in whose name is the plea for accessibility being made? On whose behalf?[4] It is unfortunate that, despite her plea that "We need to scrutinize our academic associations very carefully" in order not to stifle opportunities for "dialogue" (9), Jane Casey chooses not, at least within her brief editorial, to scrutinize her own position in relation either to the university or to those on whose behalf she is pleading. Ironically, what emerges from her argument for the unidirectional translation of theory into some other discourse is a privileging and preservation of the traditional hierarchies between theory and practice, academic and popular. When calls for accessibility come from academic women such as Jane Casey herself, what is actually being called for? And can a true dialogue take place when one group of interlocutors is required in advance not to speak or write the language of its members' lives and work?[5]

Too, one must speculate as to what other matters come into play in terms of extending this much-touted dialogue to a broader base of feminist readers. Matters also needing scrutiny include the funding, marketing and distribution of Canadian journals and magazines, the general devaluation of intellectual research and artistic practice, the relative lack of informed discussion in the media and the influence of television on reading habits. Surely it is imposing a large burden on feminist projects to insist that "accessible" language compensate for all these and other important cultural factors.

Susan Knutson also addresses the issue of accessible discourse and places her concerns about it within a concise summary of the feminist language project as a whole. She writes:

> Women's language, including that of the feminist critic, is characteristically double, inevitably complicit with the patriarchal language and culture in which we are spoken at the same time that it participates in the creation of a culture of resistance, generating codes of subversion and manifesting semiotic flight from the *nom du père*. Complexity is a condition of our engagement with a web of re-reading which, as Luce Irigaray has shown, stretches back at least as far as Plato and through which we participate in the deconstruction of western metaphysical discourse. There is not, and we should not expect to see, any singular, simple or particularly "accessible" reading of writing in the feminine in Canada. In any case singular and accessible meaning has fallen under the suspicion of being nothing more or less than the reappearance of a previously

# S(M)OTHER TONGUE?: FEMINISM, ACADEMIC DISCOURSE, TRANSLATION

> successful (patriarchal/phallogocentric) fiction. If we are attached to such fictions it is perhaps because of the pleasure we derive from the comforting and the familiar. However, feminist experimental writing can and does offer other pleasures: pleasures of utopic vision, pleasures of breaking silence, pleasures of women's body writing itself, pleasures of lesbian sexuality daring to speak its name.(23)

Women's language is always double, always both complicit and illicit. Or, in terms of translation theory, women's language is and is not a native language. It is a (m)other tongue which is not the same as our native tongue but not entirely different from the vernacular either.[6] Women's language is a simultaneous translation between language and the body, between the already spoken and the unspeakable, between the familiar and the un- and/or de-familiarized. Furthermore, this (m)other tongue is not a language that can simply be translated out of or into. No one's mother tongue, it is a language which emerges only in a complex and multivalent act of translation and can only be comprehended in two or more languages at once. The (m)other tongue is an interlanguage, a language which comes into existence only in the process of a second-language learning. An interlanguage is a separate yet intermediate, linguistic system situated between a source language and a target language and which results from a learner's attempted production of the target language.[7]

What shall I call them? Other writers/theorists/academics/feminists/women cast very specific problems pertaining to feminist issues also in terms of language-learning and translation. Here, for instance, is Alice Jardine questioning how men manage to "evacuate questions of their sexuality, their subjectivity, their relationship to language from their sympathetic texts on 'feminism,' on 'woman,' on 'feminine identity'":

> Most difficult of all is that these *few* men, our allies, have learned their lessons well. The actual "content" of their writing is rarely incorrect per se. It is almost as if they have learned a new vocabulary perfectly, but have not paid enough attention to syntax or intonation. When they write of us — always of us — their bodies would seem to know nothing of the new language they've learned ... (56; ellipses in original)

It is almost as if, according to Jardine, the "allies" have learned a new language via sleep-learning. They seem to have vaulted directly from patriarchal language to feminist language without passing through the vagaries, errors, slippages, transferred syntax, slips of the tongue, and (in)felicities of an interlanguage. Concerned about the possible effects of these athletic, triple-bypass men mastering the language of feminist discourse and "jumping on the feminist theory bandwagon" and about whether what is being staged is men's appropriation of women's struggles, Jardine writes to a colleague and friend:

> Rosi, how long before it becomes no longer a question but an *answer*, a prescription about how women should go about what they're doing, saying, and writing ... There is then a kind of streamlining of feminism — a suppression of the diversity and disagreement within the movement itself ... (57; ellipses in original)

Thus it is unreasonable to expect that while feminists are excavating, imagining, (re)inscribing, and speaking this interlanguage — translating between and among our various native languages and an as-yet-undifferentiated, unmarked, unheard foreign tongue — we be asked simultaneously to translate back into the native languages. What Jane Casey and others who hold similar views long for, in effect, is to suppress polyphonic dialogism in the name of an unquestioned valorization of dialogue as an essentially unilateral communication in a single (smothered?) tongue. Moreover, it is not clear from the repetition alone of the word "dialogue" (which occurs so often in *CV 2* editorials as to volunteer itself as a blind spot) exactly how dialogue operates as a panacea for the split Jane sees between "theory" and "activism." To press, as she does, this requirement of dialogue in what I might call s(m)other tongue is in effect to annul these feminist projects and to censor the work in the very process of its being produced. The aim of feminism is not or is not only, to create one common language of, by and for women but to multiply the linguistic potentialities, competencies and occasions in which women can speak, write, perform, analyze and celebrate their difference(s). Mary Russo describes the proliferation of feminist and postmodernist textual work as a "carnival of theory" including

> all manner of textual travesty, "mimetic rivalry," semiotic delinquency, parody, teasing, posing, flirting, masquerade, seduction, counterseduction, tight-rope walking, and verbal aerialisms of all kinds. Performances of displacement, double displacements, and more have permeated much feminist writing in our attempts to survive or muscle in on the discourses of Lacanian psychoanalysis, deconstruction, avant-garde writing, and postmodernist visual art. It could even be said, with reservation, that in relation to academic institutions, what has come to be called "theory" has constituted a kind of carnival space. The practice of criticism informed by this theory has taken great license stylistically, and in its posing posed a threat of sorts. (221)

Jane Casey's privileging of dialogue represents too, I think, an imposition onto writing of functions that are, if not more properly at least equally, pedagogical, a paradoxical imposition given her stated scepticism regarding the importance of the role of language ("Well, even if some of us don't subscribe to this 100% ...") (8).

While I am not opposed to dialogue as such (obviously translation contains, though is not superseded or wholly absorbed by, the idea of dialogue), what I am suggesting is that if academic discourse and institutions deserve careful scrutiny, and they most definitely do,[8] so do notions like dialogue. What is needed is a multiplication of tasks and approaches instead of the reduction or subordination of differences in the name of a single, artificially elevated one. In a very thoughtful and challenging essay on the ethics of feminist research, for example, Maria Lugones and Elizabeth Spelman develop the idea of "friendship" as an acceptable basis for doing theory together.[9]

What I am proposing is that in developing a model for feminist collaboration that includes dialogue but does not threaten to contradict, contract, ignore or suppress the work of some possible contributors, it may be helpful to borrow aspects of translation theory. As David Homel and Sherry Simon outline, translation has a number of traditional and brand-new functions that are compatible with feminist projects.[10] Both translation and feminism are tools for a critical understanding of language. Traditionally, the political force of translation has been in redressing the imbalance between dominant and dominated cultures. Translation is a practical and a theoretical issue in the relations between French-and English-speaking feminists in Canada (Homel and Simon, 43–4). In the same discussion, Barbara Godard adds that translation is one among many ways of rewriting within literary systems (50).

A translation model would compel us to examine the repertoires of respective systems — both so-called "ordinary" and "theoretical" discourses — rather than simply assume that the only unilateral translation from "theory" to "practice" is possible and desirable. Secondly, we might be able to deal with the problematical corollary of that assumption, namely, that theoretical feminists have a monopoly on power through a discursive advantage the non-theoretical feminists lack. Translation concepts such as interlanguages, which I have discussed only very briefly here, system interference, and translation as production rather than reproduction, for example, could be called into play to set up the conditions under which we can emerge in "a *mutual dialogue* that does not reduce each one of us to instances of the abstraction called "woman"" (Lugones and Spelman 581; emphasis added). There is a sense in which continual calls for dialogue between theorists and activists can be construed as an attempt to displace activism into the realm of discourse. I realize that in importing a translation model I am proposing to add yet another discursive strategy to the repertoire of the theoretical system. However, another advantage of translation is that it can operate both orally and in print. Dialogue, on the other hand (at least as Jane Casey valorizes the term), is a concept derived from an oral economy and transplanted into the written. If one of the unanalyzed distinctions between theory and action is that one is primarily a written practice and the other primarily oral (meetings, demonstrations, symbolic gestures, consciousness-raising groups), then translation allows for mediation between these two economies.

What must be avoided is a talking down, a speaking for, instead of, or in the name of, no matter how scrupulously. As Lugones and Spelman conclude, only friendship can constitute the groundwork of collaboration, or, in their words, a project of "joint theory-making." Theory can and does thrive outside the academy.[11] And the academy is not identical with a set of walls. A map is not the territory.[12]

♦

• S(M)OTHER TONGUE?: FEMINISM,
ACADEMIC DISCOURSE, TRANSLATION •

## NOTES

1. I would like to thank Romita Saha, a graduate student in English at the University of Alberta, for sharing with me an account of some of the discussions concerning the roles of theory and practice in which she participated during her involvement in Indian politics.
2. I must underline the call for papers in *Tessera* explicitly discouraged "academic" discourse and not theoretical language. It is in Jane Casey's editorial that theoretical language is equated with academic discourse.
3. In this connection, I should also probably acknowledge the similar influence of "I am Joe's [sic] Liver," "I am Joe's [sic] Pancreas," "It Pays to Increase Your Word Power," and the true life experiences published in the issues of *Readers' Digest* that came out during the sixties.
4. In former centuries, it was the general consensus that women, being possessed of only a weak reason and morals to match, need not be educated, or, if educated, that the women's curriculum ought only to prepare them for the extremely restricted roles they would play in society (consisting primarily of the custodianship of their "virtue"). Apparently, for example, women who *were* taught how to read, at least during the sixteenth and seventeenth centuries, were not necessarily also taught how to write. As Margaret Patterson Hannay observes, "Teaching women to read the words of men without teaching them to write their own was one effective means of silencing them"(8). History teaches us that it is necessary to be suspicious of what is perceived to be good for different groups of people.
5. This one-way translation is counter to the meaning of the word 'discourse.' In its etymological roots, 'discourse' refers to a running back and forth, to speaking at length and to running in different directions. Thus 'discourse' contains the idea not of unilateral but of mutual translation.
6. See Jane Gallop's and Madeleine Gagnon's expansions upon the idea of the (m)other tongue.
7. See Gideon Toury for development of the concept of interlanguages.
8. As Jacques Derrida cautions, the theory that has the arts as its object may be "just as useful [to the military-industrial complex as is basic scientific research] in ideological warfare as it is in experimentation with variables in all-too-familiar perversions of the referential function.... What is produced in this field can always be used. And even if it should remain useless in its results, in its productions, it can always serve to keep the masters of discourse busy: the experts, professionals of rhetoric, logic or philosophy who might otherwise be applying their energy elsewhere"(13).

Derrida claims that it is precisely the necessarily double gesture of maintaining professional competence even while engaging in the most underground thinking about the university institution which "appears unsuitable and thus unbearable to certain university professionals in every country who join ranks to foreclose or to censure it by all available means, simultaneously denouncing the 'professionalism' and the 'antiprofessionalism' of those who are calling others to those new possibilities"(17).

9. Lugones and Spelman focus on sociological rather than literary or philosophical research, but their thoughtful article exploring the nuances of the concept of friendship as a basis for a research ethics is well worth considering. See also Kathleen Martindale's critique of their article.

10. See the discussions by Barbara Godard, Kathy Mezei, Sherry Simon, David Homel, and Susanne de Lotbinière-Harwood on how feminist work is transforming the theory and practice of translation itself (Homel and Simon 43–54).

11. There is a new journal for Canadian education activists called *Our Schools, Our Selves* that has just begun publication, of which I have seen only one issue so far, that includes articles by university professors from more than one discipline, former politicians, elementary school teachers, poets, native secondary school students, a secondary school student who is also a mother, labour activists, and others.

12. In "The (eye)or(y),"*Prairie Fire* 8.2 (1987):33–9, I addressed a similar tendency, in that instance on the part of certain writers, to blur university buildings with abstract theorizing hostile to indigenous literatures. While it is indeed appalling that many university literature departments, permeated by the colonial mentality, have done very little to acquaint Canadian students with their own literary traditions, what concerns me is that, paradoxically, often those individuals in the academic community who have done the most to defend, to teach and to publish Canadian writing and writers are the ones who are maligned while the rest are left uncriticized.

## WORKS CITED

Casey, Jane. "Writing in Response." Editorial. *Tessera/CV 2* 11.2/3 (1988):6–9.

Derrida, Jacques. "The Principle of Reason: The University in the Eyes of Its Pupils." *Diacritics* 13.3 (1983):3–20.

Gagnon, Madeleine. "Langue maternelle et langage des femmes." *Tessera 4/CV2* 11.2/3 (1988):21–7. Translated by Erika Grundmann. "Mother Tongue and Women"s Language". 28-34.

♦ S(M)OTHER TONGUE?: FEMINISM,
ACADEMIC DISCOURSE, TRANSLATION ♦

Gallop, Jane. "Reading the Mother Tongue: Psychoanalytic Feminist Criticism." *Critical Inquiry* 13.2 (1987):314–29.

Hannay, Margaret Patterson ed. "Introduction." *Silent But for the Word: Tudor Women as Patrons, Translators, and Writers of Religious Works.* Kent, Ohio: Kent State University Press, 1985.

Homel, David and Sherry Simon eds. *Mapping Literature: The Art and Politics of Translation.* Montreal: Véhicule Press, 1988.

Jardine, Alice. "Men in Feminism: Odor di Uomo Or Compagnons de Route?" In Alice Jardine and Paul Smith eds. *Men in Feminism.* New York and London: Methuen, 1987. 54–61.

Knutson, Susan. "Text in Context." (f.)Lip Re-marks.*(f.)Lip* 1.4 (1988): 22–4.

Lugones, Maria C. and Elizabeth V. Spelman. "Have We Got a Theory for You? Feminist Theory, Cultural Imperialism and the Demand for 'Women's Voice.'" *Women's Studies International Forum* 6.6 (1983):573–81. Special issue featuring Hypatia.

Martindale, Kathleen. "Power to the Theorists: The Ethics of Theory-Making in Polyvocal Criticism." *Tessera 4/CV/2* 11.2.3 (1988): 54–65.

Russo, Mary. "Female Grotesques: Carnival and Theory." In Teresa de Lauretis ed. *Feminist Studies/Critical Studies.* Theories of Contemporary Culture 8. Bloomington: Indiana University Press, 1986. 213–29.

Toury, Gideon. "Interlanguage and its Manifestations in Translation." In *In Search of a Theory of Translation.* Tel Aviv University: The Porter Institute for Poetics and Semiotics, 1980. 71–8.

Williamson, Janice. "(f.)Lip Sides." Letters to the Editors.*(f.)Lip* 1.1 (1987):22.

# TO SPEAK WITHOUT SUFFOCATING

*Louise Cotnoir*

*Translated by Barbara Godard*

To construct a narration is, broadly speaking, to tell a story, a series of events making sense. Narrative questions enunciative operation and social praxis at one and the same time. What is at stake when a *woman-consciousness* produces this type of discourse? What happens when she seeks to translate her relations to the world into a form, a new one, if possible? What narrative will she offer up for reading, what hitherto ignored part of existence, its blind spot, will she set in play?

If we analyze the narratives produced by a woman-consciousness, we observe that on the level of the *plot* (the narrated story) the fictional universe is articulated around either *conflict, tension* or *paradox*. Clearly, the plot of the narrative conditions the *writing*, the expression, which are its vehicles. In each of these *narrations*, women writers question the power of symbolizing human experience by juxtaposing different emotional spaces and trying to create an "experimental ego" capable of bringing a new understanding of the entire human experience.

## NARRATIVE OF CONFLICT

The narrative based on conflict often expresses anger at what prevents a being of the feminine gender from attaining life. In this case, the story is formulated as a protest against the demented representation of a world in which women are constantly under threat. The narrative relates the contingent life of women, their exclusion, their failed destiny. The written narrative is that of a *scandal*, that is, the scandal of the indignation and revolt arising when one confronts the extravagant destiny created for women. The ensuing writing is a form of *protest* for oneself and in the name of other women. Here, one might think of Nicole Brossard's *These Our Mothers* where the text oscillates between theory and fiction, between assertive statements and anecdotal topics. These works have the great advantage of showing, of demonstrating, a coincidence between the representations of the self for a feminine being[1] and the meaning for this same being in reality, in short, they show that the personal is political. Often women writers are accused of paying homage with their imaginations to an ideology in their narratives, as if all discourse, no matter what form it takes, were not ideological ...

## NARRATIVE OF TENSION

Other narrations written with a woman-consciousness have their basis in tension; they grapple with traditional feminine submission without being able to imagine any forms of liberation. The choice of events these narratives relate is made in function of causing unbearable truths to be heard, of making the unimaginable speak. They raise questions about the abuse and injustice to feminine beings. I am thinking here of the extraordinary novel by France Théoret, *Nous parlerons comme on écrit* (We will speak as They Write). Such a problematic keeps the narrative on the brink of madness (self-destructive rage) which is one of the traditional feminine alternatives, on the point of suicide which is one way of expressing the protagonist's refusal to live in the structure of cultural narrative that would confine her to non-existence, status considered to be worse than death itself. The text is written with words choked in the throat, or else, the words escape brokenly in a flood of sobs or cries. In this sense, the text is closely related to poetry which is the supreme expression of suffering. The text denounces the hostility of which women are victims, the lies of language which cause death to be mistaken for life, which make women believe that fusion, the absence of difference, are the same thing as love; whereas the ordering (material and symbolic) of discourse leads the protagonist back to non-existence, to the abyss and death as woman-subject (*sujète*).

## NARRATIVE OF PARADOX

Finally, there are narratives structured around paradox. These are texts in which *affirmation and rejection of the feminine* are entangled. Based on contradiction, they set in play the utterances of men, plagiarize them until the violation of feminine-beings by discourse becomes visible, until they denounce the images by which women are overwhelmed. With humour, I would qualify these women writers as "double agents." They travesty and subvert language (sometimes with much irony) in order to make visible the "scandalous scandal": the primacy of the woman-subject. I am thinking here of Gail Scott's novel, *Heroine* which, in two languages (!), by creating a bridge between cause and effect, gives feminine beings access to the world, finds reasons that militate in favour of their revolt and announce their specificity. Such a narrative refuses to conform to "prestigious models," asserts the "liberty to speak otherwise" and inscribes this work in a culture in the anthropological sense of the term, that is to say, the novel questions political and social institutions, family structures, beliefs, technologies, from a point of view that is *strictly feminist*.

The writing in this novel, all fragments, digressions, paradoxes, sends us to images of "blind women" who participate in the patriarchal order just as it does to images of Amazons, of Heroines in the sense of the "principal protagonist in a literary work," but also, in that of "women gifted with a courage beyond the ordinary, having exceptional virtues." *Heroine* is a sort of kaleidoscope of the feminine universe, or better yet, a hologram of "the feminine" in hallucinated and hallucinating reality.

What we must retain from this too brief analysis is that, since writing is a form of consciousness, it must be acknowledged that all women writers (each in her own way) forms new propositions for our culture and our society.

♦

## NOTES

1. "Feminine" is used in this text in two different ways in keeping with Québec feminist terminology. Qualified as "traditionally feminine," it refers to a discourse of submission and containment. Used here with being or with subject, it designates the work of gender as a category constructed in the symbolic. This is the common term for designating sexual difference in grammar. Used in the phrase "*écriture au féminin*," feminine is an equivalent of feminist, involving a critique of the gendered order of the symbolic dimensions of culture. I have used "feminine" rather than "female" as an adjective, to emphasize this critique of cultural systems in Cotnoir's text.

## WORKS CITED

Brossard, Nicole. *Picture Theory*. Montréal: Nouvelle Optique, 1982. Trans. Barbara Godard. Montreal: Guernica, 1991.

Scott, Gail. *Heroine*. Toronto: Coach House, 1987. *Héroine*. Translated by Susanne de Lotbinière-Harwood. Montréal: Editions du remue-ménage, 1988.

Théoret, France. *Nous parlerons comme on écrit*. Montreal: Les Herbes Rouges, 1982.

# INCREDULITY TOWARD METANARRATIVE: NEGOTIATING POSTMODERNISM AND FEMINISMS

*Linda Hutcheon*

> It was conservative politics, it was subversive politics; it was the return of tradition, it was the final revolt of tradition; it was the unmooring of patriarchy, it was the reassertion of patriarchy.
>
> — Anne Friedberg

When Jean-François Lyotard defined the postmodern condition as a state of incredulity toward metanarratives, he set the stage for a series of ongoing debates about the various narrative systems by which human society orders and gives meaning, unity, and "universality" to its experience. Lyotard himself, in debate with the defender of the "unfinished project" of *modernity*, Jürgen Habermas, took on what he saw as the dominant metanarratives of legitimation and emancipation, arguing that postmodernity is characterized by no grand totalizing master narrative but by smaller and multiple narratives which do not seek (or obtain) any universalizing stabilization or legitimation. Fredric Jameson has pointed out that both Lyotard and Habermas are really, in fact, working from "master narrative" positions — one French and (1789) Revolutionary in inspiration and the other Germanic and Hegelian; one valuing commitment, the other consensus. Richard Rorty, in turn, has offered a trenchant critique of both positions, ironically noting that what they share is an almost overblown sense of the role of philosophy today.

Overblown or not, this issue of the role and function of metanarratives in our discourses of knowledge is one that demands our attention. Various forms of feminist theory and criticism have come at it from a particular angle: the metanarrative that has been their primary concern is obviously patriarchy, especially at its point of imbrication with the other major master narratives of our day — capitalism and liberal humanism. In their form of critique, feminisms have overlapped in concern with Marxist and poststructuralist theories and with what has been called postmodern art — art which is paradoxically both self-reflexive and historically grounded, both parodic and political: the paintings of Joanne Tod or Joyce Wieland, the fiction of Susan Swan or Jovette Marchessault, the photography of Geoff Miles or Evergon. Such art is ironic, not nostalgic in its engagement with history and with art history. It works to "de-doxify" the "doxa" — what Roland Barthes called public opinion or the "Voice of Nature" and consensus (47). But there is a catch here: because of its use of irony as a strategic discursive device, postmodernism both inscribes and subverts its target. From its first manifestations in architecture to the present, postmodern art has juxtaposed and given equal value to the inward-directed world of art and the outward-directed world of history and experience. The tension between these apparent opposites finally defines the paradoxically "worldly texts" of postmodernism. In response to the question of metanarrative, postmodernism's stand is one of wanting to contest cultural dominants (patriarchy, capitalism, humanism, etc.) and yet knowing it cannot extricate itself from them: there is no position outside these metanarratives from which to launch a critique that is not in itself compromised. And this sparks, just as powerfully, the no less real, if ultimately inevitably compromised politics of the postmodern. Indeed it is their compromised stance which makes those politics recognizable and even familiar to us.

It is over this paradox of postmodernism's complicitous critique of metanarrative that feminisms and postmodernism part company. Of course, many commentators have recently pointed to the maleness of the modernist tradition, and therefore to the implied maleness of any postmodernism that is either in reaction to or even a conscious break from that modernism. Feminisms have been resisting incorporation into the postmodern camp, and with good reason: their political agendas would be endangered, or at least obscured by the double coding of that complicitous critique; their historical particularities and relative positionalities would risk being subsumed. Both enterprises work toward an awareness of the social nature of cultural activity, but feminisms are not content with exposition: art forms cannot change unless social practices do. Exposition may be the first step, but it cannot be the last. Nevertheless feminist and postmodern artists do share a view of art as a social sign inevitably and unavoidably enmeshed in other signs in systems of meaning and value. But I would argue that feminisms want to go beyond this to work to *change* those systems, not just to "de-doxify" them.

But there is yet another difference between the two enterprises. Barbara Creed puts it this way:

> Whereas feminism would attempt to explain that crisis [of legitimation that Lyotard has described] in terms of the workings of patriarchal ideology and the oppression of women and other minority groups, postmodernism looks to other possible causes — particularly the West's reliance on ideologies which posit universal truths — Humanism, History, Religion, Progress, etc. While feminism would argue that the common ideological position of all these "truths" is that they are patriarchal, postmodern theory ... would be reluctant to isolate a single major determining factor. (52)

"Reluctant to" because it cannot — not without falling into the trap of which it implicitly accuses other ideologies: that of totalization. Creed is right in saying that postmodernism offers no privileged, unproblematic position from which to speak. Therefore, she notes, "[t]he paradox in which we feminists find ourselves is that while we regard patriarchal discourses as fictions, we nevertheless proceed as if our position, based on a belief in the oppression of women, were somewhat closer to the truth" (67). But postmodernism's rejection of a privileged position is as much an ideological stand as this feminist taking of a position. By ideology here, I mean that all-informing complex of social practices and systems of representation. The political confusion surrounding postmodernism — rejected and recuperated by both the left and the right — is not accidental, but a direct result of its double encoding as complicity and critique. While feminisms may use postmodern parodic strategies of deconstruction, they never suffer from this confusion of political agenda, partly because they have a position and a "truth" that offer ways of understanding aesthetic and social practices in the light of the production of — and the challenge to — gender relations. This is their metanarrative. This is also their strength and, in some people's eyes, their necessary limitation.

While feminisms and postmodernism have both worked to help us understand the dominant modes of representation at work in our society, feminisms have focused on the specifically female subject of representation and have begun to suggest ways of challenging and changing those dominants in both mass culture and high art. They have taught us that to accept unquestioningly any fixed representations — in fiction, film, advertising or whatever — is to condone social systems of power which validate and authorize some images of women (or blacks, Asians, gays, etc.) and not others. Cultural production is carried on within a social context and an ideology — a lived value system — and it is to this that feminist work has made us pay attention. Feminisms have, in this way, had a very profound effect on postmodernism. It is not accidental that the postmodern coincides with the feminist re-evaluation of non-canonical forms of narrative discourse, that a very postmodern autobiography, *Roland Barthes by Roland Barthes*, and a very postmodern family biography, Michael Ondaatje's *Running in the Family*, have a lot in common with Christa Wolf's *Patterns of Childhood* or Daphne Marlatt's *Ana Historic*. They all not only challenge what we consider to be literature (or, rather, Literature) but also what was once assumed to be the seamless, unified narrative of representations of subjectivity in lifewriting. Victor Burgin has claimed that he wants his photography and his art theory to show meaning of sexual difference as a process of production, as "something mutable, something historical, and therefore something we can do *something* about" (108). Postmodernism cannot *do* that something, however; it can *un-do* but, without a metanarrative to direct its political agenda, that is all it can do.

Feminisms, on the other hand, can do more. For instance, in granting new and emphatic value to the notion of "experience," they have given a different angle on a very postmodern question: what constitutes a valid historical narrative? And who decides? This has led to the re-evaluation of personal or life narratives — journals, letters, confessions, biographies, autobiographies, self-portraits. In Catherine Stimpson's terms: "Experience generated more than art; it was a source of political engagement as well" (226). If the personal is the political, then the traditional separation between private and public history must be rethought. This feminist rethinking has coincided with a general renegotiation of the separation of high art from the culture of everyday life — popular and mass culture — and the combined result has been a reconsideration of both the context of historical narrative and the politics of representation and self-representation.

There is, in fact, a two-way involvement of the postmodern with the feminist: on the one hand, feminisms[1] have successfully urged postmodernism to reconsider — in terms of gender — its anti-metanarrative challenges to that humanist "universal" called "Man" and have supported and reinforced its "de-doxifying" of the separation between the private and the public, the personal and the political; on the other hand. postmodern parodic and ironic representational strategies have offered feminist artists an effective way of working within and yet challenging dominant patriarchal metanarrative discourses. That said, there is still no way in which the feminist and the postmodern — as cultural enterprises — can be conflated. The differences are clear, and none so clear as the political one. Chris Weedon opens her recent book on feminist practice with the words: "Feminism is a politics." Post-modernism is not; it is certainly political, but it is politically ambivalent, doubly encoded as both complicity and critique, undermining any fixed metanarrative position. Because of their necessary notion of "truth," as Barbara Creed argues, feminisms are not incredulous toward their own metanarrative, even if they do contest the patriarchal one. Feminisms will continue to resist incorporation into postmodernism, largely because of their revolutionary force as political movements working for real social change. They go beyond making ideology explicit and deconstructing it in order to argue a need to change that ideology, to effect a real transformation of art that can only come with a transformation of patriarchal social practices. Postmodernism has not theorized agency; it has no strategies of real resistance that would correspond to feminist ones. It cannot. This is the price to pay for that incredulity toward metanarrative.

♦

## NOTES

1. I used the real, if awkward, plural here because there are as many feminisms as there are feminists and no clear cultural consensus in feminist thinking on narrative representation. As Catharine Stimpson has argued (223), the history of feminist thought on this topic includes the confrontation of dominant representations of women as misrepresentations, the restoration of the past of women's own self-representation, the generation of accurate representations of women, and the acknowledgement of the need to represent differences among women (of sexuality, race, age, class, ethnicity, nationality), including their diverse political orientations. As a verbal sign of difference and plurality, feminisms would seem to be a useful term to designate, not a consensus, but a multiplicity of points of view which nevertheless do possess at least some common denominators when it comes to the notion of the *politics* of narrative representation.

## WORKS CITED

Barthes, Roland. *Roland Barthes by Roland Barthes*. Trans. Richard Howard. New York: Hill & Wang, 1977.

Burgin, Victor. *The End of Art Theory: Criticism and Postmodernity*. Atlantic Highlands, NJ: Humanities Press International, 1986.

Creed, Barbara. "From Here to Modernity: Feminism and Postmodernism." *Screen* 28, 2 (1987): 47-67.

Friedberg, Anne. "Mutual Indifference: Feminism and Postmodernism." 1988. Unpublished manuscript.

Habermas, Jürgen. "Modernity — An Incomplete Project." Trans. Seyla Ben-Habib. In Hal Foster, ed., *The Anti-Aesthetic: Essays on Postmodern Culture*. Port Townsend, Wash.: Bay Press, 1983.

Jameson, Fredric. "Foreword" to Lyotard, vii–xxi.

Lyotard, Jean-François. *The Postmodern Condition: A Report on Knowledge.* Trans. Geoff Bennington and Brian Massumi. Minneapolis: University of Minnesota Press, 1984.

Rorty, Richard. "Habernas, Lyotard et la postmodernité." *Critique* mars 1984:181–97.

Stimpson, Catharine. "Nancy Reagan Wears a Hat: Feminism and its Cultural Consensus." *Critical Inquiry* 14, 2 (1988): 223-43.

Weedon, Chris. *Feminist Practice and Poststructuralist Theory.* Oxford: Blackwell, 1988.

# WHOSE IDEA WAS IT ANYWAY?

*Marlene Nourbese Philip*

From fireplace to desk — up and down — round and round — first the desk, next the room — back to the fireplace again he paces. The room is large, well appointed with furnishings that underscore and emphasize the owner's stability and comfort — his wealth even. Velvets; brocades; the gleam of polished wood; silver, even some gold, are all in abundance. Before the fireplace is the rug, in all likelihood Persian, but certainly of the Orient; the intensity and the depth of its colours: red, sepia, burnt sienna, beige and black are held in perfect balance by its intricate patterning. It muffles his footsteps, provides further evidence, if any is needed, of wealth.

On the panelled walls hang paintings which further bespeak their owner's station in life. The fire's energy is caught and reflected in the occasional glint of gold leaf that frames the novelty and lustre of the still-new medium, oil. Portraiture: a group of plump women in diaphanous clothing; still life: a bottle of wine — the darkest of green — luminescent, a glass, some fruit with the sheen of freshness still upon them, pastries ... all eternally ready to be consumed; landscape: a hayfield and in it a hayrick silhouetted against a red setting sun; classicism: Actaeon fleeing his hounds and the beautiful Artemis; biblical: a woman — Mary Magdalene — in deep meditation, her hand upon a skull; every genre is represented. There are, as yet, no Raphaels, Titians or da Vincis; no Pisanellos or Caravaggios; those will undoubtedly come later. For the present these are the lesser works of lesser masters, and their illusion is better served by the firelight. Their purpose is to reflect back to him who paces, as nothing else does, his solidity, his wealth, his burgeoning power — his being.

The desk, fashioned from a dark wood — mahogany perhaps — and richly coloured, faces the fireplace; its polished surfaces gleam in the fire and lamp light. As befits the man who paces, it is a large desk; on it rests a globe — a Martin Behaim globe — a hymn book, a psalter, a book of arithmetic and Ptolemy's *Geographia*.

Every so often the man interrupts his pacing to stand before the globe, and, with the tip of his right index finger he sets it spinning — gently almost at first — only to increase its speed until its outlines are a mere blur. He laughs. Abruptly he uses the flat of his palm to stop the revolutions — the globe shudders and trembles under the impact of the sudden arrest.

Can we put an exact date to the man's pacing? A time? The fire and the light through the window suggest a dying day. Did he, that morning, leap out of bed with an exclamation, a shout of surprise or discovery — of excitement? He might perhaps have echoed Archimedes — "εὕρηκα! Eureka! I have found it!" An idea the equal of Newton's discovery of the principle of universal gravitation; Galileo's discovery of the Milky Way; Copernicus' centring the motionless sun at the heart of our galaxy; the *cogito ergo sum* of Descartes. Such an idea, such a thought, such a plan that would — but as yet he had no idea of its enormous potential.

Who was he? A man, of course. Neither peasant nor serf — a nobleman perhaps — possibly a lord. Would a nobleman have sullied his thoughts with an idea so crass, yet so utterly brilliant? Spanish, Portuguese, English, French — was he any of these things? Does it matter? He was European — undoubtedly manifesting the European mind long before the word 'European' would come into vogue. Some no doubt called him blessed — a genius; generations of mothers' sons and daughters would curse him, unknown that he was, into eternity. Too many and too few would die; too many and too few live out the diabolical plan that would change the world to come ... and forever. Philosophy, medicine, jurisprudence, economics — no discipline would be left untouched; anthropology and craniology — new branches of knowledge would develop to manage the unmanageable.

## ♦ WHOSE IDEA WAS IT ANYWAY? ♦

Was it an idea that was solely his, or were there several like him, within his own nation and without, who would serendipitously conceive and nurture the same idea at the same time? An outburst — a veritable epidemic — of synchrony; a natural effervescence within national psyches that collectively manifested itself in these isolated instances of Promethean thought.

Were they all men who had risen with the morning sun from their beds of linen sheets, laundered by the many hands of their many female servants; men who had then washed themselves perhaps, dressed or were dressed — noblemen or good solid burghers; merchants with an eye for profit? Did they then shake their wives awake and, with a quietly controlled excitement, say in unison: "Listen my dear; écoute ma femme; oiga mi esposa; listen, listen, I have an idea," or perhaps, "I had a dream ... last night ... a dream, a cauchemar in which I saw one hundred thousand ships ... at anchor ... under sail ..."

They — these women — would have listened, as they had always listened to everything their husbands had to say — eyes widening under the import of what he told them — the brilliant simplicity of it all — seeing in their mind's eye larger houses, mansions perhaps, more servants, gold, jewels. Such an idea! And did he, did they then, wives and husbands all, embrace their children, flaxen or dark-haired, downy skin still damp and soft with sleep? Did he caress their youth, their innocence — their years not yet burdened with age, with doubt ... with ideas, the infinity in their gaze turned towards history — not saying much, but transferring to them his excitement — his sin perhaps? Or was it merely business?

Did he not circle? no — that would come later, but did he not note the date, record it in his diary as he would have any event on his freehold estate, or at his business? On such and such a day, in the year of our Lord, I conceived — no — the idea came upon me — no — I saw clearly how — ... *On the sixth day of January, fifteen hundred and thirty five*, A.D., he might have written, or if he wished to reveal his learning, *anno domini,* or *le huitième jour d'août, the fourteenth day of March, fifteen hundred and two, in the year of our Lord* — he could just as easily have written fifteen hundred and three, fifteen hundred and twelve or fifteen hundred and sixteen — *I sat at my desk*, he would have continued, or, *walked in my garden admiring the roses of an evening; I sat drinking port after dinner on the evening of ...; just before I rose from my bed ...; while at prayers in the chapel ... as the reverend father ... during the Te Deum Laudamus, or was it the Nicene Creed ... a blinding flash of light, a sound as of rushing winds or water, a low murmur ... almost ... a susurration of voices ... a clap of thunder and there it was — the idea. A brilliant insight it might have been called four centuries later — like Einstein's ... mine eyes have seen ... the fusion of the past, present, and future — change ...*

It would have wanted for any competition — an idea such as this — had it been *nurtured* amid smoke, grime and filth, its brilliance and luminescence lighting up, between the picking and killing of fleas, ticks and other vermin, the hovel that wombed it. It demanded light, however, space, leisure ... it demanded wealth.

Wheresoever it happened to have been conceived, it deserved to have been reported, recorded, annotated, copyrighted, data banked, chiselled in stone: on __ the __ day of __, fifteen hundred and whatever, or maybe it was fourteen hundred (the Portuguese had a monopoly by 1450), but certainly no later than fifteen hundred and eighteen — we know the Spanish crown sanctioned the idea in that year — and most certainly in the year of our Lord.

Board rooms, flow charts, bottom lines — an advertising campaign to rival Coke's and Pepsi's; an idea of such magnitude — in today's world — would call for no less than these, its purveyors pinstriped, tailored — male and female both — blonde, blue-eyed and Christian, for that was the linchpin of the idea. The full and dark flowering of the messianic, crusading spirit of Christianity.

*Idea: archetype, pattern, plan, standard of perfection; an idea the plan or design according to which something is created or constructed — 1581.*

What was the idea? To prevent further genocide of the Indian (according to Bartholomew de las Casas)? To obtain a cheap source of labour? To convert from human to thing, pagan to Christian, the African?

*Transubstantiation: the changing of one substance into another, bread and wine into body and blood ... body and blood into thing, chattel, meuble, cosa.*

The bowels of each sailing ship designed for non-human cargo would entomb approximately three hundred Africans per voyage in

♦ WHOSE IDEA WAS IT ANYWAY? ♦

their own stench and filth for however long it took to sail the Atlantic — Liverpool to the Gold Coast to the Caribbean and back to Liverpool. Equilateral triangle of trade and death. Some estimate as many as fifteen million Africans were brought across the Atlantic. And there are those who say one was too many.

*"Gentlemen, we estimate that on each voyage some of your cargo will be lost — this is unfortunate ...and inevitable, but I believe, nay am confident that we can more than recover all of our expenses through our price per chattel at the auction block. I caution you, however, to be very careful when selecting Black ivory for the voyage — be very certain to chose the fittest and strongest — it is the only way to minimize your losses and maximize your profits. If you pack closely enough, each of our sailing ships could hold some four hundred pieces of the Indies, here, you can see for yourselves, I have sketched a picture of how they would lie for maximum use of your space."*

Black ivory; pieces of the Indies; the ideas skulks and hides behind euphemisms.

*"But be prepared for losses."*
Cuffee   *African man of some 30 years — jumped overboard*
Quesaba  *Negro woman of undetermined years — died this day of wasting illness*
Quarshie *Negro man of some 30 years — passed away from dropsy*
Abena    *Very young woman — under 20 years — taken suddenly by fever*
Jumpke   *Husband to Abena — consumption, worms, and ague*
Obafemi  *Negro boy no more than seven years age — ague*
Ayo      *Negro woman — very beautiful — departed this life suddenly*
Bem      *Departed this life on account of convulsion and fits*

Did the idea encompass minutiae such as these, or did its purveyor think in broader strokes? the repopulating of not one but two continents recently decimated of indigenous populations; or of profits: hundredweights of sugar and tobacco, tons of slaves.

*"You see, gentlemen,"* he strode up and down the room, *"'I have, without a doubt, ascertained that the Old World cannot populate the New —"* He has all of their attention now, these well-fed, well-clothed gentlemen sitting around his table nursing their port as he nurses their captured attention. *'Simply put, there are not enough of us."* A low mutter of concern ripples around the table. *"Here on these spread sheets you may see quite clearly what the population of the Old World is. Our computer projections confirm that there is not one but two continents for the taking, but we need people. People! Bodies! Unfortunately the indigenous populations have proven unequal to the task ... succumbed to illnesses, indulged in useless warfare —"* A murmur of discontent and complaint eddies around him.

*"The sine qua non of the development of these areas captured from the heathen and held in the name of our sovereign is the blackamoor, the African if you will. There is nothing which contributes more to the development of the colonies and the cultivation of their soil than the laborious toil of the Negroes — Negro slaves are the strength and sinews of our New World. About that I am certain."* The murmur of approval swirls around the table. *"Now gentlemen,"* he got to his feet abruptly, *"a toast, I propose a toast,"* raising his glass and in so doing spilling some of its dark red contents onto the polished surface of the table.

*"A toast! a toast!"* The words echo around the table as the men get to their feet and hold up their glasses, the cut crystal refracting the lights from many lamps, the dark red liquid in each glass glowing preternaturally as the light is first trapped by it and then released.

*"Magnum est saccarum et prevalebit! Great is sugar, and it will prevail!"*

*"Great is sugar,"* they all replied.

*"To Black Ivory, Pieces of the Indies, and the Negro! To our profits!"*

*"Here, here!"* There was laughter; the mood had lightened and was almost celebratory.

The black skin gleamed softly above him in the candle light, tiny globules of sweat beading her breasts. In the muted light it was as if she wore a necklace of crystals, as if she had been dusted all over with crystal droplets. Roughly he buried his fingers in the short cap of hair that curled and clung to her scalp.

*"The idea, gentlemen, however, is to populate the continent with workers who have proved themselves able to withstand the work and the*

*heat with minimal costs to their owners. Furthermore, these people are also savages, pagans who have no God. We can Christianize them at the same time as they produce our sugar, our tobacco and our cotton."*

*"Surely once they become Christians we can no longer enslave them — isn't that gainsaying the teachings of the Good Book."*

*The man addressing them smiles. "We shall address that problem if and* when *it does arise. Until such time our success is assured, gentlemen." They nodded in agreement.*

She had tormented him for months with her body — nothing but a servant — a maid to his wife ... a savage really. The woman sat astride him, they both panted, she bit on her underlip drawing blood; he reached up and pulled her down so that she half lay, half sat on him his penis lodged deep within her. She washed, cleaned and served them, but oh how he wanted her! Like he had never wanted or desired his wife ... like he had never wanted anyone, or anything for that matter, before or since. And for that reason he hated her, could not reason her away: her smell, her touch. The taste of her! She made him do things he did not want to do and having done them he wished to repeat them again and again. Things that he had to do, made him no better than a rutting beast in the fields — like she was. Brought him to his knees before her, her beauty and ... their love. The word had risen unbidden to his thoughts and he felt himself flush ... with shame? embarrassment? He loved a savage!

*"Gentlemen, I have worked out the figures here — our expenses will be increased because we need to erect and maintain forts to protect our enterprises but at one hundred cowrie shells per head — we may need to include weapons like the Birmingham gun — plus the cost of transportation, and allowing for some loss of cargo, we should be making a profit of one hundred dollars per piece of Black ivory. That is a conservative estimate gentlemen!" His audience smiles and nods in approval; general conversation has broken out around the table. He holds up his hand which commands silence: "Companies are essential to the production and maintenance of our capital, gentlemen, and we must get to work immediately setting them up."*

A plethora of companies: The English Guinea Company, The Senegal Company, The Royal African Company, The British West India Company, The Company of Royal Adventurers, The French West India Company, The Dutch West India Company, The

Guinea Company. Each and every one devoted to the idea of treating human beings as chattels.

*Transubstantiation: the changing of one substance into another. Bread and wine into body and blood, body and blood into thing, chattel, meuble, cosa, thing.*

Was that where the idea started? To make her a thing — less than he? Less than human. So that he could control her ... and himself. Did that explain his fervour in getting this plan started? urging these ordinarily cautious, respectable men to get involved — risk! invest! He always managed to control thoughts such as these. Except in his dreams where she comes holding her child — savage — his child — half savage — their child ... of their love, crying and begging his mercy and generosity ... begging ... as she should.

> *The Bishop strongly recommends that when cargoes of Negro slaves arrive in the harbour, priests should immediately be assigned to instruct them in the Christian faith and to teach them the doctrine of the Church in order to baptize them, and also to see to it that the Negroes hear Mass and go to confessions and communion.* (Lopez de Haro)

Surely the progenitor and architect of this idea — if we could but identify him — should take his place alongside those who, like the Portuguese navigators, Cristobal Colon, or Adolf Hitler, have stood in the way of history and altered it.

> *It was a truly wonderful sight to see them all standing there, for some were fairly white and well-formed, some were as yellow as mulattoes, and some were as black as Ethiopians ... But who would have been so hard of heart as not to feel pity for them in their distress! Some lowered their tear-splashed faces, others bewailed themselves loudly and turned their eyes to the heavens, and still others struck themselves in the face and threw themselves to the ground. There were those who sang lamentations, and although we did not understand the words, the melodies told of their great sorrow.* (Eannes de Azurara)

Maybe the idea was happenstance, developed by small accretions of practice — a few here, a few there — as gradual as a meandering river gracefully yet inexorably eroding a shoreline. An idea that was merely the result of the accumulation of capital needing to expand — to create new markets:

> ... *it is no less than four months since traders took five hundred from Cape Verde to New Spain in one boat, and one hundred and twenty died in one night because they packed them like pigs or even worse, all below decks, where their very breath and excrement (which are sufficient to pollute any atmosphere and destroy them all) killed them. It was indeed a just punishment from God that these brutal men who were responsible for carrying them also died. The sad affair did not end there, for before they reached New Mexico almost three hundred died.* (Mercado)

A phenomenon of such gargantuan proportions and scale must have been deliberately conceived. By someone, somewhere, sometime: the man stands before the globe; his arms are folded, his head lowered as if in thought. Suddenly he throws his head back, exposing a smooth and cleanly shaved white throat, and laughs again and again. When he stops he sets the globe to a halt. Lightly, at first haltingly, he traces his right index finger down along the newly opened Indian ocean, around — the finger moves more surely now — Bartholomeu Dias' discoveries at the Cape of Good Hope, up ... along the west coast and across — now his finger is fully confident — the varnished ocean, painted blue ... to a new world not yet discovered, but which he would help to birth.

The fire is dying now; its light reddens the outline of his robe all along his right side, bleeds on to his right cheek painting his skin with a sanguinary glow as it embraces his head with its fiery corona. It is hard to tell in the dim light, but his eyes are blue, like the painted ocean, his hair is blonde, his skin fair and he laughs again and again.

♦

## Works Cited

Eannes de Azurara, Gomes. *Cronica de descobrimento e conquista de Guine.* (1410–74).

Lopez de Haro, Father Daimen (Bishop of San Juan). *Report to a Diocesan Synod.* San Juan: April 30 – May 6, 1645.

Mercado, Fray Tomas. *Suma de tratos y contratos.* Seville: 1587.

# SELF-REPRESENTATION AND FICTIONALYSIS

*Daphne Marlatt*

For the critic, the question behind autobiography seems to be first of all how does the writer represent herself? For the writer it is how do you represent others? An interesting differential which, in either case, brings up the notion of truth and how or whether it differs from fiction. The writer worries about the difference between how she sees the people she writes about and how they see themselves. The critic looks at the self that is being presented and its difference from what is known about the writer's life, the facts, say. Or "the (f) stop of act" as Annie puts it in *Ana Historic*, isolating fact like the still photo as a moment frozen out of context, that context which goes on shifting, acting, changing after the f-stop has closed its recording eye. The fact a still frame. The self framed she suspects, caught in the ice of representation.

As if there were a self that existed beyond representation as some sort of isolatable entity. And then, for company's sake, your self-representation, your self and your self-representation sitting side by side or better yet, coinciding. And without that coincidence some one can say, "Oh, she's making herself out to be ..." Oh dear, fiction as falsity.

Fiction, however, has always included the notion of making, even making something up (as if that something had never existed before), and goes back to a very concrete Indo-European word, *deigh*, meaning to knead clay. In many creation myths, a goddess or a god moulded us and made us, touched us into life, made us up. Out of nothing, out of a whole cloth as the saying goes. And so, this nothing-something, or this something that is nothing, we insist, as a species, on hanging desperately onto our Somethingness. Fact or photo or figure (even clay), separate from ground, but not ground, not that ... facelessness. Women are ground, women are nature — well, we know all this, how for us it's no small feat to be Something, given the ways our culture reinforces the notion that we are *less* Something than men. And yet we continually demonstrate our abilities to generate something out of almost nothing: a whole baby, a whole book, the whole cloth of a life.

To pick up that phrase "out of whole cloth" is to find an odd reversal, given that "whole" means healthy, undivided, intact, the whole of something. How is it that the whole phrase has come to mean pure fabrication, a tissue of lies? Whole the other side of hole, w (for women?) the transforming link. We can't seem to avoid the notion that making and the thing made — tissue, or text for that matter, since they come from the same root, have, at root, nothing: "you made it up," or more usually, "you just made it up" (as if making were easy). In our culture of ready-mades, making anything is an accomplishment, making something of yourself even more so, but add that little word "up" and you add speciousness, you add a sneer. Children learn that dressing themselves is an achievement but dressing up is only play, child's play as they say of something easy. Yet as children we know that play is not only easy, it is also absorbing and immensely serious, that play is the actual practice (not factual but act-ual) of who else we might be.

A powerful put-down that word "up." Does it imply we're trying to imitate the gods and have no business reaching a notch higher on the scale of creation, especially when it comes to creating ourselves? Or is that scale fictional too and "up" merely indicates we're getting close to something non-hierarchical and very real as in "i'm waking up"?

Perhaps what we wake up to in autobiography is a beginning realization of the whole cloth of ourselves in connection with so many others. Particularly as women analyzing our lives, putting the pieces together, the repressed, suppressed, putting our finger on the power dynamics at play. It is exactly in the confluence of fiction (the self or selves we might be) and analysis (of the roles we have found ourselves in, defined in a complex socio-familial weave), it is in the confluence of the two that autobiography occurs, the self writing its way to life, whole life. This is the practice of the imaginary in its largest sense, for without vision we can't see where we're going or even where we are. Autobiography is not separable from poetry for me on this ground i would call fictionalysis: a self-analysis that plays fictively with the primary images of one's life, a fiction that uncovers analytically that territory where fact and fiction coincide.

In *Ana Historic*, Annie and Ina discuss the difference between story and history, between making things up (out of nothing) and the facts, those frozen somethings of evidence. But what is evident to Annie is not always evident to Ina, because in each of them the seeing occurs in differently informed ways. Clearly, there are different kinds of seeing, as evidenced by another little word, "through": seeing through, which isn't prepared to take things at face value. For Annie the facts are "skeletal bones of a suppressed body the story is," and that suppressed body which can be resurrected by dint of making up is the unwritten story of who (else) each of the women in the book might be. It is through analysis, analysis of the social context each of them inhabit, that Annie can write her way through the bare bones of who they apparently are to the full sense and the full sensory body of who each of them might be, *if* they could imagine themselves to their fullest.

And why isn't the imaginary part of one's life story? Every poet knows it is, just as i know that in inventing a life from Mrs. Richards, i as Annie (and Annie isn't me though she may be one of the selves i could be) invented a historical leak, a hole in the sieve of fact that let the shadow of a possibility leak through into full-blown life. History is not the dead and gone, it lives on in us in the way it shapes our thought and especially our thought about what is possible. Mrs. Richards is a historical leak for the possibility of a lesbian life in Victorian British Columbia, which like some deep-packed bedrock continues to underlie the leather shops and tinted glass of our high-rise 1990s. We live in that context: the actuality of both. Just as we also live in the context of salmon rivers polluted with dioxins, harassed abortion clinics, Hong Kong's historic jitters, eco-islands of Sitka spruce, half-hidden memories of child abuse, and whatever hungry ghosts still pursue each one of us — to pull only a few threads of the whole cloth. The context is huge, a living tissue we live together with/in.

To write a whole autobiography, i mean autobiography in its largest sense of self writing life, not the life of the self but the life self writes its way to, the whole cloth, is to reach for what is almost unwriteable, a hole in that other sense. Yet autobiography until recently was set aside as a minor form, a sort of documentary support like letters or journal-writing, for the great texts. Its significance lay in its veracity, the faithfulness with which it followed the "life-line," the overall narrative of its writer's life, without leaving any holes or gaps, certainly without contradiction. The "life-line" after all represents a single line, just as the writer's representation of herself should be a true likeness — *like what?* Given the whole cloth, the truth of ourselves is so large it is almost impossible to write. It is full of holes, pulled threads, multiple lines, figures indistinct from ground.

Here we run up against the reductiveness of language which wants to separate —what do you mean threads? ground? Get your metaphors straight for god's sake, no for your reader's sake. Who's the creator here anyway? Maybe language after all, despite itself. But that's only if we can subvert its mainline story, that black stands to white as woman to man, that is, for the sake of definition (which language is all about) as ground to figure. Language defines Something, the subject let's say, as *different* from any thing and any other, who is always merely object. We begin to see the bias of the subject operating here and that this subject who so dominates the stage of representation is white, heterosexual, middle-class, mono-logical, probably Christian and usually male. Wherever we as women overlap with any of those aspects, inherit that bias. It leaks out everywhere in the most familiar of colloquial phrases, of idiomatic usage, in the very, indeed — and only by varying them (disrespectfully the subject might say, intent on the singular line of his story), only by altering them infinitesimally, undermining what they say, bending them into knots, into not's and un's, can we break the rigid difference between figure and ground which preserves that figure's hegemony, his "truth." No wonder women have such difficulty with the truth — such a single-minded/simple-minded truth it is, with no sense at all of the truth of the ground, of that which bears us in all our harrowing complexity: context.

Autobiography has come to be called "life-writing" which i take to mean writing for your life and as such it suggests the way in which the many small real-other-i-zations can bring the unwritten, unrecognized, ahistoric ground of a life into being as a recognizable power or agency. This happens when we put together the disparate parts of our lives and begin to see the extensiveness of that cloth of connectedness we are woven into. Then we begin, paradoxically, to weave for ourselves the cloth of our life as we want it to be. For it is in the energetic imagining of all that we are that we can enact ourselves. Every woman we have read who has written about women's lives lives on in us, in what we know of our own capacity for life, and becomes part of the context for our writing, our own imagining.

When text becomes context, when it leaves behind the single-minded project of following a singular life-line, when it drops out of narrative as climax and opts for narrative as interaction with what surrounds us, then we are in the presence of a writing for life, a writing that ditches dualistic polarities (the good guys vs. the bad guys, gays, bitches, blacks — you see how many of us there are), dodges the hierarchies (the achieved, the significant vs. the inessential, the failed, which goes to the root of our fear about life: was it all for nothing?) — it's all there in the so-called "nothing."

♦

# Tell Tale Signs

*Janice Williamson*

**1957 feminine ecriture, in english)**

Six years old, left handed, she liked cabbage. Arms and legs spread out towards the four corners of the room, she was her father's airplane swirl of low flight patterns on the carpet. After a long boozy dinner, she flew higher, born up by his sprung legs over the harvest-gold tweed sofa. Across the living room, descending, she brushed the hunting-scene curtains her brothers had set on fire last summer.

Time's up for any unwilling Icarus. Her wings crumple to the ground where she loudly reads the odd cavity in her wrist as pain. Her mother agrees temporarily. Four minutes later when the girl crosses the room towards her father, an imperceptible twist of her arm returns small bones into place. Examining her wrist, no longer hollow with memory, her father pronounces, "There's nothing the matter." The girl cries to her mother who looks away contemplating her lap. A moment later, recomposed, she explains to her weeping daughter, "Nothing, just a sprain..."

(The delirium of identity makes it possible to imagine her wrist as opposed to any other wrist broken in play. Pain and the lies of crumpled bodies sound hyperbolic truth. Another drunken fist hinges the bone.)

Later at the hospital, the girl's x-rays authorize the hairline fracture cracked through the bone. In the absence of her parents, did she sign the release form with her right hand?

♦ JANICE WILLIAMSON ♦

Thirty years later at the conference, a writer offers this unpaid signatorial advice: *Fasten on your signature before you hit the decks. You might need it. Just in case, set it into your pocket or the nape of your neck. Stitch up a little something on your left buttock in light of the others' star and stripes, big-city or just plain big-fish insignia. Flash it from under a short skirt. Body language like this makes waves of spectatorial applause only sound like appropriation.*

Remove when dancing. Snip. Snip.

(In this eventuality, *how do we tell us apart?*)

**the writer closes the book, touches up her make-up)**

Her husband wanted her to sign the papers right away in case later she wanted what he wouldn't like to provide for her. Her lawyer told her, "You're a fool." She agreed and signed. That evening, after dinner, her husband chased her around the kitchen table. Around and around, until she ran out the back door into the night losing her skirt as she scaled the neighbour's fence. In the morning, she and her husband, now composed, loaded up his car and their rental trailer for a trip north across the border to her new home. On the way, he took a "shortcut" along a different highway. The sun was on their backs, so she knew they were headed in the right direction. She dreamed about signing again with her old familiar name then ended with "son." She refused to talk with him about his work. When he turned away from the wheel to complain of her silence, he pulled over to the side of the road. His cock exposed. He told her. If she didn't. Perform. Or abandon.

Five hours later they reached her new apartment. It was small so they fit only her bed and a small table into the single room, storing her dishes in the fireplace. A small round window streamed with ruby light. He told her all she could do in that room was make love to other men. She did not lie.

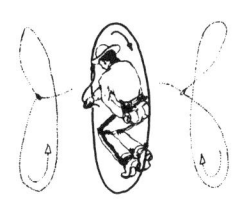

Her earrings are too long to leave behind with her wedding ring. The way the colour of everything turns feline stripped home. How this becomes t then is then his and hat too. How all the world spills into middle of the street Spadina traffic, pedestrians glowering hung up on drugs. She likes to be liked but can't help that everyone treats her like yesterday's jesus. Speechless, she has no illusions, just effects. It all boils down to this. T kettle empty this and that nothing. Sporting pricey coordinated fashions called "new exceptional freedom to roam," she drives the full length of the country day and night stopping only at the loom of primary-coloured tourist sculptures. At Thunder Bay, the dreaming princess tempts her for weeks. Twelve-foot geese, mother's shoes and condo cowboys with hard-ons make up irresistible parking-lot french toast.

### signature, the key fits, turning)

When they made love in the afternoon, his real girlfriend languished in a sterile ward suffering from twentieth-century disease. This betrayal meant that he would never "enter" her mistress body as though she were made fictive. Therefore, propped up, naked, tied to his iron bed, she tried to surprise him with yoga postures rarely displayed. Nonetheless, while she writhed quietly just beyond his field of vision, he potted and sculpted his way across lofty cat-shit floors.

In the hospital during the early evening they often visit His Love. As though it were true, having not been spoken, they all chime in about the intimacy they share. Sick with the world, His Love's gloved hands draw pictures. Deflowered women and televisions snarl to a graphite tangle.

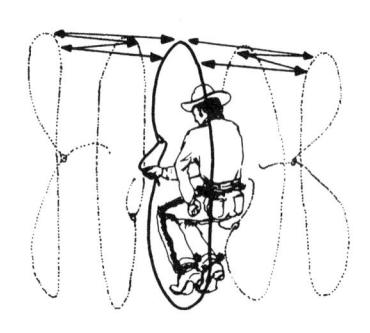

Until the artist burned himself up in polka-dot effigy, his signature had been the chignon woven through the surface of the table stippled pink *faux*-marble with dolls. A portion of his remains are laquered here and onto his fetish painting — her parting gift of slender female nude, a cut-out, air-brushed in *Penthouse*.

Practicing her full lotus headstand, she talks to the wall about his dead misery. The female nude stretched across the canvas repeats herself: *My left hand reaching beyond the frame indicates that I am eating pine nuts because I cannot resist helping myself to myself. In 1978, my thighs were thick with almonds. I have never been thick with want.*

**collaborating, reader and writer think of nothing)**

In a neo-colonial hotel on a hot Nassau evening, they dined with the aging no-longer-drunk musical comedy star who was redecorating his house with rare wood-carved panels. The gentried folly of his home echoed with the privilege of "Camelot," the refrain which zig-zagged across the continent on his trail. Snapping at his heels, content to settle for an appendage of the grate one, two women approached her in the washroom and asked her whether she was a movie star. "Which one?" she asked, curious. They couldn't remember, but they wanted her autograph "anyway." "Just in case."

That night she realized that simulating notoriety required a complete transformation of her character. She had to take herself as seriously as others would if they did. If she were no longer ignored, she had to keep up appearances and avoid sounding superficial. Later she would have to be perceived as experiencing the good time others accomplished. Would this day labour require better pay? Would psychoanalysis work through her relation to failure and power? She wanted to play a loved one returned from the dead. On a plastic beach chair, he did so convincingly. She felt herself fill up with love. Would he examine himself too carefully in the glare of her sunglasses?

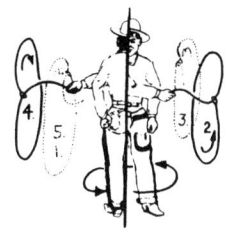

Unlike Virginia Woolf, i am not the least phlegmatic. Even though i refuse to smile on command, i have, they say, a rare though subterfuge personality. Call it — "darkly veiled ironic wit." i prefer to watch all things unfold, even myself at this very moment when my fingers move across the page, my letters bursting liquid crystal blue brilliance. i spell out this call to you. i am writing writing myself into being as though there were no tomorrow to appeal to you dear reader. and you. and you. Though tomorrow may not be the bright blue idea which brings us into being.

• JANICE WILLIAMSON •

### his memorial service speaks volumes)

Inside the covers of all of the deceased writer's Peter Handke books, there was no signature. However, on each page of Self-Accusation there were fine, numbered, fat HB-lead pencil lines under H's words. I read:

| | |
|---|---|
| 1 I came into the world | 10 I learned to be able |
| 2 I became | 11 I lived in time |
| 3 I moved | 12 I was able to want something |
| 4 I moved my mouth | 13 I made myself |
| 5 I saw | 14 I was supposed to comply with rules |
| 6 I looked I learned | 15 I became capable |
| 7 I learned | 22 I expressed myself |
| 8 I became the object of sentences | 23 I expressed myself in movements |
| 9 I said my name | 24 I signified |

38 I did not regard the movement of my shadow as proof of the movement of the earth. I did not regard my fear of the dark as proof of the earth. I did not regard my fear of the dark as proof of my existence. I did not regard demands of reason for immortality as proof of life after death. I did not regard my nausea at the thought of the future as proof of my nonexistence after death. I did not regard subsiding pain as proof of the passage of time. I did not regard my lust for life as proof that time stands still.

Number 38 was not underlined but deserves quotation in memory of her beloved dead friend, the director with the pencil and the same haircut as Peter Handke, the writer, who wrote *40 I went to the theatre*. Which he did.

**she learns to look both ways)**

Unearthed in an island jungle dig where Mayan ruins were once exposed, two jade beads made their way in his pocket to Pickering Jewellers where they were pierced with a post linking irregular gold nuggets and, after his drowning, given to his daughter and his wife. One of them lost here at the drive-in. The other at Ghost Lake.

*Every pebble looks alike along the shoulder of the road. A crack runs right up alongside the asphalt parallel to a white line (broken) running all the way to Banff. At one hundred and twenty kilometers per hour, the hood of the car rattles like wings taking off so I slow just in case. Out of the car, "Ghost Lake" sign to my right, car at my left, mountains focused in between. No problems so we get back in the car and ... "Drive," she said all along the highway. Reaching down she notices her necklace, broken open, jade beads gone. Dangling brass beads drop off one by one.*

Though it was February, it was almost hot walking along the roadside. Waiting for the jade bead to return to her hand from its resting place here or there, she sucked a stone humming her song.

*Janice*

He told her a loop-hole was an opening where small arms could be fired. It also permitted observation. He let on there was a trick he had been meaning to teach her, but she was too slow to catch on. That's what he said and that's why he never did. That's why in the Cochrane bookstore filled with spirit-line paintings and winter countstories, she bought her own *Will Roger's Rope Tricks*.

Over the years she imagines she will appreciate the reversible qualities of knots. Her roping begins with the spin of a flat look. She avoids "The Wedding Ring," and "The Butterfly" but eventually masters "The Reverse Ocean Wave." She hears that in Spanish, the wave goes around to the right. On a good day here on the prairies, the rope balloons and floats in sun dogs above her head, refusing Will's roping dream of a *perfect circle around an imaginary center*.

# The Pornographic Subject

*Claudine Potvin*

*Translated by Barbara Godard*

It is thus not lack of cleanliness or health that causes abjection but what disturbs identity, system, order. What does not respect borders, positions, rules. The in-between, the ambiguous, the composite. The traitor, the liar, the criminal with a good conscience, the shameless rapist, the killer who claims he is a savior .... The abjection of self would be the culminating form of that experience of the subject to which it is revealed that all its objects are based merely on the inaugural *loss* that laid the foundations of its own being. There is nothing like the abjection of self to show that all abjection is in fact recognition of the *want* on which any being, meaning, language, or desire is founded. (Kristeva 4–5)

a no-good girl, my mother said. She shifted in the immobility of my gesture balanced herself on the tight rope to the detriment of my vertigo her breasts brazenly on the window sills laughed at the enticing gaze of the boys. From the height of her certainty, she looked us scornfully up and down.

she consumed herself in total lucidity, wrapped up in her warmth her ardour like a wild young cat's she danced on Sundays swore at the sound of the great organ pipes.

spread shame about all tarted up. Nobody's thought her a virgin since the days she hung around the shed in the alley with the Hamel boys a band of louts spoke only about french-kissing, pawing in dark corners, screwing girls.

flaunted her desire fearless of losing/being lost only got what she deserved simplicity of a body cut in black. Resisted, so it appeared. Signs of violences traces of a rusty old iron bar stiffened on her lower ribs. Frozen by the force of wrists held on the cheek against the mouth arresting from clinging to the facts. Story of an ordinary rape in a common garage at the back of a yard so as not to be touched refuse the kindness of words. Hides herself under my wound dragged in the mire of language images of blood licked by the premature ejaculation bursts of her laughter on the blade hanging from the man's belt.

can't bear the laughter disappears under the fold of the envelope lifts his thigh touches the rising sex pushes back the lips with the right hand sucks the neck slits the body in stride a metal bar blocks the cry caught between the teeth *mordre en sa chair.*

did she really resist? Female subject to hysteria. Did she slip surreptitiously into the crack of his desire? On the subject of words confounded he speaks for her does not speak for her the reckoning is lost there's nothing. The subject is inscribed in the eye of the aggressor for worse an eye for an eye.

knows the lesson by heart knew in advance the involuntary jet from the other body tight-rope walker feather-weight girl doesn't weigh heavily in the philosophic balance judged by scent torn from her destiny a break opening.

the complicitous smile the obtuse gaze through the key hole *isn't locked* debarred/debauched and the transversal rod spreads over the female subject injured fractured it can be tended/thought. Mirna saw her bragged about it to the whole family brushed against the desire of the guys felt the burning of her agitated fingers refusal.

not given any time to breathe extinguished by force subjected a-sexuated woman under the scorn seizure of women's tails flashbacks

> licked the salt from the skin scratched the sand under the epidermis sniffed the colourless skin devoured the juices under the tips of fingernails bathed his sex in the white foam of her juices drank the ocean from his mouth tried the leap into speech cover the devil with spit

perverse was is woman depraved with knots unraveling dawn after dawn that brings her to the site of the crime thrown on a dirty old carpet right beside an old Ford recalls an old scene a game among brothers and their girl cousins sitting at the wheel pretending to drive fast straight ahead with a driver's licence licence to progress to have access to the self to the reflection of the day on the road to the thought displaced on the seat traversed by the mocking laughter the girls don't know how to drive/behave.

if Mirna had seen everything, she said nothing. Protecting the long naked body laid out peacefully raped under the leaking roof one sunny summer afternoon melting with the sweat of summer. A thin droplet of blood blackened on her scarcely bent knee the tenderness of a recent death and the assurance that everything happened somewhere else long ago. The night falls on Mirna the good girl her hand no longer blinds the gaze of those who touch her who atrophy her no longer hides the tears of Alice mingled with the echoes of Argentinian songs no longer hears the wooden clogs of the men on the bellies of the raped women recounts the obsession of giving birth a thousand times nothing the happiness of lathering girls.

she survives she he she their shameless captive ephemeral the female pupil of the assassin plays at having been/had/in the emptiness false caverns shaded by caresses arid struggles suction (action of attracting fluid — a subject — into the mouth by making a VOID) of a minute vulva inserted into the link of the ring taste of cold metal on the childish pubis the enchanted story erotic/corrupt voices insinuating take pleasure erode

the pen knife cuts moans to see herself flew off/robbed false veiled Venuses rejected derelict in the margin between the blanks the text had lost control of itself *apartheid* paper-cutter, two, bodybeings, separated, torn, red on white ground non-suit *no(WO)man's* land she survives.

the weapon took flight by the crack in the door *l'éclat de la différence comme une entrée dans la fiction* here the flash of the glazed eye subjective consciousness at work to forbid the forbidden.

Mirna observes swallows the muffled moan of Alice. Alice on the other side of the camera *fucked up* silent. Alice Malinche Madonna exhausted history snatches at vagabond sex women cling to it pleasure boats so many holes like ear rings. To listen the empty subject hung up by the bottom would mean to understand nothing taut skin of a drum reasons during the process they rape us for the pleasure of passers-by wet their eyes wash their hands of it (freedom of expression).

does Alice know when she enters the threshold of the improvised garage who she is? Does she remember her childhood? Alice star of a day the demeanour of a weeping willow took herself too seriously corruption of a minor she becomes identified with names herself cut displaces the cameras threads her words doll her low-cut dress cut trips into the decor plugs into the convertible blows up the cabin cut the pseudo filmmaker dialogue lover the flying carpet video upended ablaze CUT CUT CUT

I myself saw her sink in flames without saying anything insert myself into the rent in her flesh warm myself there in future to find again the sound lost in the obscurity of a shed there looms up the design of being the project of fabricating her death at the moment when she (he) escapes comes out of the objective graph graft

objective: merchandise, object, spoil of war, skin, obscenities, bondage, usage, orgasm, etc. Eliminate subjectivity. The appearance of exchange: giving/giving. Subject: *the thinking being considered as the seat of consciousness (opposed to) the object.* Ruinously. Besiege the subject of the film Mirna ponders all that and many other things too among others of changing the subject.

♦

## Works Cited

Brossard, Nicole. *L'Amèr ou le chapitre effrité*. Montréal: Quinze, 1977.

Kristeva, Julia. *Powers of Horror: An Essay on Abjection*. Translated by Leon S. Roudiez. New York: Columbia University Press, 1982.

# The Subject at Stake

*Carol Massé*

*Translated by Barbara Godard*

How to inscribe the feminine subject in discourse and the dominant ideology? The question is not new. It still haunts us after so many years because no one has given a satisfactory answer. Happily. This impossibility of closure is the guarantee of our liberty.

The question has already been asked in relation to literature: how to inscribe the feminine subject in writing? I am convinced that to reply to this question once and for all and for all women would be to bind the feminine subject to multiple rules and constraints. So I venture my question: how can I, a woman writer, inscribe myself as subject in language without being inscribed by a norm?

In my opinion, writing involves the abolition of any norm. Looking for the frontiers of foundations of a feminine, feminist or female writing is *maybe* seeking other limits in which to contain and repress us, for us to engage in self-censure. I have one wish to express: no limit to the imaginary of women in fiction, no edifying or reprehensible role to construct or deconstruct for the good of all women, no path traced in advance on paper that leads to a destiny for an ideal woman. Guilt over inventing outside well-marked trails is out of date.

How is the feminine subject to enter texts? Precisely, by *passing through the subject*. Is the general question not effaced by the emergence of the particular? Passing through the subject: scarcely an admissible position for any normalizing Will or globalizing

♦ THE SUBJECT AT STAKE ♦

Interpretation of the world. Nevertheless, no philosophy can protect a subject, woman or man, from her or his inalienable difference and discharge the ultimate debt: her or his life. Passing through the subject, in writing, ultimately signifies withdrawing from the collectively into intimist works where what is at stake is the re-creation of the 'I.'

The question of the subject cannot be separated from the question of the subconscious. I believe that complete freedom to explore my phantasms in literature is indissociable from my liberty to exist as a woman. Never lose sight of the relationship of the subject to language, because the world doesn't exist outside this relation. The subject will always be the privileged matter of one's own writing.

Ideology and theory, feeding sometimes on the anxiety of the individual confronting the void or the infinite, tries to fit creative activity into a grid. You want to mark the meanders of inner experience, which eludes rationalization, utilitarianism, and group consensus. Writing is the irreducible assertion of an utterance that does not know how to tie itself down to one Cause, one Meaning or one Moral, that is nothing more than protest. Writing is the demand for unremitting but contradictory recognition of the subject; recognition of the name it bears and of the unnameable inhabiting it.

Proposing a model for women's writing can only haze their liberty to imag(in)e and write themselves outside the code, outside the norm, and, multiple, playing with pleasure in fiction: women writers without origin or law, baroque, obscene, sacrilegious, orphaned; in short, inimitable because neither masters nor slaves. Working for the elaboration of a writing "conscious" of women runs the risk of blocking the emergence of writings of desire. Abandoning myself only to those drives and passions that weave the plot of my loss in writing is proving to be the object of my quest.

The force of a work rests in its singularity, in the discord it produces in the heart of a literature of entertainment or social conditioning. The pertinence of a signature stems from its power to cross out the effects of Number (in opposition to the One), of the Same and of the affected, established as mass culture.

What is the inestimable contribution of the women's movement? It restores to each woman the power to think of herself outside of norm and model and to speak of herself in terms of her own inner movement. For the paradox is none the less. Wanting a woman to take her place as subject (and not be put in 'her' place by any ideology whatsoever) means accepting that a woman may reject all allegiances and labels and want nothing else than to be, not reduced, but enlarged in her most single expression: unique, stripped of all points of resemblance to any others, invested with her exact oneness within the human species.

Changing places, for a woman, passing from the position of object of discourse to that of subject in writing, signifies gaining access to the space of her radical solitude and to the vertigoes of her own body. Then, *jouissance* of the Other and through the Other is near, the bliss for which exile from familial and social history is imperative. The *jouissances* of the body and of writing call on the same demands, for breaks with memory and community.

However, it is not only the subject who, in the search for happiness, is called upon to give things up. We know today, after the failure of the grand ideologies, that groups and movements are also called upon to exceed themselves, to move beyond.

◆

# Power or "Unpower" of the Fictional Subject: A Letter to Lise Gauvin in Reply to "What? You Too?"

*Monique LaRue*

*Translated by Barbara Godard*

Dear Lise,

Reading you in *Tessera*, I see that you find yourself divided by the desire to "capitulate" in face of what you call the "imperialism of the novel." For a long time, I have lived under the thumb of the tyrant: I want to speak to you from my side of the mirror at the same time as I respond to the invitation of *Tessera* to reflect on the question of the "subject" in fiction. Besides didn't you write that "to write a novel is to constitute oneself as subject"?

We all know that the question of the subject can no longer be raised without reference to the Derridean, post-metaphysical horizon in relation to which the traditional novel form — the very object of your love-hate relation — is out-of-date; the question, moreover, is implicated in psychoanalysis just as much as in literature, and is of a theoretical and philosophical order. Well, I am forced to admit that, addicted as I am to the novel, I cannot situate myself on this level. I'd like to but I can't. I can less and less. What prevents me is precisely the experience of novel writing. The novel nibbles away at everything of the essayist, the philosopher, even the intellectual, I might once have been. Besides what about women philosophers, about ideas and women? Apparently, that's another question. Obviously, I'm jumping from one subject to another in this cock-and-bull story. I'm not sure. I'm only establishing the facts (that's another consequence of the novelist's craft).

The novel is profoundly linked to the history of representations of woman. The more I accept to become a novelist, the more I leave behind my skill at manipulating ideas directly. I'm not speaking here of the cliché about intellectuals not writing good novels. I'm speaking of a dispossession, a loss of mastery, linked to the training of novelistic fiction without which the image of women and, hence, their experience of life, would be different. The novel appeals to me as a woman's place, and at the same time dispossesses me of the "objective" gaze, of the commanding thought which ought to be mine when I claim to write a novel. I cannot even explain or try to explain these two unimpeachable and twinned "realities." If I did so, I would cease to be what I have become, a woman novelist. I would have passed through to the other side of the fictional mirror.

Now precisely, this experience and feeling of dispossession, of "unpower,"[1] prompts me to doubt that the novel is "simply" a vestige of metaphysical thinking, an outdated, pre-modern, circular, globalizing, totalizing and, some say, "bourgeois," you say, Lise, "imperialist" form: there is always the same attempt to confine the novel in another, safely completed period, to seize it and pin it down as a fixed form, to have done with it. If the novel takes hold of me, risks devouring me, it is because the practice of fictional narrativity is grafted onto an experience of the imaginary, of narrative, and myth which is much more universal than one would like to admit. I don't want to justify my conviction. But I want to testify and affirm it: the novel, like any creation, is a de-territorialization, a loss of power. The novel is a form, and this form is more powerful than any writer. The form possesses the writer and not the contrary. For this reason, the novel continues to exist. Because every novel has been a risk. Not a repetition but an invention. In one sense, even, I would say that the greater the subjection to the novel, the greater the risk: it all comes back, as you see, to this tyrannical sado-masochistic, love-hate relationship, which obsesses you and is, in fact, that of the writer and the novel. Read the letters of Flaubert again. I'm not talking here about novels which are copies of other novels. Rather of the apprenticeship in the art of narration. Alas, I am not a poet! But I imagine the relation between a poet and poetry is freer. I'm not sure, but I have the impression there is some difference of this order in the contentious debate around the "novel."

Perhaps I am only confessing my weakness as an intellectual, as a novelist? Maybe. If I believed it, I would not write in *Tessera!* I think on the contrary that only the consciousness of this necessary and difficult loss of self can lead us to the question of the "subject" of the novel and permit its eventual transformation in writing, in particular in the writing of women. To my knowledge, one never writes what one ought or wants to write. "Writing is not a power at one's disposal" (Blanchot). I know that it looks like I'm once again jumping too lightly from one level to another. But it must be agreed that one doesn't control one's own image as a writer. That's another of the exigencies of the novel. It makes you live in total misunderstanding.

The power remaining to me when I am writing a novel is extremely slight: I do what I can. I apologize for this minimalism, but I think it is in this very sentence that is contained the entire life of "the artist." And a novel is obviously a work of art. At least, that is what I understand it to be. In this, I eliminate a great many books labelled "novels" which are not within the jurisdiction of art, of literature as such, but rather of the cultural marketplace, of sociology or pop history, which, moreover, is in no way pejorative in itself and might, in fact, confer a certain part of their power. This difference is now known to all editors, booksellers and writers, and I shan't insist on it. It seems to me then that to write a novel — the opposite of those books which, to the greatest happiness of their authors, answer to precise cultural needs — is also the contrary of "constituting oneself as subject" or of a "globalizing enterprise." Rather, it means for years each day to lose oneself as subject and to destroy the slight illusion one might have had of one's unity, of one's psychic integration, of one's capacity to think up lucid projects and to realize them. And, each day, for years to resume then one's social subjectivity. Shuttling back and forth. The form of the novel, the final result, the work of art, must have a "globalizing," "totalizing" aspect. The character must have something of an "ego," of a "subject." But this is a matter of form. To arrive at this end, all means are good. But the steps that lead to the final result are not accomplished "above the fray" in some will to speak or other, in some power. The subject of writing does not do what s/he wants and does not know where s/he is going.

I'm not surprised, dear Lise, that the person who incites you to question the power of the novel is a man, and ex-minister at that. Basically maybe, I envy the novelist who declares that "the novel is the only power" and who exercizes that power over his character, power to make it "ugly and stupid" at will. But in one sense that makes me shiver with horror, in the same way as I tremble before parents who believe in modelling their children according to their pleasure or will. Rather, I am under the impression, that characters are secret beings one must tame with tact and craft, as a photographer does his subject, on pain of caricaturing them, denaturing them, messing them up, in a relation of "unpower." Characters are shadows come from the depths of our unconscious, perhaps in what it has of the "collective." They're the walking dead, they fear the light of day and we have no power over them. This does not mean that I subscribe to the other myth, the one where the character dictates his own destiny to the writer. Nobody knows what will happen, neither the writer, nor the character.

Before a declaration like "the novel is the only power" I say to myself that I probably have no real talent for the novel. I say this without any vanity. I live in daily terror and doubt about this subject. Like all artists, probably. Because this fear of not being really "called," of not having the "vocation," the "talent," seems to me is nothing other than the quasi-sacred fear of the form itself which is the only subject of this enterprise.

I might just as well tell you that I don't know about the "imperialism of the novel" either. The novel dominates nothing at all. Like all writers, novelists grumble and suffer chronic dissatisfaction, incomprehension, scorn and indifference. Among literary types, their particular genre gets bad-press — I had proof of this once again last year during a conference at Trois-Rivières on "Poetry and the Novel" whose proceedings were published in *Estuaire* (1990). The novel was clearly on the defensive facing off with poetry, so much more noble and elevated in its apparent detachment from the literary powers. Easy, stupid genre, boring, repetitive, conventional, conformist genre. Everybody knows that tune! Serious lovers of literature scorn the novel completely.

## ◆ Power or "Unpower" of the Fictional Subject ◆

Moreover, I have never observed the magical effects you attribute to the "label of novel." Like all those who write in our time, I'm looking for readers, men and women readers. I beg people to read me, to consent to take an interest in my stories. We're all involved in this no matter what the genre, with two or three exceptions in any one country. And there are statistics to tell us that the essay, the biography are gaining and the novel losing momentum.

Finally, I have met novelists, men and women, who are successful, others who work in the shadows. This difference doesn't change very much where artists are concerned. Even a Nobel prize winner shakes in front of his or her blank sheet of paper. Otherwise it wouldn't become a great novel. If s/he knows too clearly what s/he want to do, s/he would no longer need to do it.

Certainly there is an imperialism of the novel which I think exerts itself within the genre itself. For the novel, falling within the purview of the image, is subjected to the power of its models. That is the veritable battlefield. Against this power of images, yes, I believe that one must struggle, but with the arms of the novel itself, to save the novel from fossilization, to keep it vital, alive. This mad will to go beyond (in the Hegelian sense of *aufheben* or sublation) the entire corpus of novels, this inordinate and dangerous ambition that necessarily takes hold of me as a novelist, of wanting to free characters from the empire of phantasmatic models from the fictional tradition, are these not, even unconsciously, related to a desire for power? I won't deny it. But it's only as a subject displaced, exiled from the site of the fictional utterance, without territory or sign posts, it's only by taking this multiple risk that I can perhaps earn the ultimate power of displacing the fictional subject.

As women, we are necessarily in this position of exile, of dehiscence from the novel. For the novel is linked to the traditional gendering of writing. The woman-character is the eternal object of the novel by men, the woman-reader is its eternal and silent addressee.

As a woman novelist, I am the pupil of these masculine creators who have made the fictional tradition I admire and of which I am, like it or not, the heiress. Now what do I see in their studio? The models, the subjects to be treated, are limited. For example: take a woman. Marry her off. Set in place another path of Desire, Sex, Passion. Select the way she is going to die.

Can this myth, to which the greatest women novelists have subscribed, be transformed? Can the place of woman be moved? The novelists, with their famous power over the life and death of characters have proceeded *ex cathedra* to the death of their female characters. The women readers, I have met them, they do exist. They are raising their children, got married, ought not to exist. But they do exist. The Madame Bovarys, the Anna Kareninas, the suburbs are full of them: the ones who forgot to take a lover, who forgot to commit suicide. Alone in the evening, they read novels. Do they recognize themselves in fiction? What happens when they read? Are they so mad that centuries of reading "novels" have had no effect on them? Has there not been precisely a distantiation, a certain way of taming the death drive? Are there no women survivors? Why did I begin to doubt there were? Is there another subject for a woman who wants to write a novel? Can one get out of the category of "women's writing"?

There is a fine line between the dislocation of the subject who writes and the "displacement" of the imaginary social subject in the novel. It's only by working in the crack between 'I' and 'ego' that I can make a new character come into being, be born. Every birth is a violence done to aging and death which, for the novel, occurs in the fossilization of its forms. But these models, these myths, will always be much stronger than we are. It would be presumptuous and naïve to think that because I am a woman I am not myself subjected. Also at no moment have I the impression of exercising power. To think of making novels where the woman, lost object of passion, would become the subject of her life: the enterprise is contrary, I believe, to the "guided tour" you mention. Sisyphus, David and Goliath are more suitable for describing the infernal couple novel-author which only continues to exist because literature is not everything and, not being all, must endlessly change to catch up with passing time, to be transformed. To live.

If I could, I would write poetry, free at last from the laws of the marketplace that haunt the novel. Or essays, to be equally armed for the "virile" struggle. Because it is true that in fiction, as you say, one "throws one's subject in a game of dice," in the absence of rational rules. But I am not able to change the "genre." The novel is imperialist, it is true: it requires one to sacrifice everything to it. It has become, without my knowledge, the only thing I really know how to do. Even the short story is now really foreign to me. I have fallen, like Alice, into a hole. "What to do so it holds together? How to write a transition that makes sense? Is that image inspired or sham? What did the character just say?" That's my daily bread, my obsession. I never feel any certainty, I've never found a method, I fear at every moment that my characters will break down, cease to interest me, be still-born.

Nobody asks us to write novels. Nobody is waiting for them. Few linger to understand them. The novel is an abyss that swallows up authors without giving anything in exchange, unless it is the strange pleasure, which it can never do without, of dueling with the form, which is the only subject of the novel. The sole reason for writing novels is the love of novels.

But all this, Lise, is it reasonable? Is it necessary to dedicate yourself to the novel in order to write novels? Is this not an impasse? These doubts obviously snipe at my ex-ego of the intellectual. That's why your sound position of intellectual provokes so many questions for me. Can we keep on talking?

In friendship,
Monique.

♦

## Notes

1. This neologism was first used by Madeleine Gagnon. I am borrowing the word, but not her more complex idea.

# IMAGINE HER SURPRISE

*Susan Knutson*

Thanks to *Tessera*, Teresa de Lauretis's discussion of feminist essentialist and Italian feminist theory sought me out in my *petit coin d'Acadie*, to remind me of the electric relay of neural light that feminist theory sometimes is. Thank you, *Tessera*, thank you, Teresa, and thank you, women of the Milan Women's Bookstore for responding to "the necessity to give meaning, exalt, and represent in words and images the relationship of one woman to another" (*Non credere* 9; cited in de Lauretis 14). In naming relationships between women as "the substance" of their politics, and in going further to theorize this political practice (putting it into words), the Milan Women's Bookstore has disturbed a certain sedimentation in my understanding of feminism.

*Non credere* boldly asserts that it will bring to light the "actual meaning, and therefore [the actual] name" of events and ideas which "commonly go under the name of feminism.... That name is 'genealogy.' What we have seen taking shape ... is a genealogy of women, that is, a coming into being of women legitimated by the reference to their female origin" *(Non credere* 9; cited in de Lauretis 14). I believe this corresponds to what in Quebec was named "l'émergence d'une culture au féminin" (see Zavalloni). My hope is renewed that we, too, will see our efforts "taking shape ... [as] a genealogy of women" and I think I understand the Milanese feminists when they write:

> We are not certain that the history reconstructed by this book will actually produce what we have sought, which is our

inscription in a female generation. We do not exclude the possibility that, put to the test, our experience may turn out to be just one of the many historical vicissitudes of the fragile concept of woman. (*Non credere* 9; cited in de Lauretis 14)

Doesn't Nicole Brossard express something of the same hope in the closing lines of *L'Amèr*? "*Je veux en effet voir s'organiser la forme des femmes dans la trajectoire de l'espèce*" (99).

This is one of several correspondences which appear to me to link Canadian feminism with that of Milan; not withstanding the real differences, and therefore the freshness of the Italian experience, for us. Women's friendships are addressed theoretically and are seen as central to feminist practice; Italian theory runs ahead of ours here. The Italian concept of relations of "entrustment" is a revelation permitting a more just evaluation of certain relationships between women. The interpretation of the much maligned practice of separatism as "the practice of sexual difference," the concept of a system of symbolic authorization in the feminine, elaborated as "female genealogy," "the engendering of female freedom," "responsibility to women," and the name of "the symbolic mother," strike me as important theoretical acquisitions.

Italian feminism is undetermined by the "essentialist/constructionist binarism" which has tended to structure feminist theory, particularly in the United States (Fuss 1). The Italians might simply be condemned as "essentialist," since, as de Lauretis explains, a "notion of essential and originary difference represents a point of consensus and a starting point for the Italian theory of sexual difference" (32). However, she argues that "this is not a biological or metaphysical essentialism but a consciously political formulation of the specific difference of women in a particular sociohistorical location" (31). As Adriana Cavarero put it, "For women, being engendered in difference is something not negotiable; for each one who is born female, it is always already so and not otherwise, rooted in her being not as something superfluous or something more, but as that which she necessarily is: female" (180–1; cited in de Lauretis 31).

De Lauretis argues that such an assumption "is basic ... to feminism as historically constituted" and without it, "the still necessary articulation of all other differences between and within women must remain framed in male-dominant and heterosexist ideologies of liberal pluralism, conservative humanism, or, goddess forbid, religious fundamentalism" (32). By definition, feminism is hopeful that "inscribed within the shared horizon of sexual difference, the words of all women could find affirmation, including the affirmation of their differences, without fear of self-destruction" (*Non credere* 132; cited in de Lauretis 25). The "Telling It" conference, held in Vancouver in November 1988 offers an important example of a practice —or better, *praxis*— correlative to this theory. The women who took the risk of "affirming their differences" there came, in fact, perilously close to self-destruction. However, happily, they did survive and the conference proceedings are published in an important book: *Telling it: Women and Language Across Cultures* edited by the Telling It Book Collective. I would like to explore what I understand of the Italian feminists' theory taking as a paradigm what I understand of the Telling It experience. I don't think I am simply developing an analogy; it seems that certain aspects of our practice translate over the cultural divide, and the work of the Milan Women's Bookstore collective can help us to theorize, i.e. put into words, the experience here.

One of the critical concepts developed in *Non credere* is that of the symbolic mother, a kind of transcendental signifier *au féminin*. A figure of symbolic mediation between women and the world, the symbolic mother legitimates female subjects in what de Lauretis refers to as a "female-gendered frame of reference" (24).

> As a theoretical concept, the symbolic mother is the structure that sustains or recognizes the gendered and embodied nature of women's thought, knowledge, experience, subjectivity and desire — their "originary difference" — and subjects in the social; an existence as subjects not altogether separate from male society, yet autonomous from male definition and dominance. (25)

The symbolic mother is a figure of a "female social contract" (29) which underwrites women's full social agency and accountability to other women. Among other things, the symbolic mother is the symbolic authorization for the phenomenon of debate and struggle between women which goes on in the name of, or in the frame of reference provided by, the women's movement.

I suggest that the fact that the Telling It conference was organized by the Ruth Wynn Woodward Chair of Women's Studies at Simon Fraser University is already an indication that it took symbolic authorization from what the Italian feminists would identify as the symbolic mother. Daphne Marlatt used her tenureship of the Ruth Wynwood Chair to organize it, and she conceived it in explicit recognition of difference and disparity among women, which she names "rift-lines that have become apparent in the women's movement."

> It was ... designed as a non-academic ... communities- (in the plural) focused [conference]. Limited in size, yet aspiring to showcase the writing and thought of women who are marginalized in different ways, it drew on the three largest groups of marginalized women in British Columbia ... Native Indian, Asian-Canadian and lesbian communities.... It was designed to be a celebration of the work by these writers — work which I felt to be ground-breaking in different but related ways.... It was meant to provoke discussion that seemed long overdue about difference on several crucial rift-lines, not the least of which are the rifts of race and sexual orientation.... Bringing women together in the same room implied a hope that our differences were not completely unbridgeable, that women with dissimilar, even unequal experiences of oppression, might be able to speak openly and hear each other openly, might even (and this was a wilder hope) find some sense of shared ground to enable us to help each other in our struggle against the forces of a society that continues to marginalize us. (12–13)

Clearly, Marlatt hoped that the horizon of common difference — perhaps what we used to call solidarity of women — would permit women to voice differences in a safe environment and thus begin to address the problems of racist privilege and homophobia which divide us. It was a risky affair, and it only partially succeeded. Both racism and homophobia were frighteningly in evidence. Racism is too intricately woven into western culture to be dispelled by simple good will. In the proceedings, Lee Maracle goes to the trouble of explicating one thread of that racist fabric, so that those of us who are blinded by white privilege perhaps can learn to see. She explains how one woman's well-intentioned comments, "we're all women, we're all equal, so what if you're a different colour," were "very patriarchal and very racist," denying and attempting to erase the experience of women of colour, refusing another's voice and saying "so what?" instead of listening with basic respect. Another woman challenged the presence of lesbians, the notion of lesbian culture. For her, the experience of being a woman writer, and even a feminist woman writer, was not reason enough to solidarize with lesbian writers. In the words of Sky Lee, she questioned "why white lesbians would want to connect their words and their names to Native and Asian women" (188). Betsy Warland concludes, "After the experience of the conference, I also believe that the feminist communities have not honestly confronted their homophobia" (199).

Lee Maracle, in her afterword, writes powerfully of the fact that, although the rifts of racism and homophobia were painfully in evidence, the participants risked building connections:

> We ... dug deep inside ourselves for the words, special words, that would finally begin to build the ramparts to the bridge which would allow us to meet as equals. Those ramparts are still hanging in the air in that room, dusty and unused. (163)

> TELLING IT was difficult because we are still telling it, not moving with it. I dream of the day when remarks such as "so what if you are a woman of colour?" and "is Lesbian a culture?" will stop all the proceedings, and everyone will say, "Let's thrash this out, let's settle it, let's keep going until we come to a common agreement — consensus — because we aren't going anywhere if we don't." We all struggled to build bridges at the TELLING IT conference. Too bad they weren't located in the same spot directly across from each other. (171)

It is important to honour the risks that were taken, and to understand why these bridges are not easily built. Perhaps the ramparts can still be use.

One way of naming this effort at bridge building, these lessons painfully learned and told and aching still between the pages of the proceedings, would be to refer to the conference as an important but difficult acquisition of "female genealogy." The construction of a genealogy — and the word's roots link it with gender, generation and "birth as a social event" — has to do with the symbolic placement of individual women, that is, where we place ourselves and in relation to what other realities. In patriarchal cultures, women have been invisible, silently placed in relation to father or husband. "Among the things that had no name [prior to feminist discourse] there was, there is, the pain of coming into the world this way, without symbolic placement" (*Non credere* 10; cited in de Lauretis 15). This reminds me of a feminist T-shirt I used to see at meetings and rallies: "I am a woman giving birth to myself." To inscribe a female genealogy is to construct a relationship of "belonging" which permits self-definition. For example, Sky Lee writes of her belonging in a women-of-colour context and how that supported her through the Telling It experience, which Joanne Arnott humourously renames "Yelling It: Women and Anger Across Cultures" (185). From one relationship of belonging, Sky Lee is able to illuminate others and so constructs or, in fact, *writes* her genealogy. Development of relations of belonging and construction of female genealogies is, as I understand it, a way of mediating women's access to a full humanity. To once again quote Lee Maracle:

> ... we have a great distance to travel. We have taken the first steps towards a new humanity. We look a little odd — most of us are well over thirty and ought not to be still toddling and faltering — but through the organization of such gatherings as the TELLING IT symposium, we are on our feet and on our way. (173)

The participants of Telling It — at any rate those who edited the proceedings — are clear that the problems which arose at the conference were manifestations of the same racism and the same homophobia which generates rifts between women in the first place. It is also remembered that class is another very divisive factor, a major silencer of voices, but one not dealt with in any depth by the conference proceedings. Inevitably, those without access to the gatherings and the discourse are not there represented. Nonetheless, in spite of omissions and failures, this meeting which, I am suggesting, took place in the name of the symbolic mother, made progress. What could be more important?

In attempting to read Canadian women's experience in terms of the theorization of the practice of the women of Milan — a practice of sexual difference — I may be accused of falling squarely into the trap of essentialism without even bothering to address myself to the debate. However, my strategy is intended to bring into play another aspect of de Lauretis's text — one that comes out of her framing of the Italian debate over *Non credere* within the Anglo-American debate on feminist essentialism. This is the critical importance of feminism challenging directly the "social-symbolic institution of heterosexuality" (32).

*Non credere* and its sister publications prompted a debate of remarkable magnitude within the progressive elements of Italian society. One writer raised the objection that "if the symbolic mother is the figure of a female social contract (as it indeed is), ... then the whole theory is founded on a 'radically separatist practice' and on refusing the male-female dialect" (Grazia Zuffa; cited in de Lauretis 29). This she names "homosexual fundamentalism," and condemns. "In other words," de Lauretis comments, "when the meaning of separatism shifts from the 'traditional,' socially innocuous, women's support group, in which women could let down their hair and commiserate with one another on personal matters, to a new social formation of women with no loyalty to men and intent on changing the world on their own — this is going too far" (29). It is impossible to trace all of de Lauretis's argument here, but, to summarize, she concludes that homophobia and a lesbian feminism that "dare not speak its name" are in conflict in Italy, and this conflict is raising the stakes significantly in the debate following the publication of *Non credere*. In this debate concerning the "practice of sexual difference" it is not the difference which is questioned, but the question of women's sexuality. Turning back to the Anglo-American debate through the *optique* provided by her reading of the Italian feminists, she makes the following observations:

> I would now suggest that what motivates the suspicion ... of a fantom feminist essentialism, may be less the risk of essentialism itself than the further risk which that entails: the risk of challenging directly the social-symbolic institution of heterosexuality. Which, at least in Italy, appears to be no easier said for lesbians than for heterosexual women. Here, however, the challenge has been posed, and most articulately by precisely

those feminists who are then accused of separatism in their political stance and of essentialism with regard to their epistemological claims. I do not think it is a coincidence. (32)

In other words, de Lauretis suggests that there is a kind of phantom presence in the debate over essentialism and that is the presence of homophobia. And this perhaps, after considerable thought, might explain why, when meeting with white women in the name of feminism, women of colour sometimes, and perhaps to their surprise, find themselves face to face with white lesbians. It is because of the location of the heterosexual institution in blocking the progress of women's full humanity, in thwarting any social mediation in the feminine, or, we might say, in the name of the symbolic mother. To put it the other way, feminists operating in the framework of the symbolic mother, and thus engendering "a social formation of women with no loyalty to men and intent on changing the world on their own, " — these feminists sometimes discover, perhaps to their surprise, that they are lesbians, and that the heterosexual institution is intent on silencing them, should they dare to speak their name.

To conclude, if hunting for essentialisms masks homophobic fears, if women of colour are not part of the debate, nor working class women, then surely the framework is wrong. Teresa de Lauretis — and Diana Fuss in *Essentially Speaking* — are right to try to shift the terms of the debate. I say, in this epoque, we cannot know if women are women because of nature or culture. There is, however, critical advantage in taking as a *point de repère* the notion that women are women now. Taking my hat off to Monique Wittig, I must say in spite of her that, for the same reason, we must consider lesbians to be women too. All of which is not to refuse to problematize the concept of women, but let us start, as Nicole Brossard suggests, from the paradox of women's identity in this patriarchal time (1985, 94). Because, in this patriarchal time, feminist practice, and theory which permits us to understand and to continue, is urgently needed.

◆

## WORKS CITED

Brossard, Nicole. *L'Amèr ou le chapitre effrité.* Montréal: Quinze, 1977.

———. *La lettre aérienne.* Montréal: Les Éditions du remue-ménage, 1985.

de Lauretis, Teresa. "The Essence of the Triangle or, Taking the Risk of Essentialism Seriously: Feminist Theory in Italy, the US, and Britain." *differences: a Journal of Feminist Cultural Studies,* I, 2 (Summer 1989): 3–37.

Fuss, Diana. *Essentially Speaking: Feminism, Nature and Difference.* New York: Routledge, 1989.

Libreria delle Donne di Milan (Milan Women's Bookstore). *Non credere di avere dei diretti: la generazione della libertà feminile nell'idea e nelle vicende di un gruppo di donne,* translated as "Don't Think You Have Any Rights: The Engendering of Female Freedom in the Thought and Vicissitudes of a Women's Group." Turin: Rosenberg & Sellier, 1987; cited in de Lauretis.

The Telling It Book Collective. *Telling It: Women and Language Across Cultures.* Vancouver: Press Gang Publishers, 1990.

Zavalloni, Marisa (ed.). *L'Emergence d'une culture au féminin.* Montréal: Saint Martin, 1987.

# WRITING THE RISK IN, RISKING THE WRITING

*Kathy Mezei*

We may as well begin with Virginia Woolf's *Room of One's Own*, for here we come up against a writer encountering, like a number of us, the "risk of essentialism."[1] Let's see how Woolf negotiates this encounter, for the process like the concept itself, has snared so many into immobility, anger, and acrimonious debate.[2]

Midway through *Room*, Woolf writes:

> The book has somehow to be adapted to the body, and at a venture one would say that women's books should be shorter, more concentrated, than those of men. (Woolf 78)

Then abruptly, close to the end of the book:

> It is fatal for anyone who writes to think of their sex.(102)

Now why does Woolf do that to us? After spending a hundred pages discussing the (difficult) conditions under which women write or cannot write, after explicating how Austen, the Brontës and Shakespeare's less fortunate "sister" negotiated their writing lives, she seems to cast off her carefully constructed position. How we are taken aback, for all along we have been nodding in agreement. Why must one be, as Woolf elaborates over several pages, "woman-manly or man-womanly ... before the art of creation can be accomplished"? (102–3). Why suddenly bring up Coleridge and his claim that the great mind is androgynous?[3]

As we well know, Elaine Showalter condemns Woolf's "flight into androgyny." "The androgynous vision ... is a response to the dilemma of a woman writer embarrassed and alarmed by feelings too hot to handle without risking real rejection by her family, her audience, and her class" (Showalter 286). On the contrary, I find that Woolf "risks" a great deal. She risked breaking the sentence, the sequence (Woolf 81). Toril Moi seems to understand this:

> We can read Woolf's playful shifts and changes of perspective ... as something rather more than a wilful desire to irritate the serious-minded feminist critic. Through her conscious exploitation of the sportive, sensual nature of language, Woolf rejects the metaphysical essentialism underlying patriarchal ideology. (Moi 9)

Still Showalter is right to query Woolf's flight into androgyny, but by failing to recognize the radical nature of Woolf's writing, as does Moi, she leads us astray, and the reasons for Woolf's androgyny and the reason why we, the reader, are perturbed by it remain unanswered.

Did Woolf resort to androgyny from what she already in 1928 perceived to be an "essentialist trap"? Emphasizing "fatal," she wrote: "It is fatal for a woman ... to speak consciously as a woman" (Woolf 102–3). How could she have contradicted her earlier words? Surely the only explanation is that Woolf was suddenly appalled by the implications of what we now term biological essentialism, by the limitations it can impose upon women who write, by the prison bars it can erect in order to trap women. "... I thought how unpleasant it is to be locked out; and I thought how it is worse perhaps to be locked in" (Woolf 25–6). Her only escape from an originary (and stifling) female sexuality seems to be an unsatisfactory (to us and to her) androgyny. She does, however, inadvertently offer another way out, more of which in a moment.

Woolf's entanglement foreshadows our discussion in *Tessera* — essentialism? — the positions we find ourselves taking. There are those among us who will admit that as feminists we too risked essentialism as we learned at first to understand, then theorize our always intuited "difference" from men. Only later did we re-vision this essential difference more precisely as socially constructed.[4]

Simone de Beauvoir said it best in 1949:

> It must be repeated once more that woman, like much else, is a product elaborated by civilization.... Woman is determined not by her hormones or by mysterious instincts, but by the manner in which her body and her relation to the world are modified through the action of others than herself. (de Beauvoir 682)

As feminists, teachers, writers many of us have had not only to learn to represent our experience, our selves (think of Margaret Laurence, Alice Munro, Margaret Atwood), but also to theorize them. When we began to understand ourselves as subjects constructed through language, discourse, society, we investigated whether the nature of discourse could be radically altered, seeking ways to manifest our specific subjectivity. Our differences from men interested us less. Moving beyond representation, some of us tried to reconstruct ourselves through subverting language and syntax and ideology (Nicole Brossard, Gail Scott, Daphne Marlatt, Louky Bersianik).[5]

While, for some, to write out of the experience of their bodies has been an act of liberation, for others it has seemed prescriptive, a sinister variation of the biological trap set by the patriarchy. (Not to speak of those of us feeling both simultaneously). Taking an admirably firm stand, Chris Weedon, for example, urges us to see how

> feminist poststructuralist approaches deny the central humanist assumption that women or men have essential natures. They insist on the social construction of gender in discourse ... [and refuse] to fall back on general theories of the feminine psyche or biologically based definitions of femininity which locate its essence in processes such as motherhood or female sexuality. (Weedon 167)

None of us wishes to locate our essence only in "processes such as motherhood or female sexuality." But is it not a question of who defines these processes? For, to deny myself as mother in a line of mothers would be to split myself beyond repair. How to wear my (mother) hood is fraught with consequences. "We live," Kristeva reminds us, "in a civilization where the consecrated (religious or secular) representation of femininity is absorbed by motherhood" (Kristeva 161). It is to that subject that my writing often turns of its own volition. I feel the need to talk about those limitations...real, perceived, other-defined...that our reproductive functions do impose on us. Although we may insist on legitimatizing writing ourselves through our bodies, on valuing our differences from men, the definition of "our bodies" should be elastic — "differences within essentialism" or essentialisms as Diana Fuss puts it (xii). Some of us bear children; others do not. We bear them differently: vaginally, by caesarian; we abort them, we mourn them. Each of us has a different menstruation story and tells a different menopause story, and our sexual pleasures, socially constructed or not, reflect different desires. As I write these words I think the only risk of essentialism is to deny it, to deny how we waver between positions. Writing essentially need not mean writing from a fixed, frozen position — it may mean writing out of a sense of one's essence, however troubled, variable it is, particularly because it is troubled, variable. Are we getting closer to Woolf's meaning, not a flight into androgyny, but a negotiating between positions?

Perhaps it comes down to where we locate difference. I like how Teresa de Lauretis does just this in her article "The Essence of the Triangle, or Taking the Risk of Essentialism Seriously: Feminist Theory in Italy, the U.S., and Britain," where she presents the theory and practice of the Milan Women's Bookstore as published in the co-authored text, *Non Credere*. (See Susan's thoughtful response in "Imagine Her Surprise.") De Lauretis locates difference in a dialogic relationship with its past, its representation. [Excuse the necessarily long quotation, but the idea takes a while to unwind.]

> ... the conception of sexual difference as "originary human difference" proposed by *Non credere* and *Diotima* is less an essentialist — biological or metaphysical — view of woman's difference [from man[ than a historical materialist analysis of "the state of emergency" in which we live as feminists ... this is not the sexual difference that culture has constructed from "biology" and imposed as gender, and that therefore could be righted, revisioned, or made good with the "progress of mankind" toward a more just society. It is instead, a difference of symbolization, a different production of reference and meaning out of

a particular embodied knowledge, emergent in the present time but reaching back to recognize an "image of the past which unexpectedly appears to [those who are] singled out by history at a moment of danger." (255; quoting Benjamin 27)

This may be one way out of Woolf's androgynous dilemma — to "recast" difference not through (sexual) essence, but through a dialogic relationship with the changing symbolization of gender.

When Hélène Cixous in "The Laugh of the Medusa" comes up against the trap of definition (essence), she argues that "it is impossible to *define* a feminine practice of writing ... this practice can never be theorized, enclosed, coded — which doesn't mean that it doesn't exist" (Cixous 137). Beyond the exaltation of Difference lies the Horror of the Same. Like Woolf, Cixous turns her anxiety over sexual difference as essentialist and its problematic expression through writing towards what she calls "the other bisexuality":

> It will usually be said, thus disposing of sexual difference: either that all writing ... is feminine, or inversely ... that the act of writing is equivalent to masculine masturbation ...; or that writing is bisexual, hence neuter, which again does away with differentiation ... In saying "bisexual, hence neuter," I am referring to the classic conception of bisexuality, which, squashed under the emblem of castration fear ... would do away with the difference experienced as an operation incurring loss ... to this self-effacing, merger type bisexuality ... I oppose the *other bisexuality* on which every subject not enclosed in the false theater of phallocentric representationalism has founded his/her erotic universe ... each one's location in self ... of the presence — variously manifest and insistent according to each person, male or female — of both sexes, non-exclusion of the difference or one sex ...(253–4)

Such vague bisexuality or androgyny did not seem to help Woolf or Cixous escape from the dangers they perceive within essentialism, and it worries those of us who fear it signifies merely another form in which the dominant subsumes the other. For, instead of transcending sexual difference, the concept of androgyny seems to emphasize it, falling unintentionally deeper into binary oppositions. Interestingly, Kristeva, who in 1974 echoed Woolf and Cixous, "all speaking subjects have within themselves a certain bisexuality ..." (Cixous 165), repudiates bisexuality later, in 1979, recognizing the potential for the erasure of one by the other: "I am not simply suggesting a very hypothetical bisexuality which, even if it existed, would only...be the aspiration towards the totality of one of the sexes and thus an effacing of difference" (Kristeva 209).

I said earlier that Woolf inadvertently offered another way out, one which Cixous and Kristeva, and de Lauretis in "The Essence of the Triangle," also offer in differing forms. Remember Woolf suggesting that "a woman writing thinks back through her mothers" (Woolf 96). Cixous writes, "The mother, too, is a metaphor. It is necessary and sufficient that the best of herself be given to woman by another woman for her to be able to love herself and return in love the body that was 'born' to her" (252). Kristeva in "Stabat mater" postulates a herethics of continuity, reproduction and undeath emanating from the "mother." Is it just possible that we have something closer to our desire as women and as writers than androgyny? Can we imagine a different "bisexuality"? That of mother to daughter, sister to sister, that of the nurturing symbolic Mother and of the mentoring relationship described in *Non credere*, where "the notion of the symbolic mother permits the exchange between women across generations and the sharing of knowledge and desire across differences" (de Lauretis 25). It all begins — the seduction and the resistance, the dialogic interplay essential for the locating of the self. Not flight, but honing in. In *To the Lighthouse*, Woolf's Mrs. Ramsay and Lily Briscoe, mother and artist, hand each other a gift across the divide of death, across the barrier of a different sexuality, a gift that becomes for Lily a generating vision, a creative act but also an act of defiance: mothers, sisters, mentors in love and in resistance. For we must remember Nicole Brossard's explosive, necessary "J'ai tué le ventre" (Brossard 11).

In the end, what matters is the writing itself, the fictions, the inventions, the stories, and it is to these we must turn. The writer will find her way to tell us what matters to her. Woolf's theoretical entanglement and Cixous' theoretical sleight of hand fade before the actual process of writing it out and writing us in. Look at Kristeva's personal style, her fragmented page, her typographical play in "Stabat Mater" as she takes Woolf's "playful shifts" in *Room* one step

## ◆ WRITING THE RISK IN, RISKING THE WRITING ◆

further. How can she (the writer) not risk essentialism? Writing the risk in, risking the writing.

Taking this risk becomes the subtext, the narrative grid of women's texts. Playful shifting language and narrative mirror the writer's shifting positions. It creates a dialogism between past and present, between a speaking subject and a repressed other as the self seeks to locate or define her sexual difference, her essence. In this tension lies the subject matter of so many women's texts. Jostling for position. Through the writing.

Think back to an early mother, Margaret Laurence, and the double discourse of Stacey in *The Fire-Dwellers*. Above, the constructed voice of mother and wife — the utterance; below, the inner voice preceded by a dash, speaking antithetically, authentically to the utterance. Stacey greets her husband after work:

> Mm. Everything's fine. You?
> ....
> — The automatic kiss bit. Does he actually not see me when he kisses me like that, or is it really the opposite — out of the corner of his day-beleaguered eyes he sees his life's partner, slacks and scruffy blouse, ... (55)

There is no essential self, just the dialogue between selves, wavering, working it out somehow by speaking.

Or think how Elaine Risely in Margaret Atwood's *Cat's Eye* surrealizes the conventional suburban monster mother (Mrs. Smeath) in her painting; it is her way to symbolize and distance the constructed mother. Elaine's dialogic meditation between her past, troubled girlhood and her present vacuity represents her desire to negotiate an authentic self. Only through remembering can she do so. That she fails to resolve her separation from her self may reflect the narrator's own inability to "reach back to recognize 'an image of the past,'" (de Lauretis 27) or Atwood's failure of vision or her realistic assessment of the condition of women in the 1980s.

Daphne Marlatt's dialogic process in *Anahistoric* is a more radical enactment through language and narrative of the desire to locate the "symbolic mother" in discourse. Risking her self by uncovering her selves in the past — the personal past of her mother, Ina, and the historical past of Anna Richards, the narrator, Annie gives birth to herself (and the reader) through writing it out. Here in de Lauretis's words "is a difference of symbolization, a different production of reference and meaning out of a particular embodied knowledge, emergent in the present time but reaching back to recognize an 'image of the past ...'" (27).

The writer will take her own risks in the writing. Let us look at Woolf's flight into androgyny and Cixous' other bisexuality as a way of writing the risk in, expressing ambivalence, succcumbing to the seduction of a distinct female essence, the symbolic mother, and simultaneously disclosing the fear of the devouring mother, of restrictions and definitions with their implications for the death of creativity. A writer writing her difference(s) in can frustrate a reader, as I was frustrated by Woolf's apparent abdication of her recognition of woman's difference and her recourse to androgyny. But the dialogic play and playful shifts she engages in mirror her own and our own struggles. Both and or. We can recognize ourselves in Woolf's "the book has somehow to be adapted to the body" and "it is fatal for anyone who writes to think of their sex."

We are back to where we started, but we wrote it all out or in along the way.

♦

## Notes

1. The editorial collective as they began composing their responses to this issue had a look at Diana Fuss' *Essentially Speaking* which makes the "claim that there is no essence to essentialism, that ... we can only speak of *essentialisms*" (xii).

2. Thanks to Michèle Valiquette for the dialogue that opened up this essay's essence. And I owe much of the origins of the following discussion to my graduate class who watched me skeptically while I tried to explain in sheer defiance of the printed page that Virginia Woolf could not possibly be promoting androgyny.

3. In *The Subject of Semiotics,* Kaja Silverman recounts Aristophane's story in Plato's *Symposium* (referred to by Lacan) in which Zeus bisected beings into two, male and female, leaving each half with a desperate yearning for the other. "The human subject derives from an original whole which was

divided in half, and ... its existence is dominated by the desire to recover its missing complement ... the division of the subject was sexual in nature — then when it was "sliced" in half, it lost the sexual androgyny it once had and was reduced to the biological dimension either of a man or a woman. (15–2)

4. See Julia Kristeva's two stages of (European) feminism; the first, women's attempt to insert themselves into history; the second, their "radical *refusal* of the subjective limitations imposed by history's time" (i.e. psychoanalysis) (Kristeva 195).

5. This is a whole other topic — the role of essentialism in feminist literary criticism of Canadian women writers. How have feminist critics approached women's texts? For example Pat Smart's recent study of Quebec women writers, *Writing in the Father's House*, reads the literature "from a perspective which emphasizes sexual difference." See Barbara Godard's discussion of essentialism in English-Canadian literature in "Essentialism? A Problem in Discourse."

## WORKS CITED

Benjamin, Walter. *Illuminations.* New York: Schocken, 1969.

Brossard, Nicole. *L'amèr ou le chapitre effrité.* Montréal: Quinze, 1977.

Cixous, Hélène. "The Laugh of the Medusa." In *New French Feminisms*, Eds. Elaine Marks and Isabelle de Courtivron. 1981, 244–64.

de Beauvoir, Simone. *The Second Sex.* Trans. H.M. Parshley. New York: Bantam, 1970.

de Lauretis, Teresa. "The Essence of the Triangle or, Taking the risk of Essentialism Seriously: Feminist Theory in Italy, the U.S., and Britain," *differences* I:2 (Summer 1989): 3-37.

Fuss, Diana. *Essentially Speaking: Feminism Nature and Difference.* London: Routledge, 1989.

Godard, Barbara. "Essentialism? A Problem in Discourse." *Tessera* 10 (1991): 22-39.

Kristeva, Julia. *The Kristeva Reader.* New York: Columbia University Press, 1986.

Laurence, Margaret. *The Fire-Dwellers.* Toronto: McLelland & Stewart, 1969.

Marks, Elaine and Isabelle de Courtivon. *New French Feminisms.* New York: Schocken Books, 1981.

Marlatt, Daphne. *Anahistoric.* Toronto: Coach House Press, 1988.

Moi, Toril. *Sexual/Textual Politics.* London: Methuen, 1985.

Showalter, Elaine. *A Literature of Their Own.* Princeton: Princeton University Press, 1977.

Silverman, Kaja. *The Subject of Semiotics.* New York: Oxford University Press, 1983.

Smart, Pat. *Writing in the Father's House.* Toronto: University of Toronto Press, 1991.

Weedon, Chris. *Feminist Practices and Poststructuralist Theory.* Oxford: Basil Blackwell, 1987.

Woolf, Virginia. *Room of One's Own.* London: Penguin, 1965.

# OTHER ORTHODOXIES OR THE CENTRING OF THE MARGINS: A DIALOGUE

*Sarah Murphy and Leila Sujir*

### THE MOMENT/THE PERFORMANCE

Two carefully costumed women walk up to the front of the room where a video monitor passes tape of streets filmed from a moving vehicle. Already we can tell that these streets are from a place other than here, somewhere else, moving fast, now, as the women occupy the centre, in the margins, watched, watching.

Two overhead projectors are turned on, and each woman sets onto them a group of transparencies placed, one over the other, incomprehensible. This question is asked: If you centre the margins, where do you enter the text? They wait.

The woman in black velvet, fingering the pearls about her neck, begins to speak. She speaks of waiting. Of the need to be in silence for language to arise. To form itself out of chaos, new, different. To notice itself. Finding the territory it has, unknowing, occupied.

The woman in black leather pulls off her riding gauntlets and removes all but one of her transparencies from the projector. The one that remains has no text. The space for the text is empty. But there is, in the bottom margin, a footnote. She underlines in red what is written there. Her pen moving in silence. The footnotes speak of linguistics, and folklore, and torture. They annotate a text, with us, indefinite, not yet arisen.

The tape of the streets plays on.

Now, the woman in black velvet stops speaking. The woman in black leather, slowly starts to speak. The rhythm becomes faster. She speaks of speaking. Of speaking and of speaking. Of never stopping speaking. Of speaking until language has moved to the edge of dissolution, has begun to say what has not yet been said. As she speaks, speaking.

The woman in black velvet is now silent. She takes all but one of her transparencies from the projector. On it is printed a classic feminist text. Slowly she starts to write in the margins. Ideas that challenge, and underline, and erase. Notes that change, and update and make different. Until all the space at the margins is taken up. Until the text is encroached upon. Until notes and texts start to know each other. To interact. To become in dialogue. To exceed themselves.

The tape of the streets plays on.

The women speak again. And yet again. About centres and margins. About occupied spaces. About presence and absence. About spaces yet to occupy.

The woman in black velvet will start to write marginal notes onto the current catalogues of academic publishing houses.

The woman in black leather will tell us of the title of the absent text: *Paramilitary Parafictions.*

The tape of the streets plays on.

The women stop speaking. They remove their transparencies from the overhead projectors.

The tape of the streets plays on.

♦ OTHER ORTHODOXIES OR THE CENTRING OF THE MARGINS ♦

## NOTES

1. Although she acknowledges the initiating role of his torture and the three years he subsequently spent in jail, his wife concurs in that his definitive downward spiral was set off by his inability to acquire the new language. She also reports that she cannot get through to him on any level now, even in the language they share. "He seems to think that I haven't suffered. Just because I don't have the scars on my chest from the acid the way he does. Just because I have full use of my hands. But he doesn't know what I went through the time he was in jail either. When the death squads were looking for me and I had to dress as a prostitute just to get out of the place after I visited him. You should have seen me all tarted up and with a skirt up to here, that the real whores lent me. And then once they [the death squad] followed me and I got on a bus, the number two I think but I didn't know where it went, and when I got off at the end of the line it was a market and there was a shootout where some people died but they didn't get me and I felt so sorry but what could I do, or the time I went to visit my kids, I had them hidden by then and I had to hide inside a latrine all night. But that wasn't the worst of it, not even the smell. Because the twenty-one days he was disappeared, I hunted among the corpses in the clandestine graveyards, you know about those, with my one year old on my back, I had nowhere to put her yet, and I don't know how to say it, you can't know about this, but there's a smell, so sweet, and no matter how many times you wash your clothes, you can't get rid of it."

2. *Translator's Note*: There are many figures in Salvadoran folktales that can be looked upon as weakened pre-Columbian gods or spirits of place, much the way leprechauns and fairies are the shrunken leftovers of the pre-Christian Celtic religions. One, La Ciguanava, is a *llorona* type figure, and may well be part of the same myth system as the legendary Mexican lady of that name, since the areas in which she occurs have the same myth and language base. She stands under trees crying, her *rebozo* wrapped about her. Sometimes she will follow men or walk ahead of them. One informant reported that La Ciguanava's position ahead or behind him dictated his luck in that night's fishing. Another such figure is El Cipitin, about whom less is known. He is seen as a child of about ten years who will come into the sugar cane mills to eat the ash that is left from the process of refinement, leaving his footprints in the morning. None of the informants seemed to know more about him or the reasons behind his strange diet.

♦ OTHER ORTHODOXIES OR THE CENTRING OF THE MARGINS ♦

3.  While his problems with the new language were manifest even in his classes, where he would seem to lack concentration, spending much time staring out windows or at points in space, or objects, they were apparently much worse at home, When he attempted to do written assignments, especially journal writing, he would become very agitated, complaining of headaches, screaming at his wife and children, or even hurling the textbooks across the room. "It really isn't right, to blame me, you know," his wife says. "I had to learn to speak. I was the one who went all over the city, even into the bars, to hunt down foreign journalists to make my denunciations. I told them all about him, about how he had disappeared about how he had been taken away about how I couldn't find him, it was during the civilian government when they were trying to look good internationally. That's how I started my work with the Human Rights Commission. And then I really learned. All the relevant words. Disappearance, torture, corpse, mutilation, percentage. In it seemed like at least ten languages. I probably saved his life. I didn't want to show him up."

♦ SARAH MURPHY AND LEILA SUJIR ♦

4. *Translator's Note*: It is interesting that even in the devastated Salvadoran countryside one can note the laws of applied linguistics at work. Just as the Spanish *peligro* (danger) derived from the Latin *periculum* through compression and consonant reversal, we can see the same process at work on the rather sophisticated and until now little used word *bombardeo* (bombardment). This word is now commonly said *borbandeo*, achieving greater ease of pronunciation through both the consonant reversal and the opening of the 'm' into 'n' because of its proximity to the 'd.' Both the peasants who are the victims of the act it signifies and their well-educated advocates now say the word in this manner. We can only speculate that the final monument to the 70,000 dead in El Salvador's ten year civil war may be the permanent passing of the word *borbandeo* into the Spanish lexicon. Or wonder what the effects of continued oral usage will be on the utterly foreign word *napalm* (napalm).

5. While it is generally acknowledged that first language acquisition quickly centres in one defined area of the left cerebral cortex, there is an increasing body of evidence to indicate that second language acquisition is more decentralized. Some part of the new lexicon may be located near the first language centre, while others may be located scattershot, even word by word, throughout the cerebral cortex. A secondary language centre may also develop in the brain's right hemisphere. It has been suggested that besides the words that exist in direct translation, transparent to the mind in both languages simultaneously, much vocabulary is segregated by language. Thus when the signifier is triggered into consciousness by direct or indirect apprehension (usually a visual image) of the signified, or at the end of a syntactical chain in one of the two languages, it still remains hidden, though known, in the other. The location of a word in left or right hemisphere may be tested through the blocking of one eye when the object is shown. It is the existence of two such parallel but unconnected lexicons that makes it possible for the authors to posit the existence of words or concepts so well hidden, and powerful in their effect on the subject, that they will sabotage those changes to personality and body language necessary to satisfactorily complete acquisition of a new target language, or even dictate a reactive blurring to the personality in the fully acquired language of which they should be a part. We are now beginning our search for these saboteurs in left and right brain, as the twisted bones and unseeing eyes. We will then extend it to movement, to the mind and body at one in a tiny gesture or tone, that seems to bring on silence and the aborted moment of recall.

• SARAH MURPHY AND LEILA SUJIR •

6. Although she has been helpful to us in many areas, his wife is uncooperative in the area of her husband's hallucinations. An educated woman acquainted with both culture shock and the concept of Post Traumatic Stress Disorder and how it can trigger long after the event, as it often does in Vietnam Veteran's Syndrome, she nonetheless says that she too was brought up to believe in ghosts and in her country's folkloric figures. As she puts it, "Look, I grew up terrified of my dead grandmother rattling the dishes in the cupboard on the Day of the Dead just like everyone else did. And when a neighbour told me about the dog he saw as big as a pony with glowing red eyes salivating and baring his teeth down by the graveyard, well I didn't walk on that road for a long time. Still, after so many days and nights among the dead, turning the bodies over one by one, and sleeping among them with the death squad looking for me — they didn't come to haunt me. So I'm not afraid anymore. But if he says they come to haunt him, or that the Ciguanava walks with him, or El Cipitin has come to Canada to play with his children's shiny plastic toys, Jesus Christ, man, he has better reason than most. And if they whisper and share a private language the rest of us don't know, well, they go back a long way. Who are we to interrupt a conversation between such old friends?"

7. Juan Pablo Letelier, son of assassinated Chilean diplomat Orlando Letelier, speaking in Calgary, April 3, 1989. "Although none of the casualties were inflicted in conflicts between nation states [but rather, in conflicts along the internal ideological frontiers imposed by the national security state], it can be said that in the last decade we have lived a third world war in South America. You know those casualties. They walk here among us."

# Opening up to a Lot of Pain

*Busejé Bailey*

Putting myself on the line in this work has opened me up to a lot of pain, pain that I have buried deep, deep inside my soul. Pain that I've inherited from my parents through slavery and colonialism, and them through theirs. We've lost a homeland, our names and languages. Something we must not, can not talk about even five hundred years later. This issue has never been addressed, let alone redressed, in any major way. We never own, or are in charge of media or institutions of change. Therefore, we are unable to purge our race of this legacy. So we continue to pass the effects of shame and domination down from one generation to the next. Liberals continue to refer to our past and to us as descendants of slaves. Even very educated Africans in the diaspora refer to themselves as descendants of slaves, reinforcing the fabrication that we had no past before slavery. I am not saying that we should forget the plight of our ancestors, far from it ... It is a testament to the heroism of our tenacity for survival. But we are just one of many people who at one time or another were forced into slavery. Granted we were the largest on a global scale. This should not be a place of personal or race shame. Everyone wants to keep this in the closet, the listener(s) want me to stop lest they become defensive or hurt. But everyone wants to make me over, to make me acceptable, to teach me how to speak, how to dress, how to lighten my skin, to lose my African appearance. Well all this make over still doesn't work. I am still African.

In this body of work "Body Politic," I'm not interested in providing a universal solution to the problems entailed. What I am interested in is a personal visual representation as it relates to postmodern discourse on the issue of race, gender, location, space and mainstream art practices. In this work I explore what it is to be an African-Canadian-artist-woman and an advocate of feminist politics with a social and political responsibility to the world. I follow in the footsteps of those sisters and brothers who inform and inspire my practice.

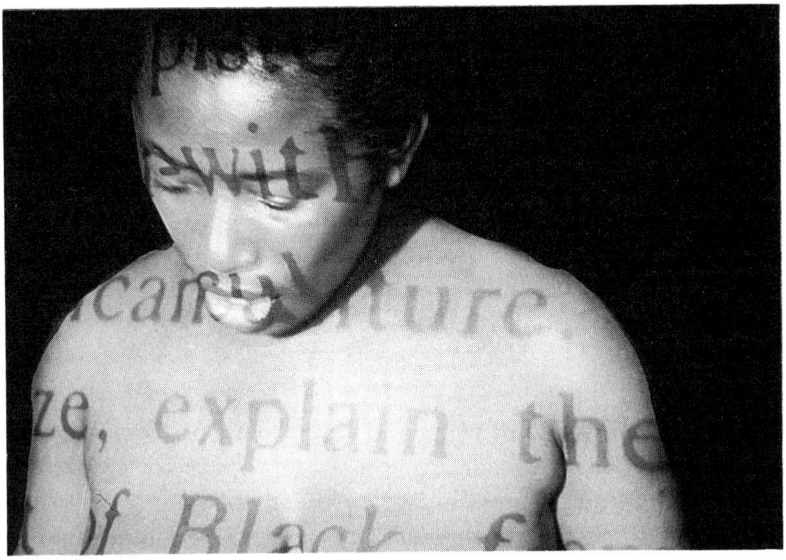
ze, explain the
Black

# WOMEN OF LETTERS (REPRISE)

*Babara Godard*

### NEGOTIATING ORIGINS

Creating a community of women of letters. This has been the project of *Tessera* for a decade, to constitute a space for women to exchange images and ideas in writing. Women writing (for) their lives, women imag(in)ing a speech or interpretive community with its distinct spaces and signifying networks, its particular modes of representation and speech genres. Such exchanges realize as "meaningful material" (Bakhtin/Medvedev 9) specific forms of social intercourse and so create the conditions of possibility for the constitution of women as speaking subjects. Through this in(ter)vention in the dominant representations of the literary institution, women reading and writing together constitute the horizon of a discursive order in which "she" is determined as "subject" or author-function. Autherity.

*Tessera* emerged from the discussions of a number of feminist writers and critics concerned about the absence in the Canadian critical institution of an appropriate frame for analyzing the exciting writing being produced by women in Canada working on language to develop a new syntax, new narrative structures, new modes of subjectivity. Haunted by Virginia Woolf's spectral 'Anon' (48), we knew that women needed to invade those library fortresses and fill up the shelves with books filed under women's names. We needed to read a narrative of the history of writing women in the classifications of library catalogues. As Woolf's literary reputation and *A*

*Room of One's Own* had taught us, putting Women and Literature together brought category trouble. How can writing be "good" if it is produced by a woman? Conversely, women writing find a dis-ease in the sentence (73-4). For women's signatures to have the truth-value requisite to fulfill the author-function under the current symbolic economy, a gendered one ordered by masculine-positive, feminine-negative, it is necessary to develop new models for interpretation that could establish as texts, as Literature — as meaningful utterance, not noise — the new forms being written by women. More than a challenge to the canon to claim significance for works by women, this approach concerns itself with signification, with systems of signs through which meaning is constructed, represented, consumed and reproduced. Signifying practices are examined for the ways linguistic and textual forms are inserted within the Literary and other systems of social conventions. What particular ordering of signs — graphemes, phonemes, gestures — composes a "good" text? How do these textual strategies become established as meaningful? What is the place of editors, of reviewers, in fixing meaning? How does gender work through this process? What is the relationship of feminist reading to the academy?

In 1980, feminist criticism was not much in evidence in English Canada: a new language of criticism needed to be invented. As Kathy Mezei summed up this imperative in the editorial to the first issue of *Tessera*, it was difficult for feminist critics to find an appropriate voice for writing about women's texts, especially one that would "illuminate a text rather than oppress it" ("Sp/elle," *Tessera*, Issue 1, 1984 12). "Illuminat[ing]" a text, finding the "appropriate" voice to give a reading *with* the text ... . What is at stake here is not just antagonism to a masculine academy, but recognition, love even, for women writers. An empathetic reading becomes synonymous with a feminine reading, one though in which is implicit a feminist critique of existing interpretive practices marked by their impersonality and apparent objectivity. What Mezei articulates here is the incommensurability of the feminist genre of criticism with the accepted modes of academic thought. There is a tension between the evaluative (critique) and interpretive (explication) functions of criticism, between judgement and embrace, which are gendered in the context of a masculine-dominated canon and academy. The exclusion of women's texts from curricula and the marginalization of women academics within the university was the norm during the 1970s (Smith). This absence of a feminist perspective in criticism, the inaudibility of the few feminist critics struggling to articulate a feminist interpretive frame to valorize women's writing, was forcefully registered for us in the personal difficulties we were experiencing establishing courses on Canadian women writers in the academy, in finding a public forum to articulate our feminist readings of texts. Into this historical moment *Tessera* inserted itself as Feminism against Literature.

The feminist criticism we imagined *was* circulating, but in marginal ways, in conversations and letters, primarily in private exchanges and impermanent oral forms. Publishing this work was difficult because the dominant form of feminist criticism, indeed of all criticism in English Canada, was what Mezei summed up as "images of women" ("Sp/elle" 9). Within this framework, woman was considered a fixed identity. Literature was understood to reflect and transcribe a pre-existing reality rather than to invent frames and establish perspectives within which to order a flux of phenomena into an image of "reality" and so inscribe relations of desire. Nor was attention paid to the ways meaning and value were produced in a specific society by the ways in which that society talks and thinks about itself. Such signifying systems of a society have a distributive function in relation to power discursively organizing social differences. They work asymmetrically to produce some groups of individuals as subjects and others as objects. Images-of-woman criticism worked as description to maintain the status quo with women as objects of knowledge rather than to raise questions about the production of women's subordination or to bring about change in their status through a theorization of representation, power and gender. To raise these questions involved exposing the illusion that language is transparent or neutral. Language is not a medium for transmitting messages about an independently existing world, but rather a semiotic system which offers possibilities for constituting such a world by differentiating between entities, so articulating identities.

Today, when everyone is presenting papers on Canadian and Quebec women writers at any and every conference, it is hard to remember the shock and incomprehension that greeted those first feminist critical analyses at conferences of the Association for

♦ WOMEN OF LETTERS (REPRISE) ♦

Canadian and Quebec Literatures (Halifax 1981) and of the Association of Canadian University Professors of English (Guelph 1984). Gail Scott recalled the first of these occasions as charged with "resistance" to Quebec "language-centred writing" ("Sp/elle" 7). Her dialogue with France Théoret about the way their writing and politics had mutually influenced them, though they came from different cultures, was part of a morning's focus on sexual difference within a two-day conference on "Otherness" in Canadian literatures. What remained problematic for the audience was that within Scott's and Théoret's feminist framework, which later would be called poststructuralist, the issue was not so much an egalitarian argument for equal representation of women's and men's experience nor, despite the dialogue form of presentation, an agonistic affirmation of differences, as it was an insistence that both these approaches were already framed within patriarchal structures or systems establishing gender as a set of (power) relations. Representation itself, with its metaphor of the mirror, its privileging of similarity or resemblance, is a patriarchal paradigm instituting the order of the one True and the many as distortion which works to eliminate difference, especially sexual difference, by hierarchically valuing the singular, the selfsame.

A feminist discourse in both creative and critical modes was emerging, however, encouraged by sporadic conferences which brought together anglophones and francophones. In such encounters, sexual difference was no longer the only consideration. Linguistic and cultural differences emerged in relations between Quebec and English Canada to complicate issues of gender. The category of "woman" became problematic for its universalizing claims as well as for its "naturalizing" tendencies. Such concerns with the differences within feminism have come to the fore of contemporary feminist theory, difference in the 1990s being articulated in more complex intersections of gender with race, ethnicity, class and sexual orientation as well as with linguistic diversity. When linguistic difference first emerged in the 1970s, within the orientation of cultural politics around Quebec's distinct identity, it was productive of transformations in literary norms in the English-Canadian literary institution, no longer subjected to a single norm of "expressive realism" but open to the Quebec literary institution and its support for "language-centred writing," as Daphne Marlatt realized

("Sp/elle" 8). Cross-cultural work against the imperialism of English was crucial to the critique of representation to produce change, for it made visible the fact that language is not a given, something natural and transparent, but a set of social conventions for relating and ordering signs to actively shape "reality." This entails political accountability in the construction of histories or narratives.

The awareness of cultural distinctions and power valences between Canadian and Quebec women made us alert to the limitations of the images-of-woman criticism with its universalization of the category "Woman" and its failure to take into account the filter of language or other sign systems in social exchange which occurs in a field of centrifugal forces unequal in relation to power. As Bakhtin points out, language is no neutral, value-free medium (293), but is charged with the ideological values of a culture, saturated with the voices and points of view of everyone who has spoken it. "The word, directed toward its object, enters a dialogically agitated and tension-filled environment of alien words, value judgments and accents, weaves in and out of complex interrelationships, merges with some, recoils from others, intersects with yet a third group ... ." Half someone else's, the "utterance arises out of this dialogue as a continuation of it and as a rejoinder to it — it does not approach the object from the sidelines" (276-7). Consequently, in learning a language, we learn relation, interrelatedness and distinction or difference within ideology.

Our understanding of cultural and linguistic difference was then limited to the Quebec question, which had been at the top of the political agenda throughout the 1960s and 1970s as one "national" group after another came to a crisis on linguistic grounds. The struggles of women writing in other cultural communities were only beginning to come to our attention — very belatedly — in the early 1980s through events such as the Women and Words Conference (Vancouver 1983), which brought Native women and Africanadians together. The histories of their oppression by the white settler society of which we are a part had been excluded by Eurocentric curricula. The marginalization of their writing was much greater than that of white English- and French-speaking women and we knew little of the history of their writing, lost in the archives and/or confined to oral circuits in Native languages. Our concern in the initial *Tessera* discussions was with the exploration of gender and colonization that had been developed by Quebec women ("Sp/elle" 11). Only briefly, and condescendingly, did our attention turn in the first editorial to the oppression of Native women and Africanadians ("Sp/elle" 11). We included texts by writers of both groups in later issues. The arrogance of insularity was not absent from our relations with Quebec feminists either, relations characterized more by abysses than by bridges. Recognizing that the "acknowledgement of difference has contributed to a cross-fertilization of ideas and mutual respect between feminists from Quebec and Canada that is quite unusual in the pan-Canadian context," Scott nonetheless asks "how much space really exists for the differences of women of other races and cultures?" In English Canada Scott senses "an imputation of exoticism to Quebecois women which leaves me feeling that, under the surface of our raised consciousness are buried less positive latent attitudes, vestiges of the conquest mentality of our history" (*Spaces* 44). This inability to hear Quebec's difference was slight in comparison to our inability as whites to hear the differences of women of colour. For the rest of the *Tessera* collective, as for Scott, "learning how not hearing the other closes space for each of us" has been an important lesson extending beyond our collective insistence on our empowerment as women in a patriarchal context. It has involved a recognition that Canadian society is divided not only by racial differences but by racism, and consequently all writers and readers have a significant racial identity. The meaning of our whiteness, the privileges it brings, the responsibility it entails, we are only beginning to learn.

With such long intervals between feminist literary conferences — Conference of Inter-American Women Writers (Ottawa 1978), Dialogue (Toronto 1981) and Women and Words (Vancouver 1983) — the opportunities for dialogue between anglophone and francophone feminist critics and writers were minimal. At these conferences, ideas were launched, conversations broached, insights flashed. Then everyone returned to their isolation. All traces of the new ways of looking and writing disappeared. This brought "frustration" since it was only at the very end of the conference that women from different cultures began talking to each other ("Sp/elle" 8). To sustain the contacts, to forge the links for a discursive community, it was necessary to produce written records, to establish forums for crossing distances and to allow people to develop new knowledges, to project new paradigms. Such a textual matrix would generate a field of discourse to produce new perspectives, new textual forms, new ways of writing. Feminist critical authority would be constituted as the effect of the new practices. Metaphors of construction peppered our dialogue, underlining our decision to found the magazine as a strategic intervention for advancing the constitution and recognition of feminist theory as a body of knowledge. That's how we optimistically framed the project of *Tessera*, a project of writing ourselves into existence, of writing ourselves with our different angle of vision into the symbolic, to write ourselves as women into the trajectory of the literary institutions, to invent ourselves as women in letters. This was a project to make a difference, to produce cultural transformation through a challenge to representation itself, more especially through work upon language.

There was an urgency and an excitement in our voices, our writing. Words like "thrilling," "wonderful," reoccur in our dialogue. A sense of discovery propelled us, naively, undoubtedly — other feminists had preceded us — but the effect of feminist ideas on our lives was profoundly empowering, personally transforming. We launched our collaborative introductions at each other, towards our readers, manifestoes seeking to disrupt the normal(izing) individualist and impersonal practices of writing and reading, to critique representation. Writing in/formed by the double slopes of our anger and joy. Hard as it is to remember the shock of novelty of the first feminist criticism, harder still is it to recall the heady optimism of these sallies in this present period of retrenchment when, through cutbacks of resources and the naturalization/neutralization of feminist discourse, the possibilities for change in the position of women in the symbolic seem ever more remote. Making difference visible — ever on the horizon. What we had to say in our initial *Tessera* editorial about the problem of women having difficulty being taken seriously as producers of truth (good writing) in the literary institution seems equally pertinent in the 1990s. For the academy's adherence to resemblance as a (patriarchal) paradigm persists in the institutional norm of "peer" decision which distinguishes (wo)men from men as (un)like subjects. These questions return inevitably to the relation of subjectivity and knowledge and the power relations that articulate it.

♦ WOMEN OF LETTERS (REPRISE) ♦

That feminist critiques of language and representation have had some impact may be noted in the masterful attempts to reappropriate them. Even that self-declared admirer of feminist criticism, Robert Kroetsch, adopts a stance of anxious male writer when reviewing feminist criticism in "My Book is Bigger than Yours." While positioning feminist criticism as the only hope for the future, making way for "a literature of the heart," Kroetsch attempts to master the theoretical text in a proliferation of containing metaphors which reassert his power to name and support the "feverish pride and genetic curiosity" (195) of his paternal interest in its conception. A phenomenon such as a man protesting his anxiety about exclusion from feminist theory could only occur in the wake of some sort of institutionalization.

Yet listening, in August 1992, to the tape recorded in July 1983 for our first editorial drew our attention to the continuing pertinency of our discussion of the problems women of letters confront with the literary institution and the production of meaning, as well as to the persistent "resistance to theory" in the Canadian literature field ("Sp/elle" 7). We wondered if we should publish the entire tape in a different forum. We decided instead to gather texts from a decade of *Tessera* into a book to engage with the literary institution in a different publishing mode. For the lesson Gwen Davies has drawn from the past is that the vast body of writing by women in Canada from the eighteenth and nineteenth centuries appeared in periodical form and, when it has not disintegrated with the paper it was published on, has rarely been taken into account by literary historians charting the periods and genres of literary production in Canada.

Optimistic we were in 1981, heartened by the example of *La Nouvelle barre du jour* in Quebec which, through the strategic intervention of feminists Nicole Brossard, France Théoret, Louise Cotnoir and Louise Dupré on its editorial board, had, during the 1970s, shifted the terrain of literary discourse into the zone of feminist issues, so that representation as desire, embodied or contingent knowledge, the strategies of the real, had become the privileged topics for an entire generation of writers, male as well as female. As Normand de Bellefeuille wrote: "Modernity does not happen only on the page: it's a relationship with writing and with *life*" (84, emphasis added). Putting the feminine into discourse, changing the system of relations to undo the order of the One, articulating a new exploded subject in the rhythms of multiple voices with new strategies of the real — this emerged in the gaps or interstices, in the in-between of texts, in dialectical relation and rupture with the Law in Quebec throughout the decade. Literary historians looking back on this period of Quebec writing have stressed the primordial influence of feminism: "On reading the entire body of work, one is struck by the fact that two major currents traversed the period [1976-1980], nationalism and feminism, and profoundly influenced literary production in Quebec" (Dorion). For Quebec feminists, institutionalization was, in the words of Meaghan Morris, "an opportunity, and a necessary condition, for serious politics" (5). In the material elaboration of feminist theory and writing, they exposed the effects of institutional realities.

Encountering these women writers was exciting for Daphne Marlatt and other anglophone writers who found both exemplary texts and supportive readers among Quebec writers for their own neglected language-centred writing ("Sp/elle" 8). Translation *from* the French, in the first phases of *Tessera* and, increasingly, *into* French, was a rewriting with a strategic difference: to transform the literary norms. At the heart of the project was the aim to denaturalize the thematics and literary realism of anglo-Canadian criticism by showing how representation produced rather than reflected subjectivity. *Tesssera*'s focus on language as language, as mediation and manipulation, would work against the instrumental view of language of the dominant thematics, a persuasive model of discourse that equates "clarity" with the correct representation of the "one true." The order imposed by such unambiguous "expression" advanced the literary institution as an order of homosociality.

What was political about this project was the "We," the determination to work collectively, collaboratively, to establish a network of women speaking, writing, thinking. This was an attempt to stage the possibility of a different sort of continuity through reading and its performatives or provisional positions. "We" is, of course, exclusionary as well as inclusionary. The four founding editors of *Tessera* shared an interest in francophone cultures, Gail Scott as an anglophone working in Quebec, Daphne Marlatt, Kathy Mezei and Barbara Godard (later Susan Knutson) as comparatists by academic formation. Working across cultural and linguistic lines, translating from one language into another, was to take up the position of translator as code-switcher, as go-between, culture-broker and potential traitor. Shape-shifters bringing about change. For the boundaries are where the movement is. The issue raised by Quebec feminists before us was the consideration of gender as a crucial category of symbolic value and intellectual capital: it matters who is establishing the norms of the Literary, who is exercising the "gate-keeping" functions making decisions about what is a "good" text, the decisions that regulate the fictions producing the "real." These fictions are a function of desire, as Brossard has argued, which sets in play certain relays or networks of images informing interpretive (hermeneutic) conventions and reading practices within complex gendered economies. So men's "realities" are not the same as women's "realities" (*Letter* 149). For the "real" is nothing else than a code of representation which exceeds the lived or the performed. What is taken for the "Real" is a particular network of signs that valorize men's fictions — the monetary system, for instance — whereas women's "realities" — sexual harassment or domestic violence — are taken as "Fiction." Such fictions or "as-if" statements are well-established modes of address: they constitute the normative force of discourse which is produced as a semiotic system and constructed in language. Currently, the heterosexual contract regulates relations between men in groups, positioning women only in relation to the maternal function. If the project of *Tessera* as a group of women in the public space, thinking and talking together and producing a truth-effect through symbolic exchange among women — that is manipulating signs and producing knowledge, value being constituted through exchange — was to proceed, it required a rethinking of the thinking being. Also necessary was a reconfiguration of the economies of symbolic exchange from the present order wherein women are constituted as lack, bearers of opinion, under the hegemony of masculine presence or subjectivity. We needed to exit from the family romance as narrative structuring criticism, leave behind the story of he(subj.)-loves-she(obj.). This necessitated a disruption or parallax where, through a negation of negation, feminism might be turned into a speaking stance or angle of vision that would creatively elaborate the different or unexpected. As a creative as well as critical discourse, feminism may imagine fictions, hypotheses, models of potential relations between women, to open the possibility of a horizon mediating relations between women. For Luce Irigaray, the absence of such symbolic forms has meant the inability to conceptualize women in the plural: there is no modality for facilitating exchange between women. When "the goods go to market" in the current symbolic economy which, like the discourse of philosophy, is ordered by the masculine imaginary, women go as objects, not subjects of exchange, as the sign or token (tessera) exchanged to make meanings between men. They have social value only in as far as they as are so exchanged for they are the empty space or gap to be negotiated in the drive to make sense. Within this order, "public space" is constituted by men in the plural. What *counts* as public space, that is. Developing a public space for women in which their exchanges may circulate entails reconceptualizing the symbolic so that it no longer functions within the model of representation or resemblance, a perspective which, since Plato, has favoured the transcendent over the embodied. Women would no longer be caught as non-subject, non-object in the indifferentiation of suffocating oneness or violent rejection of each other, but as women, both the same and yet different, mutually recognizing the sameness and otherness of the other woman, would participate in an exchange of reciprocal differences. No longer would this be an exchange in which the Subject absorbs or incorporates the Other.

Central to this imaging of an other symbolic that encompasses diversity, flow and change has been Brossard's project of articulating the "thinking body" as that which jams the discursive order of "hom(m)osexuality" (Irigaray, 172) or order of the masculine selfsame. "Each [textual] figure is a relay centre, a transmission device. We read in the relay. In fact, we participate in the relay as if at an abundant feast of sense, for sense figures in the relay; it evokes image. Thus we participate in the emotion of figures that are familiar to us ..." (*Letter* 151). Exploding the economy of relations of the closed signifying system of the selfsame founded in the primacy of likeness or metaphoricity (the representational order of phallogocentrism) proceeds through undoing the laws of (linear) narrative, of anecdote, of syntax, to allow for the circulation of mobile signifiers in unfinalizable networks of relations. This would weave the open, the diverse, into the narrative as the locus of possibility, make visible the contingencies of economies of desire in the ordering of signifying networks, the situatedness of knowledge, and write into the text what is normally written out, namely the conditions of its articulation within the gendered (and racialized) production of meaning.

The constitution of a community of women writing and reading, engaged in an exchange of letters, is a crucial feature of identity formation: theory and form of self-identification, it figures as necessary fiction of collective activity and its legitimizing tool. Strange, though, that it took women so long to become aware of the need to establish collective spaces — periodicals, publishing houses, book stores, art galleries, film collectives, recording labels — in order to inflect the production and reception of the unspoken rules and conventions of culture so as to make meanings *for* women not *on* women. For a number of generations in Canada young men have seized the means of production to found little magazines and publish their own work. Eventually, this is taken up by mainstream publishers and the young men become the Establishment. Charles G.D. Roberts and Bliss Carman published each other in periodicals at the turn of the century. In the 1920s, A.J.M. Smith and F.R. Scott collaborated on *McGill Fortnightly Review*, Louis Dudek and Irving Layton on *First Statement* in the 1940s, while George Bowering and Frank Davey founded *Tish* in the 1960s. Too many of us as young women have waited for the acknowledgement of the Establishment rather than taking the floor and making a space for ourselves. Who would listen to us without public authority? Participation is not a matter of choice: such authority is constituted by the recognition of an audience which is granted only to those whose discourse aligns with the dominant. An authority effect maintains itself in an absence of the person, in the force of a signature. A woman, however, inserts the personal into discourse, unravelling the author-effect.

In the late 1970s, several groups of aspiring women writers started literary magazines where women wrote for other women. Unlike *A Room of One's Own* and *Fireweed*, *Tessera* has focused on feminist poetics or "theory" rather than on "creative" texts by women, though the borderlines between these two genres are what it seeks to blur in emphasizing the creative or aesthetic dimension of thinking. It differs from them also in its commitment to bilingual publishing as critique of the imperialism of English within a cross-cultural project. Writing *through* has been *Tessera*'s concern, through the marked binaries of feminist debate displacing the opposition itself: mind/body, theory/criticism, theory/feminism, psychoanalysis/materialism. Another boundary *Tessera* erases in its work on the in-between is that separating the academy from the literary institution at large. With two literary critics — Kathy Mezei and Barbara Godard (later Susan Knutson) — and two active writers — Daphne Marlatt and Gail Scott (later Louise Cotnoir) — on the first editorial collective, a balance was struck. In theory, that is. In practice, the different priorities we gave to reading and writing made more complex the contradictory identities we had as feminists and as literary practitioners. This tended to polarize around debates as differences *between* us what were in fact contradictions *within* us between feminism (politics) and literature (poetics).

We constantly debated the issue of feminist criticism. What exactly did we mean by the term? How does textuality relate to the political of literature? Should we be doing readings of texts? Which texts? Women's or men's? Could the work of pre-1970s writers be "feminist"? Should texts be more generally theoretical? Or more interpretive? Or more "creative"? What were the interrelations of the literary and the theoretical, the aesthetic and the scientific? How long should texts be? Should we have any such norms? These issues surfaced in our first editorial. A call for criticism to become "a writing in its own right" ("Sp/elle" 12), theory with a transformative intensity, was followed by a call for criticism to be "discussion of texts and language and syntax" ("Sp/elle" 13). That this might turn into a "dualist split" between reading specific texts and engaging in generalizing theorizations was a problem raised subsequently. To avoid the tendency for theory to work abstractly avoiding texts and for criticism to cling too closely to texts and forget about theory, it would be necessary to work theory through specific texts ("Sp/elle" 14). After all, our concern was with Canadian and Quebec writing. Any feminist theory we elaborated must address the specificities of this geopolitical situation. Could theories generated within other literary institutions speak to the particularities of women's writing in Quebec and English Canada? The matter was not settled once and for all at this meeting, but remained subject to ongoing debate with the selection of texts for each issue.

What was clear to us all was that along with the need for recognition of women as knowing subjects within the literary institution as writers or as readers/rewriters, we were under an imperative to change the social structures of the institution itself, that is to change the structures and forms in which knowledge is produced. This was a double imperative, both interrogative and assertive, critical and creative. That we succeeded to a certain extent in forging a new way of writing about women's texts is suggested by a recent call on a computer bulletin board citing *Tessera* as model in its request for contributions to a book about criticism as life-writing. This underlines the within/without situation *Tessera* has held in relation to the academy, advancing a form of writing that breaks with academic norms for essays but which is ultimately an object for academic analysis. Combining an aesthetic activism with a social collectivity that sees itself acting in society and history, *Tessera* has investigated literary form and social discourse to contribute to the revitalization of an avant-garde sensibility, the potential of radical feminism in the post-modern era (Russell 251).

The last decade has seen the establishment of women's studies and feminist theory as academic specialities. This general realignment of the disciplines has stimulated and enabled *Tessera*'s questioning of critical norms. The effect of this energy has been marked in terms of the numerous theoretical fictions produced by Scott and Marlatt, for instance, and the explorations of voice and subjectivity in the criticism of Mezei, Knutson and Godard. Marlatt has commented on the importance of *Tessera* in stimulating her "theoretical pieces" and in providing what is so necessary for a writer, "a sense of writing into an ongoing dialogue" (Butling 123). What the longer term effect might be is as yet unclear for it is a "cumulative effect," Marlatt suggests, one which "established a reference point that wasn't there before" and "extended the range" of the sayable (Butling 122).

Extended the range, changed the possibilities for writing criticism, these are some of *Tessera*'s effects, according to Frank Davey, who notes that its articles would look decidedly out of place in any other of the Canadian literature criticism periodicals (74). This difference has manifested itself not only in the "communal purpose" of the periodical, but also in its rejection of the usual focus on "authors, on the already-written" emphasizing instead "writers, current participation and future production" (75).

Difference, purpose, community, future — these are key terms that situate *Tessera* as feminist pro-ject.

## DERIVATIONS

"Language-centred writing," post-structuralist linguistics, socio-semiotics, these have informed *Tessera*'s focus on language play, on power and silence. A feminist critique which takes this linguistic turn emphasizes the way language as a sign system works to produce gender as a set of meaningful *relations*. It is intriguing, in light of these concerns, that no member of the editorial collective can recall how the title *Tessera* was chosen. This amnesia may indicate how our relations were developing: *Tessera*, attached to no individual name, is imbricated in a collective project.

The narrative of the name we almost selected, "Sp/elle," is well known to the collective. Related at our first editorial meeting, in a ritual iteration of the history of our coming together, it is a story that speaks to the venerable Canadian topos of communication, the power of (cross country) networks. What the telephone system privileged, in the absence of physical proximity, was an awareness of language as a system of sound images. The tenuousness of the connection is most notable, a mobility that also marks our ultimate choice. The story unfolds an episode in our initial discussions when Daphne Marlatt, passing through Toronto, talked with Barbara Godard on the telephone, exchanging acronyms, bilingual puns and other forms of word play. Of these, "Sp/elle" held our interest because it would function bilingually ("Sp/elle" 5). We liked "Sp/elle" enormously for the relays of images it activated — "the speaking elle" or the issue of subjectivity; "the 'e' ending" of the feminine articulated and made visible or the work upon language and syntax to change the rules wherein the masculine as generic category takes precedence over the feminine; the casting of "spells" or the work of transformation and validation of covert feminine knowledges. We liked the name enough to use it for our first editorial "SP/ELLE: Spelling Out the Reasons."

♦ WOMEN OF LETTERS (REPRISE) ♦

Why did we decide to change it? Clarity was not the issue, unless, perhaps, that "Sp/elle" was too explicit and potentially limiting. That the name spoke directly to the topic of women and words was demonstrated when Judith Fitzgerald adopted the title for an anthology of feminist poetry. Thanking *Tessera* for the title, Fitzgerald underlines its "appropriateness" for her anthology. Her research into the term connects it to the Old English *spe(l)l* from the Gothic *spill*, meaning tale, story, statement. In Old French, *espel(l)er* meant discourse. As she elaborates: "If we cast spells, we tell the tale, we make spellbound ... . This is the feminine case: we name, we create and recreate; we write our alphabet correctly. We imagine, we compose. Incantations." *Tessera* has proved to be anything *but* clear, as constant questions indicate. With hindsight, however, the shift in title indicates a turning in our thinking about language and gender during the process of putting together the first issue, "Duplicity in Language," on the "double-voiced" character of feminist discourse, its intricate work of resistance through critique *within* the prevailing discourse. This was a turning away from archetypes and magic towards the politics of exchange.

"Sp/elle" invoked a web of images around the figure of the witch, important in radical feminist discourses of the 1970s in connection with the oppression/repression of female power. In English, the figure was closely associated with alternate feminist religious practices developing from Wiccan rituals within such frames as "Witchcraft as Goddess Religion" (Starhawk). Among the types of exorcism for such institutional misogyny as the "european witch-burnings" or "goddess murder," Mary Daly identifies "spooking" and "spinning" in "un-creation," unravelling the social premises implicit in accepted discursive practices, undoing the (k)nots of meaning through ludic play with language (24). This play involves making up words, hyphenating them to make their gendered presuppositions explicit and/or to expose alternate or archaic meanings, drawing attention to the pleasure of the sound of words — the kind of language play evident in the word "Sp/elle."

In contrast to the onto-theological field of the "witch" in English, *sorcières* in French was linked to an historical discourse of social change as well as to a symbolic discourse of disruptive bodily speaking. *Sorcières* was the title of a periodical edited by Xavière

Gauthier, which in 1978 published a special issue, "La Jasette" (gossip), involving Quebec feminist writers. Adopting the analysis of historian Jules Michelet, Gauthier considers the witch to be the negative trace of women's economic and social power during the Crusades and the witch-burning a retaliatory violence against women to contain it, to "wall up women's speech" (164), on the return of the men after the Crusades. Gauthier extends the implications of both symbolic and historical frames, connecting subversion in the political and economic register to writing in the symbolic through surrealism, an artistic movement which affirmed the subversive force of eros whose economy of permanent change in the encounter of heterogeneous objects of desire undermines the fixity of ordered sociality, disrupting the status quo and producing revolutionary art. This potential of the witch has been most extensively articulated in the dialogue of Cathérine Clément and Hélène Cixous, where the witch is figured as open-ended desire, in a discourse of excess. Unlike the hysteric, who also speaks with her body, the witch is not a symbol of individualism, but a public spectacle which the culture takes into account and makes an object of transmission (8). As "incompatible synthesis" and "imaginary transition" (57), she marks the limits of social struggle and figures the desire for structural transformation. Madeleine Gagnon in Quebec mapped the intersections of transformation, writing and witchcraft in "Écriture, sorcellerie, féminité," drawing a parallel between the situation of women and witches who both present bodily ills mediated as metaphor in language. Writing re-moves women from a kind of silence or exile by recreating them (359). The point of exit or flight from masculinist discourse is a space of risk, of free play, a space in constant mutation, opening continuously as the gesture, always excessive, slips through the constraints of interpretation.

We were displaced from this terrain of incipient feminist archetypalism, with its emphasis on a pre-existent feminine power to be *expressed* in language, on identity claims, by "tessera," a signifier connecting to feminist *strategies* in language that would constitute a woman-in-effect. If Sp/elle exists in our memories as narrative, "tessera" lingers as quotation(s), as fragments assembled to form mosaics, collages. It connects thus to the collage form privileged in *Tessera* editorials with their dialogic model of discourse, the one

## ♦ Women of Letters (Reprise) ♦

within the other which is simultaneously one about the other, and so highlights the partial nature of the perspectives or knowledges advanced. Fragments. Connecting at many angles. The need to begin over and over again ... . Not metaphor as figure of discourse, a carrying across. Anaphora, rather. Stuttering, repetitive. Attempting to put together a narrative of naming, a creation story, we came up with questions, then scattered definitions and quotations which individual members of the editorial collective circulated in response to a word possibly proposed by Marlatt. The importance of the fragment for conceptualizing women's writing had been raised in her conversations with Barbara Godard. Someone introduced the metaphor of the mosaic and of tessera as a piece of the mosaic. But, as Kathy Mezei reminded us, the word has "several different meanings" ("Sp/elle" 6).

> **tessara'**. also tessera. a Gr. neuter pl. of tessares and comb. form of FOUR used in Gk. compounds, and forming the first element in a few English words adopted from or formed on Greek.
>
> **tessaraglot**. Of, in, or pertaining to four languages. *tessaraglot* bible. *Complutension Bible* (1517). (OED)

At first we were four ... . This, though, was the last of the meanings we learned about, but it confirmed the appropriateness of our choice.

> **tess'era**. Pl. tesserae. [L., f. Ionic Gr. = Attic four.]
>
> 1. Anc. Hist. A small quadrilateral tablet of wood, bone, ivory, or the like, used as a token, tally, ticket, label, etc.
>
> b. *fig.* A distinguishing sign or token; a watchword, a password. (The earliest use in English.)
>
> 2. *spec.* Each of small square (usually cubical) pieces of marble, glass, tile, etc. of which a mosaic pavement, or the like is composed Usually in pl.
>
> b. *transf.* Any one of the quadrilateral divisions into which a surface is divided by intersecting lines; e.g. by the lines of latitude and longitude.

c. *Zool.* Each of the plates of which the carapace of an armadillo is composed.

**tesseract.** *Math.* Also tessaract. [f. tessara- + Gr. ray.] A four dimensional hypercube. Also *fig.*

**tesse'rarian,** a. *Obs. rare.* [f. L. tesserarius pertaining to tesserae or dice +-AN.] Of or pertaining to dice or gaming. *tesserarian art*, the art of dice-playing. (OED)

In the editorial collective's discussion about the connotations of our title, we focused on its phonetic links with *texere*, weaving or constructing, foregrounding textuality, as well as on its subversive potential as "password." This connection to cabals and undercover groups through the secret "password" spoke directly to our editorial process of taking over other established periodicals to disseminate feminist discourse more widely, a kind of *noyautage* or revolutionary cell-building. Several of us had backgrounds in left-wing political movements and this metaphor of infiltration was very resonant for us. As well, there was the call for change with the opening of the "fourth dimension" or "tesseracts." This movement into new frames of perception was dicey, however. An open-ended itinerary. The stakes in the game we were playing with such boundless space were high and potentially contradictory, as this figure of the curvilinear rectangle (tessera) made tangible. Paradoxical as well as subversive, our project.

We were also alert to the network of meanings established for "tessera" in contemporary literary theory, especially in Lacan's conceptualization of language in the subconscious.

> ... however empty this discourse may appear, it is only so if taken at its face value: that which justifies the remark of Mallarmé's, in which he compares the common use of Language to the exchange of a coin whose obverse and reverse no longer bear any but worn effigies, and which people pass from hand to hand 'in silence.' This metaphor is sufficient to remind us that the Word, even when almost completely worn out, retains its value as a *tessera*. Even if it communicates nothing, the discourse represents the existence of communication; even if it denies the obvious it affirms that the Word

constitutes the Truth; even if it is destined to deceive, here the discourse circulates on faith in testimony. (Lacan 13)

As Gail Scott commented, "tessera" is the "fragment that leads into and *out of* silence!" ("Sp/elle" 7). The empty sign exchanged in discourse, "tessera" signifies the meaningfulness of the act of exchange itself over and above any referential "content" exchanged. Filling in the sign entails interpretation of the connections between the "parts," producing partial truths that are traces of desire for completion or meaning. To mark the significance of this figuration of subjectivity in language to the *Tessera* project, we chose as our logo a mosaic with stones or tesserae missing, an incomplete woman's head waiting to be filled in or made up, to become woman as the effect of that actualization/completion. Interpreted or invented, that is, in an exchange.

The connection of *tessera* to the exchange of signs and the constitution of meaning and community as partial or interested is underlined in Anthony Wilden's *System and Structure*, where *tessera* is introduced in a discussion about metaphor and metonymy as different modalities of relating signs, the one foregrounding resemblance and acts of substitution, the other contiguity and acts of combination.

> The concept of the 'symbol' as a communication and of the Symbolic as a system of communication finds its support in anthropology and in the history of religion. Besides its legal sense of 'pact' or 'contract,' the word *sumbolon* is probably equivalent to the Latin *tessera* — the two halves of a broken potsherd whose fitting together served as a token of recognition or password in the early mystery religions. Like the verb *sumballo*, the etymological source of the word symbol is that which implies a LINK ... . Charles Sanders Peirce pointed to these correlations in 1897 in his "Logic as Semiotic: The Theory of Signs." In the complex systems of exchange examined by Mauss in the *Éssai sur le don*, or by Malinowksi in his *Argonauts of the Western Pacific*, the gifts exchanged can be called symbols. But they do not stand for what they 'represent' in some fixed relationship to an unconscious' meaning.' They are the symbols of the act of the exchange itself, which is what

ties the society and its neighbors together. Thus they cease to be symbols in any important sense; it is the ACT of exchange ... . In Lévi-Strauss's terminology, these objects of exchange are often referred to as "signs," which are exchanged like words in a discourse. (Wilden 32)

To be underlined here is "tessera" as "link," as "act." *Tessera* as a space of interconnection, as a place for exchange to make meanings between women.

What went unmarked in our interchanges, though was crucial in our choice of "tessera," is that, with its classical connections, the title looks and sounds the same in both French and English. Its resistance to the domination of English is heightened in that "tessera" is also a word in a contemporary "foreign" language, Italian. Here the architectural resonances are less pronounced. The semiotic valences "tessera" introduces from Italian into French and English augment its political effect. For "tessera," meaning "card," is hyphenated with terms marking identity and belonging. *Tessera-di riconoscimento* means "identity-card." Most tellingly, though, *tessera di partito* means "party membership-card," while the cognate verb *tesserare* means "to provide with a membership-card" and the adjective *tesserato* means "member (of a party)." This sideward move into Italian marks *Tessera* as a space of adherence, as a site of symbolic exchange forged in political connections, in a collective will-to-become. Identity and subjectivity are hence affiliative, not filiative, produced within a political rather than familial formation. In a desire for transformation of social structures of belonging. That *tessera* also commonly means "bus ticket" reminds us that this is a political adhesion in motion.

From figures of woman, we moved through a weave of quotations and discourses to the act of exchange itself as the site of political in(ter)vention to constitute a woman-in-effect. This entails less a desire to recover a lost origin than a consideration of effects or (political) fallouts of diverse perspectives with their various modes of address and styles of discourse. The concern with feminist strategies in language is a tactic legitimating a demand for recognition of a diversity of angles of vision that would take difference, both sexual difference and differences among women, into account in the constitution of knowledge. A shift from identity to meaning making, from being to acting. Making connections — or faces. Mimicry instead of mimesis, re-presentation drawing attention to the conditions and processes of speaking. What vectors orient the relations of signs and sociality in respect to community and power? How does gender as a system order values? How are the contingencies of gender imbricated in the conditions of enunciation? What points of exit do the interconnections provide from a system of masculinist values and styles of writing and reading (reception and interpretation)?

Such a perspective posits a process of becoming woman which, from the point of articulating woman-as-subject through a collective will-to-become-women, opens up a field of possibilities for alliances among women through which to change political and theoretical practices. Through a collective recognition that being-a-woman is the result of an historical and linguistic construction of femininity which has in the past positioned women as different, as Other, a discursive community or collective subject is constituted which functions to empower the subjective becoming of each woman and make her an agent of change. Within this model of history and subjectivity, language as a chain of signifiers constructed relationally along an axis of metonymic displacements is an open-ended field of possibilities for action whose manipulation will bring into being certain kinds of relations, enable certain modes of subjectivity. The lack-of-being in such relations, a lack of identity between signifier and signified and between subjects and objects, generates both signification and desire. The realization or actualization of these possibilities depends upon the strategies adopted, the choices made, the desires in play. A feminist politics of language would make visible woman-in-effect through relays of images redefining the rules of the game so as to make a difference and to make the difference felt effectively, that is, as effect, in-deed. Difference here is not negation but relation, the introduction of alternative perspectives. A parallax. Possibly a pro-ject or casting forward.


Derivation may also be written dérivation, which opens a wor(l)d of difference. In English, "derivation," refers to the "formation of a word from a word or root, the tracing or statement of this; theory of evolution" (OED). In French, "*dérivation*" refers to this grammatical procedure of forming words from a root, but has many other meanings in a variety of discursive fields. In calculus, it refers to the derivative (variable) of a function, while for the military, it means the displacement or rotation of a projectile's trajectory in relation to shooting angle. In a totally different register, it relates to "drifting with wind or current" (Robert). If in English we are invited to understand the tracing of words and their signifying networks in association with that which is derivative from a *fixed* point of origin, in French we are encouraged to examine the process of such tracing as a formation of meaning by a *movement* of deviation or displacement. *Dérive* is a term much used by Nicole Brossard for feminist discourse: setting meaning adrift, unmooring prevailing codes. *Détournement*, a synonym of *dérivation*, is the principle technique in the French Situationist cultural and social praxis, a shifting of relations through the reuse of preexisting artistic elements in a new ensemble where the double meaning of their convergence produces a "negation of the value of the previous organization of expression" (SIA 55).

Such recontextualization introduces "violences in a system of rules" to produce what Foucault terms an historical "event" or "reversal of a relationship of forces, the usurpation of power, the appropriation of a vocabulary ..." (154). Events occur in tangled profusion, for origin or "emergence" is never singular and visible, but occurs in interstices at different non-identical points, producing a heterogeneous "unstable assemblage" (146). Approached through the prism of genealogy, an examination of descent would not attempt to go back in time to a fixed point beyond dispersion in order to "restore an unbroken continuity" but would focus on dispersion, "the minute deviations — or conversely, the complete reversals" (146). Seeking the subtle traces that might intersect to form a network, a genealogy would "sort out" lapses, differences, piecemeal fabrications, fleeting articulations, numberless beginnings (145). Between (contradictory) versions, different constructions or assemblages might be produced.

Numberless beginnings ... . *Dérivation*, or deviation. Genealogy, or dispersion. The cumulative effect of such detours, shifts, wanderings, repetitions, is to extend the relays of images, multiply the angles on the signifer "tessera" and produce a tangled web of meanings.

## ♦ WOMEN OF LETTERS (REPRISE) ♦

### *THINKING MEETING, NOT OPPOSITION*

Editing a journal with the project of destabilizing conventional distinctions between the "literary" and the "theoretical, the "aesthetic" and the "scientific," central to the constitution of literary studies as a discipline is potentially an ins*urgent* project. Editing a collection of essays from the production of a decade of that journal is a project with a difference. *Re*surgent? Writing less with an eye toward the future than cast backward over the shoulder raises questions of a different order. This text is less manifestory — its enunciation both declaration and promise, performing a language act of disruption — than memory work — repetition covering over the time-gap or lack in a play of substitution. Psychoanalytic anemnesis or remembering seeks to fix the affective content of such a substitution around an absent object of desire centripetally, to close the gap with a singular narrative giving continuity, fullness of meaning. Can feminist memory-work disengage critically the strands woven by memory? Scrutinizing the assemblage of networks and signifiers would bring inside what is usually left outside — the moment of enunciation with its temporal disjunction and embodied speaking subject — to bear/bare witness. It would extend the inquiry into the relations *between* texts and cultural practices, into the processes by which meanings are constructed and socially validated. Not just the writing but the body and the organization of the reader's reading informed by historical, economic and intersubjective factors. Can memory work through the traces of the past and make a place for anOther speaking within one before one, simultaneously present and absent? Memory's substitution as centrifugal motion: memory work as the production of *differences* over/as time?

The dilemma in putting together an anthology is selection: moments in an ongoing process are frozen as representative. Representation, that contentious field in contemporary feminist theory, is indeed a pressing issue. Representation-as-persuasion, a speaking as proxy *for* another in the political arena? Or representation-as-trope, the repetition of images through which, in writing or by actors on a stage, one speaks for oneself obliquely? These modes of representation as persuasion or petition are unstable and colliding, for representation is always re-presentation, something staged for a specific audience, relating seer and seen within political and economic networks. Representation, moreover, is the mode whereby individuals are constituted as subjects in that they are addressed and come to identify with the Subject of a representational or discursive practice, legitimated by some relations of production (Althusser). To select a few texts to re-present a history of *Tessera* inevitably reduces the complexity of positions, subjectivities, voices, which have been elaborated over time in response to changing conjunctures, to a singular *Tessera* Auth*er*, situated in one narrative line. Moreover, this narrative is constituted from the present moment which reconstructs a past in function of where "we" are now. However, this "we" is no longer functioning as a collective: its work has been taken up by other women, while "we" pursue our individual projects as theorists/writers/critics/activists. Looking back, what seems most important to each of us may tell more about how we hope to shape the future from our present diverse geopolitical and personal locations. Contradictions between the one and the many amplify.

To some extent, the future is traced in advance by the intervention of a publisher, Second Story Press, with a specific project of reaching out to an academic audience. Nonetheless, an audience is no pre-existent entity but a potentiality or virtuality. Nor is the academy necessarily a set of walls. The future toward which this text is moving is not just a future present. When one takes a re-presentative position, one becomes aware of possibilities for representation of oneself in areas that are totally inaccessible to one. This is to become open to the trace of the other, to the dialogic, where texts are considered as dynamic interactive processes constituting social relations. Working to interrogate the binary opposition between writer and reader, one imagines a reader responding to one's text, an invitation launched as broadside into a public forum. Like all letters, however, the invitation is open to interception. "[P]eople turn up in other places for other occasions with that invitation," with that text (Spivak 153). Purloined letter. Refusal to draw a sharp line between the positions in play opens up lines of variation, a dispersion of points of "subjective" observation throughout images of movement. The occasions in which this particular invitation is taken up may make it speak in excess of *Collaboration in the Feminine*. A speaking beyond the cover's borderline.

♦ WOMEN OF LETTERS (REPRISE) ♦

Most certainly, though, there is in *Collaboration* ... a speaking of collaboration as process, one that foregrounds the exchange of the signifier and the instability of all language practice. *Collaboration* ... is in excess of itself: it finds meaning in precisely that which a limited economy of meaning expends or writes off, the moment of its enunciation, the contingencies of its coming to speak. In its endless repeatability, moreover, it is never wholly determined by that moment which, written in, speaks on, speaks elsewhere ... . Making this second selection has foregrounded the activity of selection itself as a work of re-membering, of re-ordering inside and outside, so calling into question the classifications and epistemological categories in which the "meaning" of *Tessera* has been made and through which the traces and values of its past (re)circulate. Can *Tessera*'s cultural functions once fixed, be re-mobilized?

Who, then, is the "we" who is re-presented in this selection? For what "you" is this re-presentation ordered? Though unfinalizable, the "you" is figured within language as a reader of English. A crucial feature of this selection process has been a decision to produce a unilingual English text, a major swerve from *Tessera*'s practice of foregrounding the work of translation as the (re)reading of one language through another by placing French and English on facing pages, or by framing a text in one language with a précis in another. These practices write into the text the passage between languages, between cultures, a passage elided here.

The "we" selecting and the activity of selection are more readily circumscribed within a process this introduction restages. Following established editorial practice of collective decision making, *Tessera* editors past and present were asked in the spring of 1993 to send a list of their preferences to include in an anthology. Responses ranged from a page of texts selected on the grounds of those "I like and use with my classes" to a list of three pages framed by four pages of analysis on the implications of making a selection and an articulation of the salient questions to ask in the decision-making process. These lists were combined with overlaps, points of consensus, highlighted, then recirculated for further comment, addition or deletion. Some texts appeared on all lists, others on most lists. Since our editorial policy has always been decision by majority vote, these texts formed the backbone of the anthology. Selection of the remaining texts has followed the usual process of negotiation, horse-trading and some strong-arming by the coordinating editor of a particular issue.

An attempt has been made to work out a balance between the particular focus of individual issues of *Tessera* and the longer trajectory of the magazine over a decade, between timely text and cumulative effect. Elusive, this latter is introduced obliquely by editors in defense of their choices: "a text central to what *Tessera*'s all about." What "what" is has been matter for both speculation and disputation. Every time we had to make decisions about texts or titles, we realized that each of us understood *Tessera*'s project in very different ways. Some of this related to our different institutional locations as writers or critics and their accepted conventions, some to the different ways feminism was being articulated regionally, and some to the different ways it was being lived passionately. Different lines of desire establish divergent modes of relation as meaningful. A certain tension prevailed between ironic and romantic narratives: the former seeks through an antagonistic dialogue with a patriarchal academic institution to affirm women's status as writers and critics where the locus of interaction is between feminism and patriarchal culture. In the other narrative, the locus of interaction is between women in a discursive practice that sees criticism itself as lesbian, women reading expressing passion for women writing. There was also divergence between a frame of "difference," where woman is a category from which to begin writing, and one of "*différance*," where sexual difference is to be constituted in discursive practices.

These differences provoked much writing. Our letters and discussions where the debate was staged became, with rewriting, our collective editorials. This process has been materialized in the collage form of this retrospective introduction: the individual editors have each written texts that frame the differing political and emotional stances which colour their choices. Rather than drawing a line sharply between inside/outside, collage locates the differences *within* the text, not broken down but layered to expose the internal incoherence of absolute categories, categories in which hierarchical oppositions such as man-woman, straight-lesbian, ironic-romantic, fiction-theory, real-representation, text-effect, are produced by bringing together interactively the different locations and measures of social validation around these categories. Realigning boundaries, theoretical practice en*corp*orates the contradictions of writing subjects.

To give a sense of the excitement we felt over the years on reading the texts submitted and seeing them exfoliate as they resonated interactively with other positions on a given topic was another objective guiding this particular selection of texts. Such a clash of perspectives underlines the importance for *Tessera* of a sense of event. Preference was given, however, to texts from earlier issues, long out of print. Another major objective was to highlight the quality of the texts published, many of which like Lorraine Weir's "'Wholeness, Harmony, Radiance' and Women's Writing" and Godard, Marlatt, Mezei and Scott's "Theorizing Fiction Theory" have become reference points in Canadian feminist literary debates. To reconcile a topical intervention with a project aiming to produce movement — these are contradictory aims which this textual assemblage sets in play.

Since one of the crucial features of *Tessera* has been the dialogic element of the writing in the constitution of a discursive community, it has seemed important to group the texts chronologically around particular issues to set in play a diversity of angles of vision. Texts which appeared in one number are responded to in a later one where the question is framed differently. So, Lise Gauvin's "What? You too?" (Issue 5, 1988), a fictional dialogue on the contemporary tendency to novelize all genres, specifically the essay and life-writing, is queried and set aslant by Monique LaRue's personal letter to Gauvin, "Power or 'Unpower' of the Fictional Subject," (Issue 9, 1990) which analyzes the lack of author-ity, subjectivity as lack, of the auth*er* of narrative.

One strategic matter, the resistance to theory in the anglophone Canadian literary institution, in contrast to the literary institution in Quebec, and how this works to marginalize feminist attempts to theorize gender in that institution, has been a thread interweaving many texts from the first issue where the problematic was lucidly articulated by Weir's "Wholeness, Harmony, Radiance and Women's Writing" (Issue 1, 1984). The debate centres around the privileging of realism in fiction and "images-of-women" criticism that presupposes an understanding of literature as a *reflection* of society not a *production* of subjectivity and consequently masks the ideological work of the literary in support of an order that is "capitalist, bourgeois, patriarchal" and "Anglo-Protestant." The twinning of mimetic realism and critical clarity is taken up again as a persistent problem within feminist theory in Valerie Raoul's text "Is Feminist Theory Anti-Feminist? (Reprise)" (Issue 4, 1988), which outlines the debates within feminist theory in a list of contradictory maxims such as feminism's concern for abolishing traditional false sex-role stereotyping alongside its concern with revalorizing what has been dismissed pejoratively as "feminine." It is reframed as yet another set of contradictions by Pamela Banting in "S(m)other Tongue?: Feminism, Academic Discourse, Translation" (Issue 6, 1989), who sees this as a problem in intersemiotic translation, an attempt to transport into a register of language termed "authentic" and "accessible," with no apparent "slippage" or "loss," concepts that have been worked out within another discursive system. Attempts to elide the inevitable slippage and to fix meaning by overlooking sign systems as systems of distinctions or differences works to support the same, similarity. This call for accessibility functions to limit, to censor even, feminist innovation rather than to "propel readers to exceed themselves." Clarity functions as metaphor for unity or universal sisterhood, while Babel signifies the potential for the many.

In developing her argument, Banting refers to work by Maria Lugones and Elizabeth Spelman on the importance of conditions of "mutual dialogue that does not reduce each one of us to instances of the abstraction called 'woman'" (Lugones and Spelman 581) in order to advance feminist theory as a "project of 'joint theory-making'" between activists and academics, between Spanish- and English-speaker. Such collaborative work is the ethical project of feminist theorizing, according to Kathleen Martindale in "Power, Ethics and Polyvocal Feminist Theory" (Issue 4, 1988), who also analyzes the text of Lugones and Spelman in developing her concept of "polyvocal theory." For Martindale, as for Lugones and Spelman, there is no opposition, no sharp line drawn between feminist activists and theorists, but rather a collaborative project approached from different locations with respect to power. Martindale notes how the project began with "complaint" about exclusion and silencing to become an engagement with the politics of theory and language around exclusion by false universalization, the feminist "we," as a political and ethical issue. The project charts relations between women in language, the power valences constituted around colonized differentiations between Spanish and English. Unilingualism in the language of the colonizer is the condition of the powerful. How can Lugones, a bilingual Spanish speaker, engage in theoretical work with Spelman *in English* as an equal?

These meditations on the hierarchical relations of language(s) ring ironically in the context of the colonizer/colonized status of English/French relations within the Canadian feminist community. *Tessera*'s policy of bilingualism gestures (vainly?) toward undoing these power relations. This irony is not lost on Madeleine Gagnon, whose text "Mother Tongue and Women's Language" (Issue 4, 1988) gains resonance from juxtaposition with Martindale's. For Gagnon too advocates the "polyvocal." She articulates the urgency of looking not for Truth in fiction or in theory, in one thing or another, but for the "truths to decipher *between* theory and fiction," "polyphonic truths." Writing not to "substantify characteristics," Gagnon sees the questions for feminist theory and discourse as "a matter of thinking meeting" not opposition. Martindale's and Gagnon's metaphors of duplicity and foreignness echo backwards to Louise Dupré's text, "The Doubly Complicit Memory" (Issue 1, 1984), which articulates the dilemma of the hierarchy of languages posed for her as a Quebec feminist. She offers a pact of friendship as a commitment to an (anglophone) Other in the "richness of differences" as the resolution to the dilemma. The cumulative effect of such dialogues and cross references extends the discursive fields and relays of images, multiplying the angles on pivotal signifiers such as "translation," "rewriting," and "polyvocal" to produce an expanding web of meanings.

The problem of language and power is phrased differently by Donna Smyth in "Gnosis" (Issue 4, 1988), a passionate and fluid text about women's struggle to create a new sign system. Refusing castration or silencing under the current symbolic order like Dupré (the "Logos" as "She"), Smyth also refuses the binary of activism/theory. Her poetic text moves through feminist struggle to image a new relation with language, a new society, as women engage in civil disobedience resisting nuclear armament. An ethical project of attentiveness to the trace of the Other transmutes into a discursive project of innovating an art of approach, a way of writing theory that works the space *in between,* opening up a wedge in dominant discursive forms. Such zigzag paths between theory and activism, between fiction and theory, between poeïsis and mimesis, between sites of intervention, places of publication, have been taken by these writers. Intertexts and textual effects are brought into the weave of the texts situating them within a network of reversible relations. As such, they perform displacement, stage the instability of the letter. Postcards going off in all directions at once, posted forward, or sent back to guard the posterior, or halted at the relay ... . Words, images, concepts, repeated exfoliate so as to destabilize any fixed coherence, or monumentalizing gesture.

The horizontal tendencies of heterogeneous series are at play *within* as well as *between* texts, as evidenced in the various collaborative editorials included here. "Theorizing Fiction Theory" (Issue 3, 1986), despite its ostensible focus on defining the concept "fiction/theory," opens up many levels of discussion and dissent. The framed borders attempt to cerne the definitions, to keep them in place, but they start to move, any certainty is unravelled, as each editor introduces a new metaphor: a scramble "over the barrier/slash" (Mezei); "a 'telling' telling" (Marlatt); a space "through" (Scott); transformative "work" (Godard). This troping unsettles the fixity of the letter as signifier. Meaning(s) proliferate. The abyss between francophone and anglophone feminisms yawns.Disjunctions within a text are perhaps most evident in "Versions con-verse: A Sequence of Translations" (Issue 6, 1989) which introduced "Translating Women" with seven different versions of "espaces vers," one in French by Lola Lemire Tostevin and six variants Englished by the *Tessera* editors. Serialism as translation strategy is announced in the title by "sequence." Dispersion reigns from the first line where "vers" is rendered variously by "green," "lines," "where," "vers-ions." The shifts between one text and another perform the slippage or contamination of language(s) that Tostevin's introduction welcomes as the "possibility of a relation of differences" displacing an "illusion of authenticity and purity." This dynamic view of translation undermines the conventional onto-theological conception of the translator's task as "introversion" or self-effacement to become a transparent window between source language and target text. Translation moves beyond the (impossible) dream of total identity or equivalence to recognize the translator's poetic creativity and the possibilities of enhancive (or propagandistic) translations productive of difference.

Desirous/delirious speaking in tongues is one image of "conversation" as "openness," exploring the "betweenness" the "mutual listening" of "woman-to-woman" meetings found in "In Conversation" (Issue 5, 1988). The possibilities for establishing relations between women on dialogic, rather than hierarchical monologic lines, are the utopian hope that conversation holds forth for subverting the unidirectional codes and norms of patriarchal discourse. Participants in this *Tessera* editorial exchange disagree on whether women's textual forms are predicated on some fixed identity to be recovered by another woman or are forged through social struggle against a prevailing masculinism. Consequently, "dialogue" is inflected differently. There is no unity in the editorial, no single feminism articulated, but a discursive struggle over the potential meanings of feminism. Such encounters of the discordant, the unexpected, are legacies of surrealism and productive of the dialogic mode of feminist discourse, according to Suzanne Lamy, whose theory is analyzed by Sherry Simon in "Suzanne Lamy: 'Talking Together'" (Issue 5, 1988). Dialogism relativizes languages and subjectivities. Within a weave of texts, questions of authenticity, of identity, are approached sideways through the oblique angle of another and so displaced by the question: in relation to what? The other turns up unexpectedly at the heart of one's (self)reflection.

Such differences in articulation of key terms are introduced again in the editorial to "Essentialism(e)?" (Issue 10, 1991), of which two texts are included here, Susan Knutson's "Imagine Her Surprise" and Kathy Mezei's "Writing the Risk In, Risking the Writing." One angle of investigation evident in these two essays turns on the "risk" involved in locating the "symbolic mother" which engages "a difference of symbolization, a different production of reference and meaning out of a particular embodied knowledge." Knutson examines the stakes of making "relationships between women" the "substance" and "practice" of feminist politics to give shape to "a genealogy of women" ("une culture au féminine" in Quebec parlance) through a symbolic practice of sexual difference;

the "Telling It" Conference, organized in Vancouver by Daphne Marlatt in her role as Ruth Wynn Woodward Chair of Women's Studies, is given as an example of such an "authorization" of the "symbolic mother." Though inscribed in a relation of "belonging" within a female genealogy, the identity politics during the conference exposed the "racist fabric" as well as the "presence of homophobia" within Canadian feminism. Mezei takes up this "paradox" of women's identity through the mother within the frame of sexual difference, the mothers to "think back through" (Woolf), who constitute one model of a female genealogy in generations of feminist writers and theorists. Considering both the impossibility of escaping the culture's representations of femininity as motherhood and of denying her own involvement in mothering, as well as the necessity of recognizing that "woman is determined by her relation to the world" and that "mothering is a metaphor," Mezei suggests that writing from one's sexual *difference* "out of a sense of one's essence" is writing from a variable and troubled position of "bisexuality" with its emphasis on "exchange between women."

A *différend* is enacted also around the term "post-modernism," another mobile signifier in contemporary feminist debates. Different stands on the interconnection of postmodernism and feminism multiply among Quebec writers and friends, Louky Bersianik, Nicole Brossard, Louise Cotnoir, Louise Dupré, France Théoret and Gail Scott, who regularly meet for "Theory on Sundays." "What We Talk About on Sundays" (Issue 5, 1988) produces disequilibrium through intensification and recombination of signifiers. Each poet-critic articulates the relation to post-modernism differently, ranging from the negative stance of Théoret, who rejects the "nihilism" of postmodernity and calls for feminists to write out their very different version of history, to the positive stance of Louise Dupré, who finds openings in postmodernity's "post-historical consciousness" for a feminist project of reinscribing the embodied subject in textuality.

The serialism of these collectively signed texts is amplified in each individual issue, where different perspectives are brought into play on a topic or problem. So, from the first number of *Tessera* (1984), Weir's "'Wholeness, Harmony, Radiance' and Women's Writing," a cautionary tale of the embattled state of feminist language-centred writing and theory in the patriarchal English

Canadian critical institution, is set aslant by Dupré's "The Doubly Complicit Memory," a poetic meditation on doubleness in the French language, of being spoken for when as a woman she tries to speak, which prompts her to reach out through other languages to a community of women writing. Gail Scott's "Red Tin + White Tulle" works the interval, comparing the situations of feminist theorizing in anglophone and francophone communities. She writes of "[t]he inexpressible pain of contradiction" of being spoken for in patriarchal discourse, being muted by the repression of anglo-Protestant culture, then struggling in her acquired French to challenge syntax along with French-speaking women like Dupré.

Intensification through modulation and recombination is at work again in the selections from the second issue, "Writing as Reading/Reading as Writing" (1985), which examines the meaning-making activities of reading which, like writing, is the adventure of a desiring subject engaged in a narrative of quest for the fullness of meaning working through the maze(ment) of language. Whereas Marlatt in "Writing our Way Through the Labyrinth" focuses on the maze, Brossard in her ironically titled "Certain Words" emphasizes the way words or other signifiers function as relays for creative wandering, from one woman's image and words on a postcard through improvisational riffs animated by desire, rewriting her text in a palimpsest. Tostevin, in "re," foregrounds the work of desire for completion in language itself, as signifier stretches toward signifier, ordering language and text according to the contiguity of sounds, through repetition and rhyme, not syntax. This produces unexpected connections, ungrammatical meanings. Slipperiness in the heart of the letter, sound teasing out sense, institutes transformations, contaminations, that set a system of meaning caroming, introduce lines of metamorphoses, dispersion of points of "subjective" observation through images of movement inhibiting closure or completion. "Re" in its title signals the re-versibility of the processes of reading and (re)writing, the commutability of signs, in short of translation. "Re," a text which Tostevin translated into French herself, launches a line of flight to Issue 6, "Translating Women" (1989), where Tostevin wrote about the richness of difference(s) when she translates herself into the thought of another language.

In "Coming to Terms with the Mother Tongue" (Issue 6, 1989),

Dôre Michelut analyzes the way her languages, Furlan, Italian and English, order the world differently and are marked by different orders of experience, different periods in her life, these separate registers of culture incommensurable, hence, seemingly untranslatable. The feeling of fragmentation disappears when she begins to translate herself while writing, for this requires a "reciprocal flow" between languages. In her drifting among languages, she dismantles the distinction between mother tongue and foreign language, making them available as languages presenting different possibilities for articulation, instituting different views, making different wor(l)ds. In this contamination of languages or translation, the logic of the first and the second, the Platonic logic of original and representation, of the one and the many, the pure and the impure — the logic of identity —, is upset: mother tongue can no longer claim priority as a discourse of truth, nor writing assert priority as a "primary text." The hierarchical relations of firstness and secondness which have supported metaphysics with its focus on a singular disembodied subject have given purchase to discourses according primacy to the masculine over the feminine gender. So too, they have served as prop to the binary distinction between activism and theory, which Pamela Banting challenged with her metaphoric extension of translation as "turning" and her interest in "systematic interference."

## *Theoria, or Rewriting Narrative*

It is such an insistence on intervals, continuities and contiguities that fiction/theory reemphasizes in its focus on a mutual traffic in signs. Theory can no longer claim priority as a discourse of truth but is continuous with the readings it produces and with fiction which, in turn, loses its claims as "primary text." Relations are established not from some fixed original point as it radiates outward, but within the processes through which diversity constitutes itself in many mutual interactions. Inside and outside are not absolute terms but are situated reciprocally in relation to the moment of speaking within specific institutional constraints.

The possibilities of reversibility are entertained by Smaro Kamboureli in "It Was Not a Dark and Stormy Night" (Issue 3, 1986): "Does theory (re)tell what the writer has left untold? Does it express without creating? Does it tell a parallel story?" Her text performatively answers these questions by arbitrarily drawing a horizontal line across the page and placing numbers for footnotes below the line to separate primary text from secondary references according to the norm in academic discourse. A distinction is notated. But the images and concepts are written across the line, the "content" ignoring this "formal" distinction. Reading violence in the field of the symbolic that hierarchizes relations of knowledge, of gender, Kamboureli responds subversively by cutting into the very space of division constituting the one to make it a place of connection and contradiction among the many. The metaphor she generates for fiction/theory is that of the embrace, produced from the polysemy of "to behold," English for the Greek *theoria*, and to "Be. Hold," folded in the arms of the story "I-love-you." As a passionate fiction, Kamboureli's text fantasizes a mode of relation where the one true idea of the philosopher and the writer's representation or copy are confounded in a scene of looking and a process of narrating informed by desire. Critical fictions, this text proclaims, are always interested and partial, yet, contradictorily, in their mixture of genres lack self-coherency. As the story of "she-loves-he," this text inverts yet maintains the matrimonial metaphor, linking the feminist critic to the patriarchal institution.

As Kamboureli's metaphor of the embrace intimates, what is being written into the network producing meaning is the gendered body. Line McMurray's fiction/theory, "Impunity: Distance as an Ethic" (Issue 3 1986), takes up this question of an ethics of embodiment or contiguity differently, by writing in the rhythms of her body as she makes the text. Verbally, this is framed as the particular work of fiction/theory: a "going beyond" in "an energetic/apprehension" of the written word. Going beyond for McMurray entails going beyond the limits of the word, the logos, to contaminate it with the sensible — the visual image — and the tactile — the hand writing. Her fiction/theory explodes the binary text/image, verbal/visual, to inscribe reading as a physiological process — looking at black marks on a white page — as well as a hermeneutic activity of interpreting traces. The "body's woven mesh" is concretized in a metonymy of the production process of the text which has been drawn/written by a particular hand, transmitting "an energetic charge" of a subject in an embodied "discourse." The controlling ego is displaced by a series of mechanical writing strategies that constitute writing as "musculature" and "morphosis," as simulation and transformation of the real.

It is just this corporeality, ascribed to the feminine, written out of the production of knowledge in Western metaphysics with its privileging of the true original over the lying representation, the intelligible over the sensible, that McMurray and others want to write back into the weave of the text. Breaking down the boundaries between verbal and visual is one such strategy of work on the interval, the occluded passage, metonymically to en*corp*orate relations of knowing and make visible the marks of gender, the partiality and locatedness of "truth." A number of texts in *Collaboration in the Feminine* extend the possibilities of such work. Brossard's "Certain Words" considers the photographic image as a relay opening up connections between women. Persimmon Blackbridge's collaborative text, "Doing Time" (Issue 5, 1988), exposes the ways discourses of the Logos, of the Law, have marked women's bodies so as to incarcerate them as outlaws, and demonstrates the struggle to break free, a struggle that is documented in her installations and in accompanying texts written by women in prison. So too, Bussejé Bailey's "Opening Myself Up to a Lot of Pain" (Issue 12, 1992), exposes the way discourses of white privilege have written over the black female body, to stamp it out, erase it. Visual metaphors of tattooing in her photos from "Body Politic" show how language and the gaze work to produce racial outcasts. Her images also move through a sequence from resistance to domination as the body becomes, metonymically, a raised foot. Black looks. Re-turning the gaze. While mixed visual and verbal texts have been included in every issue of *Tessera*, the question of their interaction was specifically theorized, in "Talking Pictures" (Issue 13, 1992) which addressed the topic from a number of angles ranging from a consideration of photo-textual narratives, to the layering of words on visual images by visual artists, or the collaborative processes of filmmakers and writers.

Work across the cleavage between verbal and visual image, like that across the border between fiction/theory, intersects around a series of concerns that have traversed many issues of *Tessera,* namely those of subjectivity and narrativity, interconnected around questions of Law and desire. The most direct link is forged in Issue 8,

"Auto-graph(e)" (1990), as evident in the two texts from the issue included here. Janice Williamson's "Tell Tale Signs" weaves a biographical narrative about the visual signs manifested in x-rays of a fractured wrist that witness, silently, to paternal violence. Signs expose a secret. This text introduces other ways of graphing the body, other kinds of signs of identity, not just those done to one, but those one performs oneself: images of a lassoo sequentially modulate into the shape of the capital J of "Janice." In its progressive unwinding of the loop from strangling noose into free-flowing signature, the text performs the struggle for Williamson as a woman to produce a position from which to write. The tension between the proper name and the common noun enacts a struggle between lending oneself authority to write, to make a name for the self, and losing the self, the name, in the process of writing, between speaking and being spoken by discourse under the Father's law/name. The signature stages the textual split between "I" and "she," the split which is written out when the authorial subject is masculine and perceived as normal, hence neutral (Benveniste).

Marlatt takes up the same issue of the location of a space in discourse through the angle of narrativity. "Self-Representation and Fictionalysis" (Issue 8, 1990), articulates the problem of how the writer represents herself through the visual metaphor of framing. Identity is a still photo "frozen out of context," isolated from a shifting and changing network of relations. This presupposes an understanding of a self existing prior to or outside representations of that self, as an "isolatable identity," buried under cultural repression and waiting to be re-covered. Against this logic of the one and the many, of the self as autonomous self-presence, Marlatt writes of a self produced as textual effect through "our own writing, our own imagining." In this view of identity, the feminine (lesbian) subject has been excluded from the symbolic, from sociality, and remains to be created. Noting the self is for Marlatt a rusing with fiction, understanding a subject not "as *different* from any thing and any other, who is always merely object" but as a continual web of overlapping selves. Writing out the "self" means shifting from writing autobiography, as the re-presentation of a singular life story making distinctions, to "fictionalysis," which plays imaginatively with the "ahistoric ground of a life" to invent possibilities of becoming and relating. Marlatt's project of notating the self overlaps with Kamboureli's reworking of "I-love-you" (characteristic of the romance genre or the heroine's tale) into the genre of the fantastic or theory, which connects the unconnectable, conjures up the unthinkable. It becomes a story of theoria, of "I" embracing "I" who is also "she." Marlatt displaces the conventional articulation of "I-love-you," namely "he-loves-she," with a new grammar of narrative, "she-loves-she," unsettling the heterosexual contract of the dominant matrimonial metaphor to fantasize the "unthinkable," the ghostly, abject lesbian, both object and subject of women's desire, autoerotically doubled, yet split from itself and invested in pursuit of the other woman. Simultaneously, the subject is engaged in a different kind of specularization in which she sees herself reflected in the act of seeing oneself, in the very representation of desire. The move from love story to theory via passionate fiction is a shift from a tale of absorption/incorporation of the other by the masculine to explorations of doubling, repetition, the uncanny.

Issue 9, "Changing the Subject" (1990), extends the implications of Marlatt's argument to look at strategies for thinking and writing the question of subjectivity to enable women to locate themselves as speaking subjects within a discursive community of women. Many texts submitted focused on the subjection of the feminine under the violence of the Father's law, subjection produced in the rhetorical violence that makes "I" identical with "he," and in the way the violence of the paternal name is marked on the daughter's body by regulatory acts of voyeurism, incest, pornography. Resistance is less an issue for these writers than the horrors of pain, the power of horror in the ambiguous position of the feminine, caught in the in-between, where one is neither subject nor object but abject (Kristeva), as Claudine Potvin develops it in "The Pornographic Subject." Carole Massé in "The Subject at Stake" considers the "outlaw" position of the female subject dispersed across a number of contradictory positions and unable to coalesce into a coherent identity, as a place of possibility, of opening, to the unnameable, to radicality and vertigo, refusing the constraint of a singular meaning. This is the place of writing as investigation or research where a decentred subject, both subject and object of (self)knowledge, is constituted in the play of language, within the infinite reversibility of those shifters, the reciprocal pronouns "I" and "you." In the interstices of the movement between the dispersed subject and a utopian imaginary subject of difference is positioned a virtual female subject, articulated provisionally in the conditional tense as a textual effect to be actualized.

Change involves projecting virtual woman *in effect*. This is a project of changing symbolic and cultural forms to make it possible for women to become (writing) subjects. It is above all a project for making visible the effects of power, to write them out so as to write them in. To take up such a regulating position, one must adhere to a discursive community institutionally sanctioned. The image of a complete narrative, Hayden White argues in agreement with Hegel, is based in a concept of law, legality and legitimacy (14). Only a subject aware of a central social and political ordering principle is capable of full narration.

The feminist project draws attention to this narrative function through its focus on the conflict between desire and the law. It shows, by way of contrast through its lack of totality and coherency, the extent to which narrative strains for the effect of having filled in all the gaps. As Scott suggests, feminist narrativity makes use of "spaces like stairs" in the open weave of text, the work of the middle ground. Incompletion, gaps, digressions, parentheses — so many strategies point to an awareness that there are still other meanings beyond what has been included.

Eminent male narratologists have read the conventional narrative sentence of the Western quest or metanarrative of epistemological conquest (*Aufhebung* or incorporation) as paradigmatic of the trajectory of male sexual arousal (Brooks). In this system, woman-as-text/text-as-woman (the "blank page" (Gubar), the "plot-space" (de Lauretis)) functions as object of exchange between authors and readers, an enabling position organizing the social fiction of heterosexuality through homosociality. Feminist writers resist this entire erotic metaphorics of the literary text, built on the figuration of the feminine as passive and empty receptacle for masculine conception and creation. Some take up narrative with a vengeance, exaggerating narrative conventions in order to denaturalize them, to make visible their work in the reproduction of social codes of gendered relations. These are the strategies of "conflict," "tension" and "paradox" which Louise Cotnoir identifies as protocols for contemporary Quebec feminist writing in "To Speak Without Suffocating," (Issue 7, 1989). Such strategic uses of "parodic and ironic representational strategies" are adopted by contemporary women writers and artists to work "within," while "de-doxifying," patriarchal narrative discourses as well as "metanarrative discourses," such as the discourses of postmodernism. Feminists have developed this sceptical stance towards postmodernity, Linda Hutcheon argues in "Incredulity Toward Metanarrative: Negotiating Postmodernism and Feminisms" (Issue 7, 1989). Hutcheon's text elaborates the possibilities of metafiction to engage in critique of social systems of power in the representational modes through which they operate.

Such a challenge to metadiscourses is mounted in Marlene Nourbese Philip's "Whose Idea Was it Anyway?" (Issue 7, 1989) which reframes quotes from Spanish and Portuguese chronicles of the conquest of the Americas in a narrative that interrogates the historical record of imperialism by personalizing it. The transportation of slaves from Africa to America is an idea as revolutionary as the scientific discoveries of Newton, or Galileo, or Descartes, the narrative suggests. Yet, the one who conceived of the slave trade remains anonymous, while the names of these scientists are celebrated as founders of the systems of modernity. Asking the question "Who was he?", rewriting the official records as a narrative of masculine desire, this is the wedge of "fantastic" narrative or theoria Philip forces into the gaps and intervals in "factual" narratives of domination and exploitation. This exposes their secret workings, writes them out, so as to write the narrative of racial genocide into the cultural narratives of European "Enlightenment" discoveries under a (its) proper name. The text challenges the dominant quest story by shifting it to a narrative of the quest for narrative (knowing), a quest for a proper name around which signs will cohere to form a narrative. Through its lack of closure, this narrative functions to expose the strategy of the central social and political ordering principle of narrative completion in Canadian society, one that advances white privilege as well as masculine dominance. Realigning the boundaries, shifting the frames, fiction/theory brings into the shape of narrative the dislocating work of theorizing, to expose the "matter" of fiction as gendered (heterosexist) and racist conditions of production and reproduction.

### ◆ Women of Letters (Reprise) ◆

The dialogic mode of Philip's fiction for riffing and changing frames is used too by Leila Sujir and Sarah Murphy in "Other Orthodoxies or The Centring of Margins: A Dialogue" (Issue 11, 1991). This text began as a collaborative performance with video and sound track of streets supplemented by transparencies on which the text was printed. Framed by the question, "If you centre the margins, where do you enter the text?", one woman speaks about silence, chaos, the emergence of a new language. The other projects her text, a blank text, except for footnotes at the bottom of the printed page. The footnotes, part of the paratextual apparatus of the absent "Paramilitary Parafictions," themselves speak of military torture, introducing a fragmented narrative of a woman looking for her tortured husband, alternating with translator's notes which give information about Salvadoran culture and the Spanish language. The usual order of texts is inverted so that the peripheral is made central: the translator's performance as cultural mediator, the trauma of the witnesses of violence, are made the key features of the "story," the secondary implicit in the primary. Unsettling notions of anteriority, and hence of (narrative) causality, this questions the narratives of imperialism and their politics of non-translation.

This is one particular performance among a number documented or analyzed in Issue 11, "Performance/Transformance." For the area of performance has, among contemporary art practices, been one where women have been particularly visible. The novelty of the art form with its discursive conventions less solidified, allowing for the inflection of its material and styles of address by feminist concerns, is one reason for this interest. But performance is also one way in which the critical project of feminism has been framed. The use of repetition by Philip and Sujir and Murphy is strategic re-presentation as *mimicry*, which is, as articulated by Irigaray, a ludic repetition that exposes the operation of representation as the production of exchange value, in contrast to the conventional understanding of representation as *mimesis* or similarity, the copy that masks its status as produced under the fiction of "being." Re-presentation is the construction of fictions of provisional identity, subjectivity as becoming. Performance destabilizes fixed subjectivity by setting in play the "fictive body" manipulated by the player in rehearsing her own staging of the imaginary as a subject in process, moving between the

♦ BARBARA GODARD ♦

positions of being spoken by and speaking social discourses. Crucial here is a theory of enunciation that considers a textual event as process inevitably incomplete and open to interruption, rather than finished product with a fixed meaning, within the constitution of social subjects. Performance is not confined to the stage but spills over into performances of social and behavioural strips in the everyday. Femininity itself is understood as performance, a playing out of the gendered social scripts. These modes of address, styles of performance, and genres of discourse constitute "technologies of gender" which (re)produce subjects in their "proper" place (de Lauretis).

## OTHER GENEALOGIES

Thus far, I have been reconstituting *Tessera* within a historical narrative, presenting issues chronologically. There are other ways to remember these texts by moving sideways and tracking particular "topics." Despite what might seem an exclusive concern with strategies of writing otherwise, signalled in the titles of issues, so called "activist" agendas have been interwoven in each issue of *Tessera*. Dispersion of these texts works to unsettle the binary activism/theory which has contributed to the marginalization of "cultural feminism" within feminist discourse. Politics and writing are not opposed but coterminous as these texts demonstrate. "Be holding" and "holding," or theoria, involve up-holding a position or taking a stand. A cluster of concerns, grouped around questions of linguistic and ethnic or racial differences, have been of both more general and more focused concern. While the major interest of *Tessera* in its first two years was in relating francophone and anglophone feminist criticisms with their divergent concerns and potential to interrogate the parameters of a totalizing literary institution, the dialogism or agonistic interplay of differences of a comparative framework alerted us to the very different traditions developing in each language group, and in different countries using the same language. Feminisms in Canada were distinct from those in France and the United States if, for no other reason, than that they were situated within this transatlantic axis at an oblique (northern) angle. What this might mean in a multilingual and multiracial society like Canada was unclear to us in the beginning. How many different feminisms might there be?

♦ WOMEN OF LETTERS (REPRISE) ♦

How might a frame of differences interact with our focus on signification to relativize languages? Should there be a more extensive application of a translation model to all communicative exchanges? That it most certainly entailed a more complex struggle to come to writing was demonstrated in Anne-Marie Alonzo's "Ritual" (Issue 3, 1986) which in a fiction/theory interweaves a meditation on the amnesia and aphasia of her immigrant condition with another on the stasis of her body, its memories of childhood mobility in Egypt no longer active traces in her present caged paralysis. Writing it all out, sheet-upon-sheet, in a ritual of remembrance, trying to conjure that child back by paying the accounts, Alonzo probes the immigrant's dispersion between a country scarce remembered and one barely inhabited, through the figure of nostalgia and souvenir. Caught in contradiction, write though she will in the French language, what she says remains incomprehensible in Quebec. This is the greatest loss, the interruption of the speech exchange when there is inequality between languages and when cultural translation does not occur.

Jam Ismail figures this stereoscopic vision of the racially different not through the doubling of incommensurable landscapes or narratives, but through the interruption of Chinese ideographs into an English language dictionary to make strange both the act of seeing and that of interpretation. "Diction Air" (Issue 4, 1988) is a resistor's dictionary which refigures the language of feminist theory to bring together under the category "words" both the definition "chinese characters" and "the idea of race ... [as] autonomous, scientific and legal status." Ismail's glossing of race as "leak of nations" emphasizing boundaries made leaky through immigration, is accompanied by a visual image of a classical coloseum or olympic race course wherein occurs "a contest of speed," overlaid as palimpsest on fragments of words beginning with "rack," an instrument of torture. She plays with collage as a mode of "metonymy" to establish new connections, new relations that make of the space between cultures, languages, races, a productive space, one of invention and critique. "Making up" meanings foregrounds the constructedness of looking and interpretation, the way these are inflected by a particular location, one which is ordered along hierarchical lines of race as well as gender. Ismail's project engages the "making" of history as making stories, fictions to be circulated in an ex-change of cultures undermining the power of the imperial One.

In recent years, following the critiques of exclusion in the discourses of Euroamerican feminisms, race has become a major category for the consideration of the production of meaning and value. Issue 12, "Other Looks: Race, Representation and Gender" (1991), demonstrates a range of strategies for writing the syntax of race and ethnicity, an oscillation between reclaiming "home" through memory, or a syntax of "retentive" particularity, and an in(ter)vention in a new country through dissidence, one of "restitutive" particularity. Some texts also manifest a third strategy, a transformative project that seeks to read one cultural and racial text through another to conflate old and present topographies and languages in a syntax of "syncretic" particularity. This entails subjecting an underread or overwritten category to an intensive gaze to expose oversights. Such re-turning the gaze changes the angle of vision, produces a new set of relations between subject and object of vision and, potentially, a new value for the excluded, the marginalized, the in-between.

## *BETWEEN RE-MEMBERING AND BE-COMING*

An oscillation between "retentive" and "syncretic" syntaxes of identity, between past and future, recalls the tension within feminist theories of subjectivity even within *Tessera* between an identity which has been buried and need only be recovered, remembered, and potentialities that have never been conceivable socially and remain to be actualized, invented. The opposition between past and future is not marked, as the relation of recovering to inventing might suggest: memory work persistently links past and present, connecting images within different networks to make something different in the process and intervene thus in the future. A sign is launched as promise of (im)possible meaning: memory produces re-collection repeating the sign as citation, the voice of another speaking in one, before one, so confounding questions of interiority and anteriority (primacy). Readers project themselves interpreting, to bequeath a different future. Memory work*ing*. The compulsion to repeat is not the rote learning of childhood with its focus on producing the same, but an active selection and connection. Rememoration as possible

◆ WOMEN OF LETTERS (REPRISE) ◆

threshold. Writing from, writing through. Memory resists the nostalgia of fixed relations even as it rejects the future as catastrophe. Recurring memory reframes and so casts ahead or throws forward images that are in the process of becoming.

Project in turn is interested in missing lines. Reading or interpretation is to project oneself into the lines which are reframed, reanimated by desire. Images relay desire producing lines of affiliation, of adhesion. Networks constituting a community of women of letters. Project thus joins memory in a double movement of casting forward as well as backward, simultaneously. It is a movement that (re)plays the contradiction of memory, namely the confounding of interiority/anteriority with exteriority/posteriority. For just as remembering empties out in the letter to another within and prior, formerly internalized and lost to view, project writes in, in reaching for the future, what it will send out as forecast. Project, too, specializes in the doubled signification of interpretation and anticipation. Conceived as a movement of extension, project is also paradoxically interiority, to conceive or imagine, to put before oneself in thought. What does it mean to have feminism as a project? This is to conceive of a collective subject of feminism, a "we," in the tension of the still-to-come and the already-in-process. As becoming. What does it mean to project oneself as a feminist? *She* projects a virtual image of woman-in-effect. To think of the project of the project is to confound the economy of the one for it is to participate in an economy of thinking one thing through another, of conceptualizing the space between as differential relation or movement not yet completed.

### *READING IN COLLABORATION*

Memory. Project. In the oscillation between past and future, in some conditional present, *Collaboration in the Feminine* occupies a space and sets out future relations. Reframing the texts of *Tessera* through the changed angle of hindsight, it projects a virtual image of a textual effect and makes it available for a different reading. Its subject is never completed and fixed in the words of a single text because it is situated in the (dialogic) space between texts. It is into this space that the reader must project herself, throw herself into the speculative activity of interpretation. Leave behind her romantic fictions of familial romance to "be hold" herself and the future, theorizing (in theory). To combine thus a position of specularized object of theory and that of speaking subject of knowledge. To become accountable for her own partial perspective in relation to other similarly situated and interested perspectives.

These are the strategies which any reader may use to investigate the texts in *Collaboration in the Feminine.* Sent forth, these letters run the risk of intelligibility: one cannot be sure that among those others we address, the readers of this book, there will be someone who is in that particular subject position to receive, to theorize. The letters, moreover, will be read backwards as traversed by the message of another somewhere else, so that absence and presence, sender and receiver, are confounded. Look at the texts, look around and through them. What you see in them is what you bring to them. Speculate. Re-play the specular scene of self as reader. Read the book backwards as well as forwards. Read it sideways, to see what each text borders on, and what differences that touching might make. Turn it upside down too. The words might well come out in another rhythm, in another dialect or even another alphabet. If that is your desire, your "wont" ...

♦

## Works Cited

Althusser, Louis. "Ideology and Ideological State Apparatuses (Notes towards an Investigation)." *Lenin and Philosophy.* London: New Left Books, 1971: 124–173.

Bakhtin, Mikhail. *The Dialogic Imagination.* Trans. Caryl Emerson and Michael Holquist. Austin: University of Texas Press, 1981.

Bakhtin, M.M./Medvedev, P.M. *The Formal Method in Literary Scholarship: A Critical Introduction to Sociological Poetics.* Trans. Albert J. Wehrle. Cambridge: Harvard University Press, 1985.

Benveniste, Emile. *Problems in General Linguistics.* Trans. Mary E. Meek. Coral Gables: University of Miami Press, 1971.

Brooks, Peter. *Reading for the Plot: Design and Intention in Narrative.* New York: Vintage, 1985.

Brossard, Nicole. *Aerial Letter.* Trans. Marlene Wildman. Toronto: Women's Press, 1988.

———, Louky Bersianik, Louise Cotnoir, Louis Dupré, Gail Scott, France Théoret. *La Théorie, une dimanche.* Montreal: Editions du Remue-ménage, 1988.

Butling, Pauline. "Magazining: Interview with Daphne Marlatt." *Open Letter.* 8th ser. 5–6 (Winter–Spring 1993): 113–124.

Cixous, Hélène and Cathérine Clément. *La Jeune née.* Paris: Union Générale d'Edition, 1975. Trans. Betsy Wing. *The Newly Born Woman.* Minneapolis: University of Minnesota Press, 1986.

Daly, Mary. *Gyn/Ecology: The Metaethics of Radical Feminism.* Boston: Beacon Press, 1978.

Davey, Frank. "English–Canadian Literature Periodicals: Text, Personality, Dissent." *Open Letter.* 8th ser. 5–6 (Winter–Spring 1993): 67–78.

Davies, Gwen. "'Dearer than His Dog': Literary Women in Pre-Confederation Nova Scotia." In *Gynocritics/Gynocritiques: Feminist Approaches to Canadian and Quebec Women's Writing.* Ed. Barbara Godard. Toronto: ECW Press, 1987: 111–129.

de Bellefeuille, Normand. "La modernité." "Vouloir la fiction." *NBJ* 141 (1984): 84.

de Lauretis, Teresa. *Alice Doesn't: Feminism, Semiotics and Cinema.* Bloomington: Indiana University Press, 1984.

———. *Technologies of Gender: Essays on Theory, Film and Fiction.* Bloomington: Indiana University Press, 1987.

Dorion, Gilles, ed. *Dictionnaire des oeuvres littéraires. 1976–80.* Tome VI. Montreal: Fides, 1994.

Foucault, Michel. *Language, Counter-Memory Practice: Selected Essays and Interviews.* Ed. Donald F. Bouchard. Trans. Donald F. Bouchard and Sherry Simon. Ithaca: Cornell University Press, 1977.

Gagnon, Madeleine. "Ecriture, sorcellerie, fémininité." *Etudes littéraires.* 12, 3 (1979): 357–362.

Gauthier, Xavière. *Surréalisme et sexualité.* Paris: Gallimard Idées, 1971.

Gubar, Susan. "'The Blank Page' and Female Creativity." In *The New Feminist Criticism: Essays on Women, Literature and Theory.* Ed. Elaine Showalter. New York: Pantheon, 1985: 292–313.

Irigaray, Luce. *Ce sexe qui n'en est un.* Paris: Editions de Minuit, 1977. Trans. Catherine Porter and Carolyn Burke. *This Sex Which Is Not One.* Ithaca: Cornell University Press, 1985.

Kristeva, Julia. *Powers of Horror: An Essay on Abjection.* Trans. Leon S. Roudiez. New York: Columbia University Press, 1982.

Kroetsch, Robert. *The Lovely Treachery of Words.* Toronto: Oxford, 1989.

Lacan, Jacques. *Speech and Language in Psychoanalysis.* Trans. Anthony Wilden. Baltimore: Johns Hopkins University Press, 1968.

Lugones, Maria C. and Elizabeth V. Spelman. "Have We Got a Theory for You! Feminist Theory, Cultural Imperialism and the Demand for 'Woman's Voice.'" *Women's Studies International Forum* 6.6 (1983): 573–81.

Marlatt, Daphne and the Telling It Collective. *Telling It: Women and Languages Across Cultures.* Vancouver: Press Gang, 1990.

Michelet, Jules. *La sorcière.* (1862) Paris: Garnier–Flammarion, 1966.

Morris, Meaghan. "in any event..." In *Men in Feminism.* Eds. Alice Jardine and Paul Smith. New York: Methuen, 1987.

Russell, Charles. *Poets, Prophets and Revolutionaries: The Literary Avant Garde from Rimbaud through Postmodernism.* New York: Oxford University Press, 1985.

Scott, Gail. *Spaces Like Stairs.* Toronto: Women's Press, 1989.

SIA. *Situationist International Anthology.* Trans. and ed. Ken Knabb. Berkeley: Bureau of Public Secrets, 1981.

Smith, Dorothy. "An Analysis of Ideological Structures and How Women are Excluded: Considerations for Academic Women." *Canadian Review of Sociology and Anthropology.* 12, 4 Pt. 1 (1975): 353–369.

Spivak, Gayatri Chakravorty. "In a Word. Interview." With Ellen Rooney. *differences.* 1, 2 (Summer 1989): 124–156.

Starhawk. *The Spiral Dance: A Rebirth of the Ancient Religion of the Great Goddess.* San Francisco: Harper & Row, 1979.

White, Hayden. *The Content of Form: Narrative Discourse and Historical Representation.* Baltimore: Johns Hopkins, 1987.

Wilden, Anthony. *System and Structure: Essays in Communication and Exchange.* London: Tavistock, 1972.

Woolf, Virginia. *A Room of One's Own.* (1929) London: Granada, 1977.

# CONTRIBUTORS' NOTES

ANNE-MARIE ALONZO, editor of *Trois* and author of more than twenty-two books of fiction, plays and poetry, won the Emile-Nelligan Prize for *Bleus de Mine* (1985), published as *Lead Blues* (1990) in the translation of W. Donoghue. Her collaborative work has appeared in *Liens/Linked Alive* (1990), a collection of Renga. A recent collection of poetry is *Tout au loin la lumière* (1994).

BUSEJÉ BAILEY, MFA from the Nova Scotia College of Art and Design in Halifax, has worked in different media including printmaking, sculpture, video and installation. Her work which critiques the representation of African-Canadian women has been exhibited in solo and group exhibitions across the country.

PAMELA BANTING, poet and critic, is the author of several books of poetry including *Running into the Open* (1985) and *Bareback* (1993). Her book on translation peotics will appear with *Turnstone Press* (1995).

LOUKY BERSIANIK, filmmaker, poet, novelist, is the author of the celebrated feminist dystopia, *L'Euguélionne* (1976) translated by G. Denis and collaborators as *The Euguelionne* (1982), and *Le Pique-nique sur l'Acropole* (1979) as well as several volumes of poetry, most recently *Kerameikos* (1987). Her feminist essays were collected in *La Main tranchante du symbole* (1990).

PERSIMMON BLACKBRIDGE has been involved in a number of collaborative projects combining texts and images including *Still Sane* (1985, with Sheila Gilhooly and Kiku Hawkes) and *Her Tongue on My Theory* (1994) with the Kiss and Tell Collective. She is a graduate of the Vancouver School of Art. Her collaborators in this project, Geri

### ◆ CONTRIBUTORS' NOTES ◆

Ferguson and Michelle Kanashiro-Christiansen, are graduates of Lakeside Women's Correctional Centre and Lyn MacDonald of Madame Vanier Women's Correctional Centre.

NICOLE BROSSARD has published more than thirty books — poetry, novels, essays and theatre. She has twice received the Governor-General's Award (1974 and 1984) and the Athanase-David Prize of Québec (1991). Her most recent titles are *Langues obscures* (1992) and *La nuit verte du parc labyrinthe* (1992). Her feminist theory appeared in *La Lettre aérienne* (1985, *Aerial Letter* trans. Marlene Wildeman).

LOUISE COTNOIR who teaches at the Collège de la Région de L'Amiante in the Eastern Townships has been a co-editor of *Tessera* since 1989. Playwright (*Si Cendrillon pouvait mourir!* 1980), she has published a number of books of poetry following *Plusieures* (1984), the most recent, *Des nuits qui créent le déluge* (1994), preceded by a collection of short stories *La déconvenue* (1993).

SUSANNE DE LOTBINIÈRE-HARWOOD won the John Glassco and the Félix Antoine Savard Prizes for her translations which include Lise Gauvin's *Letters from An Other*, Gail Scott's *Héroine* and Nicole Brossard's *Mauve Desert*. Her work as a feminist translator is the subject of *Re-Belle et infidèle: La traduction comme pratique de réécriture au féminin/The Body Bilingual: Translation as a Rewriting in the Feminine* (1991).

LOUISE DUPRÉ, writer and critic, teaches at the Université du Québec à Montréal. She has published several books of poetry including *La peau familière* (1983, Prix Alfred Desrochers) and *Noir Déjà* (1993, Grand Prix de poésie de la Fondation des Forges) as well as an essay on feminist writing in Québec, *Stratégies du vertige* (1989).

MADELEINE GAGNON's pioneering works of feminist theory appeared in *La venue à l'écriture* (1977, with Hélène Cixous and Annie Leclerc) and *Retailles* (1977, with Denise Boucher) and were collected in *Autographie 2, Toute écriture est amour* (1989). Her fiction *Antre* (1978) appeared as *Lair* (1990) in the translation of Howard Scott. Most recently she has published *Les cathédrales sauvages* (1994).

♦ CONTRIBUTORS' NOTES ♦

LISE GAUVIN, writer, critic, professor at the Université de Montréal, is author of *Lettres d'une autre* (1987) published in the translation of Susanne de Lotbinière-Harwood as *Letters from An Other* (1989) and a collection of short stories *Fugitives* (1991). She has recently edited *Écrivain cherche lecteur* (1991, with J.M. Klinkenberg) and *L'Âge de la prose: romans et récits québecois des années 80* (1992, with F. Marcato).

BARBARA GODARD, a founding co-editor of *Tessera*, teaches at York University. Her translations include France Theoret's *The Tangible Word* (1991) and Nicole Brossard's *Picture Theory* (1991). She is the author of *Talking About Ourselves: The Literary Productions of Native Women of Canada* (1985) and *Audrey Thomas: Her Life and Work* (1989) and editor of *Gynocritics/Gynocritiques: Feminist Approaches to the Writing of Canadian and Quebec Women* (1987).

ERIKA GRUNDMANN teaches French and works as a freelance translator in Victoria, B.C. She has translated poetry by Jeanne Hyvrard and chapters of Louky Bersianik's *Pique-Nique sur l'Acropole*, writers included in her thesis "Louky Bersianik, Jeanne Hyvrard et Assia Djebar prennent leur place de sujet dans la langue colonisatrice" (1990).

LINDA HUTCHEON, professor of Comparative Literature at the University of Toronto, is author of many works of theory including *The Canadian Postmodern* (1988), *The Politics of Postmodernism* (1989), *The Poetics of Postmodernism* (1989). *Irony's Edge: The Theory and Politics of Irony* will be published by Routledge (1994) and her work with Michael Hutcheon on gender and opera will appear in 1995.

JAM. ISMAIL was born in Hong Kong and lived in India before moving to Vancouver in 1963. She has published her work in a number of periodicals and anthologies including *Many-Mouthed Birds: Contemporary Writing by Chinese Canadians* (1991). Recently she collaborated with Jamelie Hassan on a visual text *Jamelie/Jamilia Project* for Presentations House Gallery, Vancouver (1992).

SMARO KAMBOURELI teaches at the University of Victoria. She is co-editor of *A Mazing Space: Writing Canadian Women Writing* (with Shirley Neuman, 1986), and author of *in the second person* (1985) and *On the Edge of Genre: The Contemporary Canadian Long Poem* (1991).

♦ CONTRIBUTORS' NOTES ♦

SUSAN KNUTSON, a former co-editor of *Tessera*, teaches at Université Sainte-Anne in Nova Scotia where she writes about Canadian and Québec women writers.

MONIQUE LARUE, who teaches at the CGEP Edouard Montpetit in Montreal has written several novels including *La cohorte fictive* (1979), *Faux fuyants* (1982), *Copies conformes* (1989) as well as criticism, *Promenades littéraires dans Montréal* (1989).

DAPHNE MARLATT, a founding co-editor of *Tessera*, is author of more than twenty books of poetry and a novel *Ana Historic* (1988). Active as a conference organizer and editor, she co-edited *In the Feminine: Women and Words* (1985) and *Telling It: Women and Language across Cultures* (1990, with Sky Lee, Lee Maracle, Betsy Warland). Her recent publications include *Salvages* (1991), *Ghost Works* (1993) and *Words with You* (1993), collaborative essays with Betsy Warland.

KATHLEEN MARTINDALE teaches at York University. She has published widely on feminist pedagogy, feminist ethics, and lesbian theory including "The Unfeminist Figure of Melancholy: Gail Scott's Heroine" in *Woman as Artist* (1993). She is currently working on *Unpopular Culture: Lesbianism in the Postmodern* (1995).

CAROLE MASSÉ, after studies at the Université du Québec à Montréal, works in publishing. She is the author of five books of poetry (*Rejet, L'Autre, Je vous aime, Los, Les Petites-filles de Marilyn*) and of four novels (*Dieu, L'existence, Nobody, Hommes*), all published by Les Herbes Rouges.

LINE MCMURRAY, founder of l'Académie Québécoise de 'Pataphysique and organizer of *La 'Pataphysique, d'Alfred Jarry au Collège de 'Pataphysique* (1989), has published a number of fiction theories since *Bluff* (1983), */Fiction, as/Phixion, Trans/fixion* (1985), *Miss Morphose* (1988), as well as several essays with Jeanne Demers, *L'enjeu du manifeste/Le manifeste en jeu* (1986) and *Montréal graffiti* (1987).

KATHY MEZEI, a founding co-editor of *Tessera*, teaches English at Simon Fraser University. She has published on feminist narratology, Canadian literature, translation in Canada. Her children's book *Cuthbert and the Merpeople* appeared in 1992.

## • CONTRIBUTORS' NOTES •

DÔRE MICHELUT, born in Friuli, Italy, grew up in Canada, was educated in both countries, has published several books of poetry: *Loyalty to the Heart, Ouroboros: the Book that Ate Me* and, in collaboration, a book of renga *Liens/Linked Alive* (1990).

SARAH MURPHY, social activist, teacher, translator, visual artist, writer, lives in Calgary. She has published a number of works of fiction including *The Measure of Miranda* (1987), *Comic Book Heroine and Other Stories* (1990) and *The Deconstruction of Wesley Smithson* (1992).

MARLENE NOURBESE PHILIP was Guggenheim Fellow (1990). Her third book of poetry *She Tries Her Tongue, Her Silence Softly Breaks* (1989) won the Casa de las Americas Prize in 1988. Her fictions include *Harriet's Daughter* (1988) and *Looking for Livingstone: An Odyssey of Silence* (1991). Her collected essays *Frontiers: Essays and Writings on Racism and Culture* as well as *Showing Grit: Showboating North of the 44th Parallel* appeared in 1993.

CLAUDINE POTVIN teaches Québec and Latin American literatures at the University of Alberta. She is co-editor of *Women's Writing and the Literary Institution* (1992) and has published a number of essays on Québec and Latin American women writers. Her short stories appeared in *Détailles* (1993).

VALERIE RAOUL teaches French at the University of British Columbia. She is the author of *French Fictional Journals* (1980), *Distinctly Narcissistic: Diary Fiction in Quebec* (1993) and editor of *Anatomy of Gender: Women's Struggle for the Body* (1992, with Dawn Currie).

GAIL SCOTT, a founding co-editor of *Tessera* and *Spirale*, lives in Montreal. She is the author of several works of fiction, including *Spare Parts* (1981), *Heroine* and *Main Brides* (1993) as well as works of feminist theory such as *Spaces Like Stairs* (1989) and, in collaboration, *La Théorie une dimanche*.

SHERRY SIMON, a co-editor of *Spirale*, teaches French at Concordia University, Montreal. She is the author of *L'inscription sociale de la traduction au Québec* (1989) and *Fictions de l'identitaire au Québec* (1991, in collaboration) and editor of *Mapping Literature: The Art and Politics of Translations* (1988, with David Homel).

## ♦ Contributors' Notes ♦

DONNA E. SMYTH, writer, critic, professor at Acadia University, is the author of several plays, *Giant Anna* (1993) and novels, *Quilt* (1982), *Subversive Elements* (1986) and most recently *Loyalist Runaway* (1991). With Margaret Conrad, she is author of *No Place Like Home* (1988), a study of Nova Scotia women's diaries.

LEILA SUJIR, Calgary writer and video artist, recently exhibited "Working Portraits" at the Nickle Arts Museum (1992), "Archival Moments in an Ongoing Set of Power Relations" at Artspeak Galley, Vancouver and Ace Art, Winnipeg (1992-3). She is working on a video "The Dreams of the Night Cleaners" (1994) and an installation "River of Tears".

FRANCE THÉORET has published poetry *Bloody Mary* (1991, collected poems), *Étrangeté, l'entreinte* (1993), two fictions *Nous parlerons comme on écrit* and *L'homme qui peignait Staline* as well as a collection of essays *Entre raison et déraison*. Her work has appeared in English translation as *The Tangible Word* (1991) and *The Man Who Painted Stalin* (1991).

LOLA LEMIRE TOSTEVIN is the author of four books of poetry (*Color of Her Speech* 1982, *Gyno-Text* 1983, *Double Standards* 1985, *'sophie* 1988) and of a novel *Frog Moon* (1994). A collection of her critical texts *Subject to Criticism* will be published in 1995.

LORRAINE WEIR teaches Comparative Literature at the University of British Columbia. She is the author of *Jay MacPherson, Her Life and Work* (1989), *Writing Joyce: A Semiotics of the Joyce System* (1989) and editor of *Margaret Atwood: Language, Text, and System* (1983, with Sherrill Grace).

JANICE WILLIAMSON teaches at the University of Alberta in Edmonton. She is the editor of *Up and Doing: Canadian Women and Peace* (with Deborah Gorham, 1989), *Women's Writing and the Literary Institution* (with Claudine Potvin, 1992) and *Sounding Differences: Conversations with Seventeen Canadian Women Writers* (1993) and the author of *Tell-Tale Signs: Fictions* (1991) and a poetry chapbook, *Altitude x 2* (1992).

♦